The Good Book

Peter J. Gomes

The Good Book

COMPASS PRESS

Published in Large Print by arrangement with
William Morrow and Company, Inc.
in the United States and Canada.

Compass Press Large Print Book Series;
an imprint of Wheeler Publishing Inc., USA

Set in 16 pt. Plantin.

Grateful acknowledgment is made for permission to use the following material:

Page 253: These lines of Anna Russell comprise the third verse of "Jolly Old Sigmund Freud," THE ANNA RUSSELL SONG BOOK, 1960, and are published by arrangement with The Carol Publishing Group.

Page 336: Excerpt from "Little Gidding" in FOUR QUARTETS, copyright 1943 by T. S. Eliot and renewed 1971 by Esme Valerie Eliot, reprinted by permission of Harcourt Brace & Company, and Faber and Faber Limited.

Library of Congress Cataloging-in-Publication Data

Gomes, Peter J.
    The good book : reading the Bible with mind and heart / Peter J. Gomes.
        p. (large print) cm.(Compass Press large print book series)
    ISBN 1-56895-451-4 (hardcover)
    1. Bible—Criticism, interpretation, etc.   2. Large type books.   I. Title.
II. Series
[BS511.2.G66   1997]
220.1—dc21   97-019159
                                                         CIP

TO

ARCHIE CALVIN EPPS III
OLDEST OF COLLEAGUES
CLOSEST OF FRIENDS

"A friend may well be reckoned the master-piece of nature."   —Ralph Waldo Emerson

Contents

APOLOGIA

SOME writers begin their books with an Introduction or a Preface, sometimes titled simply From the Author, in which the origins of the book are briefly stated, and something, but not so much as to make reading the book unnecessary, of its intentions disclosed, and necessary acknowledgments made. Such an opening is meant, in part at least, to attract the reader's attention, with the hope that what follows will sustain it, while giving something of the author's method, clearing away wrong expectations, and positioning a few useful clues and landmarks by which the reader may make way through a form of argument and prose which has become far too familiar to the author. Some readers routinely skip such introductory matter to get on to "it," the real heart of the book. I have been guilty of this, for I am one of those who, in driving, for instance, refuses, at least at first, to spend much time in consultation of a map. I am convinced that I can find my way on my own with just my common sense, my not always justified sense of direction, the urgent good intentions that tell me that I must or wish to get to my destination, and the naive faith that that is enough to get me there. I, and the waiting friends on the other side of my travels, have discovered over many years that this is not a sound system.

The front matter of a book is something of a road map. It tells the reader not only where the author intends to go but in some measure how the author wants the reader to get there, and why the journey is worth taking at all. Obviously such an enterprise is more than a mere map—it is also an explanation, a justification.

Secular readers will notice that this front matter bears a slightly unfamiliar title, and in a foreign language. I say "slightly unfamiliar," for even those with no Latin will recognize in the sonorous term *Apologia* something that looks remarkably like our word *apology*, and we all know what that is. Or do we? The third meaning in *The Oxford English Dictionary* comes closest to our unexamined sense of what an apology is: "an explanation offered to a person affected by one's action that no offense was intended." It is in this sense that we understand the remark attributed to the Duke of Wellington, "Never apologize, never explain." Charles I, who knew much of these things, said, "Never make a defense of apology before you be accused," and Ambrose Bierce, the cynical author, earlier in this century, of *The Devil's Dictionary*, said, "To apologize is to lay the foundations for a future offense." The best of these aphorisms about apologies in the popular meaning of the word is that of Elbert Hubbard, who advised, "Never explain: your friends do not need it, and your enemies will not believe it anyhow."

All of this notwithstanding, this is neither

the oldest sense of the apology nor the sense in which I use it. The oldest usages describe an apology, or *apologia*, as a formal argument to speak in defense of anything that may cause dissatisfaction. It is more explanation than excuse. It does not ask for pardon but rather seeks to offer light to those who may need it but may not want it. That is what an *apologia* is, and one who makes such an argument is known as an apologist.

There is a risk in embracing so ancient a term with such an ambiguous contemporary resonance to it. One thinks of hapless presidential press secretaries, usually called by critics "shameless apologists for the bankrupt policies of the present administration," and it doesn't take a degree in linguistics to recognize that apologists, in the evolution of the species, became public relations experts, then press officers, and now spin doctors, who, together with pollsters, have become the court astrologers of modern politics and industry. To begin one's work with the title *Apologia*, to call oneself an apologist, and to consider one's argument as an apology is at once to risk confusion and to court disaster.

Yet the term as I am using it has an ancient literary and specifically Christian lineage. *The New Dictionary of Christian Theology* defines apologetics in the history of Christian theology as "the defense, by argument, of Christian belief against external criticism or against other world views," and gives as an example of such apologetics Paul's sermon on Mars Hill, in Acts 17:22–31, in which he argued the Christian faith against the Greek secular philosophy. Saint Augustine's *The City of God*, written in reply to pagans who blamed the fall of Rome in a.d. 410 on the Christians, is counted as one of the most magisterial of apologetics. In modern times Paul Tillich and Hans K;auung are so styled, and it might be argued that Pope John Paul II's remarkably successful book, *Crossing the Threshold of Hope*, is a vivid example of a contemporary apologetic. Given such company I do not mind that Karl Barth was dogmatically opposed to all forms of apologetics, although, ironically, his works have seen considerable use as fodder in the apologetics of others.

My *apologia* is an argument in favor of taking the Bible seriously, and it is addressed in part at least to those who either trivialize it or idolize it, and who thereby miss its dynamic, living, and transforming quality. It is an argument addressed as well to those who are in search of spiritual and moral grounding in their chaotic lives, and who may have heard of the Bible but know little and want to know more. It is also an argument that condemns the lazy, simpleminded approach that many are tempted to take when considering the serious matter of Bible study and interpretation. Finally, it is also an invitation to enter into the Bible and to let it enter into us, all of us, and most particularly into those who have been excluded from the faith of the Bible by the use of the Bible. The summary of such an argument may be found in the aphorism of the early biblical scholar Bengel, who said, "Apply yourself closely to the text; apply the text closely to yourself." As my own new class of Harvard Divinity School students began New Testament studies now thirty-something years ago, we were instructed to write this on the flyleaf of our Bibles.

There is a certain inevitability about this book. Henry Ward Beecher used to tell of the Free Will Methodist preacher and the Predestinarian Presbyterian preacher who agreed to exchange pulpits. As they met on the road, each on the way to the other's pulpit, the Presbyterian said, "Brother, does it not give you pleasure and glory to God that before the earth itself was formed, we were destined in the mind of God to have this exchange this morning?" To which the Methodist replied, "Well, if that is so, then I ain't going," and he turned his horse around and went home. I know how he felt. We all want to feel that we are masters of our own fate, at least of our intellectual fate, but I know otherwise. I have been an apologist in the sense that I hope that I have rehabilitated scripture for general use for over twenty-five years. The day that I accepted duty as a Christian minister at "godless Harvard" I became one, and willingly, even gladly, for I was not ashamed of the gospel and wanted to present it with all its power to a time and a place that badly needed it. In my view, to be a Christian is by definition to be an apologist, for not only are you obliged to present your view to a world that is no longer, if it ever was, Christian, but people want to know why, in such a world, you would continue to hold allegiance to something so out of harmony with it. Conviction on the part of the Christian, and curiosity on the part of others, are essential ingredients in the apologetic for the faith. One offers one's own life as the immediate and ultimate "explanation," remembering that Christian truth is advanced not by postulates and formulas, the bone-crushing logic of arguments point and counterpoint, but in the living flesh of human beings. Jesus Christ remains the ultimate apologist for the faith not because of the sublime logic of his teaching but by the undaunted example of his life. I take enormous consolation in the precedent of one of the great apologists of the last century, John Henry Cardinal Newman, who in 1864 published his now classic autobiography under the title *Apologia pro Vita Sua—A Defense of His Life*.

This book began a very long time ago with the conviction that intelligent people seemed to know less and less about the Bible, and that religious people revered it and would defend it to the death but seldom read it with any industry or imagination. The fact that we preach regularly from the Bible to congregations that know so little about it means that we have a fundamental task of reeducation before we can relate the Bible to the world in which we live. This task is further complicated by the fact that the Bible has become an American cultural icon with enormous influence, both symbolic and substantial. Thus, for me, the Bible and the social and moral consequences that derive from its interpretation are all too important to be left in the hands of the pious or the experts, and too significant to be ignored and trivialized by the uninformed and indifferent.

The theme of this book is the risk and the joy of the Bible: risk in that we might get it wrong, and joy in the discovery of the living Word becoming flesh. It is around this theme that I formulate three basic questions which the thoughtful reader brings to the Bible: What is it? How is it used? What does it have to say to me? The three-part structure of the book is designed to address these questions. The first part, "Opening the Bible," is didactic; it discusses what the Bible is and how it came to be as it now is. The second part, "The Use and Abuse of the Bible," is more polemical. It is concerned with the interpretations of scripture, as well as with the reappropriation of scripture on the part of those who feel excluded from it. The third part, "The True and Lively Word," a phrase drawn from Thomas Cranmer's description of the Bible in the Book of Common Prayer, has a pastoral function and seeks to discover the relationship between the human condition and the biblical witness. This pastoral ambition, however, is not only the driving force behind this final section of the book but is the spirit that animates the whole book.

My debts are many, and yet responsibility falls fully to me. I am grateful to my publishers, and particularly to my editor, who had enough confidence in me and in the idea of this book to wait for it with the patience of Job and the perseverance of the Saints. I thank Will Schwalbe for his conscientious collaboration, his many trips to Cambridge, and his genuine interest in the substance of this book. I thank as well John Taylor Williams, the best of all literary agents, without whom none of this would have happened. A sabbatical leave of absence at Duke University Divinity School provided me with a season of refreshment, stimulation, and research, in addition to boundless hospitality. I thank Dean Dennis Campbell for his many kindnesses while I was his guest. I thank as well my Duke colleagues and friends William H. Willimon, Stanley Hauerwas, and Samuel DeWitt Proctor, whose conversation helped refine many an idea. The assistance of Donald Polanski at Duke was invaluable, and I remain ever grateful to him for the benefit of his extensive knowledge of the resources in the Duke library.

Closer to home, I thank the President and Fellows of Harvard College, by whose kind permission my leave of absence was taken. This book had its origins in the imagination of my colleague and friend Daniel Ayers Sanks, whose insistence on its writing is equaled only by his support along the detours: I owe him much. I owe a significant debt to Dr. Eugene Clifford McAfee, who joined this enterprise at its earliest stages and while pursuing his own academic work found time to help me. As a teaching colleague in the fields of Church History, Interpretation of Scripture, and Preaching, and as a friend, his worth to me is beyond measure. There would literally be no book without the consummate skills of Cynthia Wight Rossano, who prepared the final manuscript and all of its prior permutations, gave encouragement in moments of despair, and lavished upon me much for which I call her blessed.

My colleagues and congregation in The Memorial Church have borne my absences and fits of authorial despondency with great Christian forbearance, and they, more than anyone, will be relieved to see this project finally accomplished. I am grateful to all my friends, and record here and now my most especial appreciation to those friends who, after a decent interval, stopped asking me, "How's the book coming?" I owe a great debt of gratitude to my old and late friend and colleague, John Robert Marquand, long in the service of Harvard College. He knew of the earliest stages of this book and followed them with his characteristically keen and pungent interest. Much of this I did for him.

Finally, I must remember my mother, Orissa Josephine White Gomes, daughter of preachers, who first taught me the Bible, and the people of the First Baptist Church and the Bethel AME Church of Plymouth, Massachusetts, my first community of interpretation. In the end we are where we came from.

Johann Sebastian Bach used to write at the top of the first page of every new composition the Latin words *Soli Deo Gloria:* Glory to God Alone. I adopt his device as my own.

Peter J. Gomes
Sparks House
Cambridge, Massachusetts

The Good Book

PART ONE

OPENING THE BIBLE

"The study of the Bible is
the soul of theology."

CHAPTER 1

WHAT'S IT ALL ABOUT?

MANY years ago when I began my service as minister in Harvard's Memorial Church, an anonymous benefactor offered to present as many Bibles as were needed to fill the pews. No particular translation was specified, and no objections were made to the Revised Standard Version. Before proceeding too far along the road of this benefaction I felt it wise to take the advice of some colleagues, and I found their reaction to be apprehensive, and in fact quite suspicious of the motivation behind the gift. "What does the benefactor want or expect?" I was asked, and warned that placing Bibles in the pews would create an invitation to steal them. Further, I was warned that "people will think that this is a fundamentalist church. If they see Bibles in the pews you will have an image problem." My colleagues and counselors meant well, I knew, and wished only to protect the church from secular and religious zealots. These concerns notwithstanding, however, we accepted the gift, placed the Bibles in the pews, and, happily, over the years we have lost quite a few to theft.

One of the more embarrassing social situations, upon which even Miss Manners and other arbiters of social etiquette have failed to provide a useful strategy, is the one in which you have more than a nodding acquaintance with someone. At the point of introduction you got the person's name, forgot it, asked it again, and forgot it again. Meanwhile you go on meeting this person, chatting and being chatted with, but you have clearly passed beyond the point where you can ask for the name again. It is easy enough to maintain the facade of friendship until that awful moment comes when you are required to introduce your nameless friend to a third party. What to do? I have seen artful evasions such as "Surely you two know each other?" followed by a discreet withdrawal while they got on with the job themselves, leaving you unexposed. Another stratagem is to avoid the risk of introduction altogether by declaring emphatically, "Ah! Here's an old friend!" What we should know, pretend that we know, and wish that we knew, we don't. Worse still, we do not know, without risk of embarrassment, how to ask about what we need to know.

This, I suggest, is the way it is with so many people and the Bible. Once, perhaps a long time ago in childhood or in early youth, or even as late as in college, you were introduced. You have a nodding acquaintance with the Bible, or at least you feel you ought to, and you can recognize some familiar phrases, especially if they "sound" like the King James Version of the Bible; yet, to all intents and purposes, the Bible remains an elusive, unknown, slightly daunting book. It is awkward to concede that you don't know very much about the Bible, given its cultural prominence, and it is difficult to figure out how to get reintroduced without conceding your illiteracy. Perhaps the lament I have heard more and more frequently in recent years is the one that says, "I wish I knew more about the Bible."

Poll after poll continues to find the Bible atop every best-seller list, and one survey after another confirms the fact that an astonishingly high percentage of American households claims not only to own a Bible, but to read it on a regular basis. Hardly a hotel room in the world is without a copy of the Bible in the bedside table, placed there courtesy of the Gideons; and through the unremitting efforts of the Wycliffe Society the Bible has been translated into nearly every language on earth. There are Bibles for women, Bibles for children, Bibles for Asians, Bibles for African Americans. There are so many translations, paraphrases, revisions, and editions now available, many of which are the products of the last twenty years, that the market for the Bible may well be saturated. In the introduction to their 1983 study of twentieth-century English versions of the Bible, *So Many Versions?*, Sakae Kubo and Walter F. Specht observe, "Some people are of the opinion that there is a 'glut' of translations on the market today. Some feel it is time to call a halt to the work of translation for a while until we absorb the flood of recent translations."

Despite the ubiquity of the Good Book, it is increasingly clear that the rate of biblical literacy has gone down rather than up. A recent American poll conducted by the Barna Research Group discovered that 10 percent of the sample of more than one thousand persons polled said that Joan of Arc was Noah's wife, 16 percent were convinced that the New Testament contained a book by the Apostle Thomas, and 38 percent were of the view that both the Old and New Testaments were written a few years after Jesus' death. These replies are worthy of the old Sunday school howler in which the epistles are defined as the wives of the apostles. The president of the polling firm commented, "Clearly, most people don't know what to make of the Bible. Adults constantly gave us answers which contradicted or conflicted with previous replies." It is not that people lie about their knowledge of the Bible; it is that they often feel that in order to maintain their moral credibility they must reply in the affirmative when questioned by pollsters, since most believe that they ought to read it. Many of these modern Christians are much like the Emperor Charlemagne who, it is said, slept with a copy of Saint Augustine's magnum opus, *The City of God*, under his pillow in the hope that this passive proximity to a great but difficult work might be of some benefit to him.

Hearing the Bible in church presumably helps people become better acquainted with it. In fact, hearing the Bible in church was the way in which most Christians for a thousand years became familiar with scripture, and in most Christian churches today pride of place is still given to the reading of appointed passages from the Bible. In the Anglican and Protestant traditions these readings are called "lessons" because it is believed that they are not merely liturgical acts but have a moral teaching function as well. This tradition of hearing the Bible read aloud in public is as old as Christian worship. When Saint Paul instructs the Christians in the Corinthian church on a suitable order for worship, he tells them: "When you come together, each one has a hymn, a lesson, a revelation, a tongue, or an interpretation. Let all things be done for edification." (I Corinthians 14:26)

In my naïveté as a pastor I thought that this tradition of edification in church was alive and well until I once said as much to a regular churchgoer who every Sunday hears a psalm and at least two lessons, one from the Old Testament and one from the New Testament, and has done so for years. Her response caught me up short. She said that listening to the lessons in church was like eavesdropping on a conversation in a restaurant where the parties on whom you are listening in are speaking fluent French, and you are trying to make sense of what they are saying with your badly remembered French

101. You catch a few words and are intrigued, trying to follow, but after a while you lose interest, for the effort is too great and the reward too small. That is a pretty vivid image of a fairly common modern dilemma, and most people find themselves too embarrassed to confess that this is their situation. It used to be said that most Christian adults live their lives off a second-rate second-grade Sunday school education, and that the more they hear of the Bible in church, the less they feel they know about it.

Many people want to do something about their biblical illiteracy. There is something there that they feel they ought to know about, and yet they are frustrated in their attempts to read the Bible and to make sense of it for themselves. Because it is unlike any other book, reading the Bible is an intimidating enterprise for the average person. To remind the reader that the Bible is not a book but a library of books, written by many people in many forms over many years for many purposes, is to further complicate the ambition and add to the frustration. Bound in its authoritative black leather and gilt-edged pages, with, in some editions, the words of Jesus printed in red, the physical artifact of the Bible has a certain aura. Add to this the powers attributed to it, with its designation as "holy" and therefore suitable for use in oath-taking and in sanctifying proceedings both civil and sacred, and the Bible is much more easily reverenced than read.

It is not its status as an icon or holy object, however, that inhibits the reading of the Bible. It is the sense as well that the Bible is a technical book, requiring a level either of piety or of knowledge not available to the average reader. There are also admitted obstacles. What does a person who has no knowledge of the biblical languages, no formal theological training, and no experience in the very technical fields of translation and interpretation do with the Bible? An ancient answer was to submit oneself to those who did possess those qualities. The image of formative Christianity as a "Bible-centered community," one continual scripture seminar for the faithful, is an appealing one, but totally false. Saint Augustine, for example, opposed Saint Jerome's heroic project of translating the Greek Bible into the more accessible Latin because making the Bible more accessible would be more likely to cultivate a conceit on the part of those who, because they could understand the language, would now also assume that they could understand the book. Vernacular translations of the Bible were forbidden to those few premodern Christians who could read, and English translations of the Bible up to the time of King James's version of 1611 were generally regarded by the religious establishment as doing more harm than good.

Ironically, it was the tremendous explosion in scholarship about the Bible itself, an enterprise whose highest motivation was to make sense of the Bible and to clarify its complexities, that made it harder rather than easier for the average person to read the Bible with any degree of self-confidence. By the close of the nineteenth century, a period of unprecedented attention to the complexity of biblical scholarship, the frustration of the average reader was represented by no less a figure than Grover Cleveland. In some exasperation, the twenty-second and twenty-fourth president of the United States said, "The Bible is good enough for me, just the old book under which I was brought up. I do not want notes or criticisms or explanations about authorship or origins or even cross-references. I do not need them or understand them, and they confuse me."

A century later we can understand his frustration and his desire to return to what the scholars call a precritical stage, and in fact many have attempted to do just that. After all, we should not have to be a certified electrician in order to enjoy the benefits of the lightbulb.

Suppose, however, that that lightbulb does little to illumine the dark places in which we find ourselves in these last days of the twentieth century? What are we to do with a Bible about which we know less and less, and which itself would appear to have less and less to say to us in language that we can understand? The question is not a new one. In 1969, in a small book with the provocative title *The Strange Silence of the Bible in the Church*, James D. Smart addressed the gap between the fullness of modern biblical scholarship on the one hand,

and the poverty of biblical literacy on the other. In an America racked by the intensities of the struggle for civil rights, the battles of the counterculture, and the depredations of the Vietnam War, the Bible seemed unequal to the morally demanding times, and its silence was deafening. How could this be? In his Preface, Smart, a Presbyterian minister and biblical scholar, attempted an answer:

> Responsibility for this strange silence of the Bible in the church does not rest upon preachers alone. Much too often they have borne the whole reproach without there being any recognition of the complex character of the dilemma in which they find themselves. Rather, there had been a blindness which scholar, preacher, teacher, and layman alike have shared—a blindness to the complexity of the essential hermeneutical problem, which, in simple terms, is the problem of how to translate the full content of an ancient text into the language and life-context of late 20th century persons.

Contemporary Christians tend to avoid complexity as being hazardous to their faith, and are thus unprepared to cope with complexity when it confronts them. In April 1996, for example, all three major U.S. weekly newsmagazines featured Jesus as the cover story for Holy Week. What was the reason? This was hardly an outbreak of newsroom piety, but rather the "discovery" that scholars were debating yet

11

again the relationship between the Jesus of history and the Christ of faith, and that many of the words and actions attributed to Jesus in the New Testament were in fact, in the view of much of modern scholarship, the work of writers of the early Christian movement. "Some scholars are debunking the Gospels," ran *Time*'s cover headline. "Now traditionalists are fighting back. What are Christians to believe?"

I was asked by many sincere believers as well as by the vaguely curious what I thought of *Time*'s story. Would it do damage to the faith? Hardly. As the sign in the old antique shop reads: nothing new here. Questions about the nature of the gospels and of their place in the life of the church are as old as the gospels themselves. Questions about the resurrection are as old as the Apostle Paul's writings on the subject. These are matters that have always belonged to the church, and always will. *Time*'s discovery of Christianity's two-thousand-year-old debate suggests only how far *Time* is removed from the intellectual life of biblical scholarship. But alas, the story also revealed the large gap between the basic working assumptions of biblical scholarship long held by the scholarly community and the conventional wisdom or general knowledge of a less and less biblically literate Christian population. To make a story there must be winners and losers. The not too subtle implication of this Holy Week Special is that what the scholars believe they know and what the believers believe they believe are seen to be at odds, and if the scholars are right, then the believers must be wrong, and the Christian faith folds like a house of cards.

What Are We Doing?

What can be believed about the Bible? What do we need to know about the Bible? Can the Bible survive the efforts to interpret and understand it? Can we? Is it wrong to ask critical questions of the Bible? How do we reconcile the parts we understand, and perhaps dislike, with the parts we do not understand but which may be salutary? When we speak of the authority of scripture, as certain Protestant traditions delight in doing, does that mean that we suspend all of those faculties of mind and intelligence which we apply to all other books and all other instances of our life? How indeed do we, as James Smart suggested, "translate the full content of an ancient text into the language and life-context of late 20th century persons" without risking our intelligence or the integrity of that text?

Over the years of my ministry in a university and well beyond it, I have come to the conclusion that most sincere Christians are curious in these matters, unlike Grover Cleveland, and want to become better acquainted with the Bible. I am further convinced that the more importance one attaches to the significance of the Bible both for the self and for society, the more one is driven to a consideration of questions which in an earlier day might either have been ignored or left to the competence of the experts. As making sense has as much to do with formulating useful questions as it has to do with developing useful answers, the thoughtful but uninformed reader will want to know how to go about doing both.

The Episcopal Church, while not known as a "Bible" church in the sense of those evangelical and free churches that advertise themselves as such, nevertheless exposes its worshipers to a great deal of scripture on Sunday mornings. There is a movement to do something about biblical literacy among what one social historian of the Episcopal Church has called "God's frozen people." *Understanding the Sunday Scriptures,* a release of Synthesis Publications, is designed to provide help to people who have finally reached the awareness that they need it. The Reverend Dr. H. King Oehmig, editor of the first volume in a series on the Episcopal lectionary, says of it, "The Episcopal Church has more scripture on Sunday than any other denomination in America. After listening to the desires of the people in the pews for a responsible yet inspiring study resource to prepare them to hear the Word on Sunday morning, we have produced this unique resource."

The United Methodist Church, America's second-largest Protestant denomination after the Southern Baptists, is also attempting to respond to the felt needs of biblical literacy. It has produced not only a series of books and study aids but a series of films utilizing the most sophisticated of contemporary biblical scholarship. When I asked some Methodist pastors how this worked, nearly all of them were pleased with the results in their churches. The study program is organized into small groups that pledge to meet during the week for nine months, and are meant as bonding fellowships as well as study groups, designed to combine the best elements of the old adult Sunday school class, the Methodist class meeting, the prayer meeting, and the support groups that have become the local units of our secular therapeutic culture. Apparently these groups help in developing a better knowledge of the Bible, and provide an informed lay leadership which enriches the work and the life of the local congregation at the same time. As one of the pastors said to me, "The church is in bad shape when the only person who knows anything about the Bible is the pastor."

These are clearly new initiatives taken to meet what is generally recognized to be the crisis of biblical illiteracy. We might well ask how this illiteracy came to be, given that the Bible has always had pride of place in Christian worship and particularly in American Protestantism, but any of us who have had experience of what passes for "Bible study" in recent years in most churches can answer that question. For many the Bible served as some sort of spiritual or textual trampoline: You got onto it in order to bounce off of it as far as possible, and your only purpose in returning to it was to get away from it again. It is the lay version of what Willard Sperry, one of my predecessors in The Memorial Church, used to lampoon as "textual preaching." The preacher who was keen to practice what he preached would follow this formula: "Take your text, depart from your text, never return to your text."

Bible studies tend to follow this route. The Bible is simply the entry into a discussion about more interesting things, usually about oneself. The text is a mere pretext to other matters, and usually the routine works like this: A verse or a passage is given out, and the group or class is asked, "What does this mean to you?" The answers come thick and fast, and we are off into the life stories or personal situations of the group, and the session very quickly takes the form of Alcoholics Anonymous, Twelve-Step meetings, or other exercises in healing and therapy. I do not wish to disparage the very good and necessary work that these groups perform, for I have seen too many good effects and have known too many beneficiaries of such encounter and support groups to diminish by one iota their benefit both to individuals and to the community. I simply wish to say that this is not Bible study, and to call it such is to perpetuate a fiction.

Bible study actually involves the study of the Bible. That involves a certain amount of work, a certain exchange of informed intelligence, a certain amount of discipline. Bible study is certainly not just the response of the uninformed reader to the uninterpreted text, but Bible study in most of the churches has become just that— the blind leading the blind or, as some caustic critics of liberal Protestantism would put it, the bland leading the bland. The notion that texts have meaning and integrity, intention, contexts, and subtexts, and that they are part of an enormous history of interpretation that has long involved some of the greatest thinkers in the history of the world, is a notion often lost on those for whom the text is just one more of the many means the church provides to massage the egos of its members.

Opening the Bible is the easy part. What to do with it once it is opened is more difficult. At the start of Lent each year, when the time for taking up a Lenten discipline is upon us, invariably a number of people will tell me that they intend to read the Bible from cover to cover. They mean to start at Genesis 1:1 and stop when they get to Revelation 22:21. The enterprise is not as easy as it sounds, and people begin to waver in their resolve when their expectations of narrative inspiration are not sustained by genealogies, codes of Jewish law, and ancient Jewish history. The New Testament is somewhat easier to digest, in part because it is smaller and its subject more easily identified as Jesus and the early church. Nevertheless, it is not always clear what is going on in the Acts of the Apostles; the expectation that the letters of Paul provide a systematic correspondence is often disappointing; and while they find it fascinating, not many know what to make of the book of Revelation. Those who get through usually feel as if they have run a marathon, where the object of the course is to finish and not necessarily to observe the landscape along the way. Those who do not cross the finish line often feel like moral failures

17

who have broken their diet or fallen off the wagon and taken a forbidden drink.

The risks of discouragement notwithstanding, I think there is something to be said for taking on the Bible in this way. It is a bit like total immersion in a foreign language; eventually, if you stick with it, you will get some sense of what is going on, you will see and feel the shapes of the language, and you will acquire a sense of those places to which you wish to return, and those places you wish to avoid. This is not a bad thing.

The Construction of Scripture

The Bible, however, is more than an endurance contest, and one may know better how to make a useful reading of it if one has a sense of what the Bible actually is. At the risk of appearing to offend those who already know what they need to know in this regard, I begin by stressing the fact that the Bible is not a book but a collection of books, in fact, a library of books. Sixty-six separate books have been collected from the writings of ancient Hebrews and early Christians, and by a rational editorial process have been brought together over a period of centuries to form the book we now know as the Bible. The first thing the reader must remember upon encountering the Bible is that it is a result or consequence of a complex process that is both human and divine. The relationship between the human and the divine in this process is an intimate one. These are writings by human beings who are themselves believed to have been inspired by God. It is further believed that it is by the inspiration of God that human agency is given the wisdom and the will to organize these books, and it is believed that through these books the divine word of God is to be communicated. Thus it is not sufficient explanation of the Bible to say simply that it is either the Word of God or "merely" a human book, such as *The Iliad* or *The Odyssey*. The Jews who gathered together these books from a whole range of their writings and called them "scripture" did so in the firm conviction that God spoke through these human writings, and that these human writings brought the people of God nearer to God. Thus, when they call the first five books of the Hebrew scriptures— known as the Pentateuch—the Books of Moses, they mean that here Moses speaks of his understanding of God, and through Moses God speaks to his people.

Although Hebrew scripture takes different forms—poetry, history, law, and wisdom—the subject is always the same: the relationship between God's people and their God. The human element in this relationship is significant and important to understand, for scripture is always understood to be a human response to the initiative of God. The scripture of the Jewish people does not simply record historical facts, but by its interpretation of history, the Jewish scripture seeks to ask and to answer the fundamental questions of human existence. Who am I? Why am I here? What is the purpose of life? What does it mean to be good? What is evil, and how do I deal with it? How do I deal with death? These are both individual questions and, with regard to the Jewish people, also public and communal questions. It must never be forgotten that it is a community of people chosen, beloved, and willful, to whom the Law, for example, is given, to whom the land is promised, and to whom a future is offered. The sacred literature of the Jewish people reflects this conviction, and that literature is therefore regarded as sacred because God is seen to be revealed in it. The determination, however, of what is sacred and what is scripture is a human and rational enterprise, and it tells us as much about the people of God as it tells us about God. As Wilfred Cantwell Smith points out in his book, *What Is Scripture?*, "Scripture is a human, and an historical fact. We may say: it is a human, and therein an historical, fact intimately involved with the movement, the unceasingly changing specificity of historical process, its grandeur and its folly."

Thus the narrative history of Genesis, the legislative tedium of Leviticus, the books of history—Samuel, Chronicles, and Kings—the lyrical book of Psalms, the salacious, to some, Song of Solomon, the saga of Job, the wisdom of Proverbs, and the salutary story of Esther are all regarded as authoritative and inspired because each in its own way has been proven useful in the people's attempt to understand themselves and their relationship to God. The Hebrew Bible is not merely a book of history or a book of devotion but a library of writings of proven worth, self-consciously composed, collected, and preserved as the repository of wisdom both human and divine. These writings reveal both the nature of the people who wrote and collected them, and the nature of their God. These writings are of course not God, and the writings themselves are not substitutes for God. That would be a violation of the first commandment, which forbids idolatry and false gods.

The Hebrew Bible is organized somewhat differently from what Christians call the Old Testament. The first five books are called The Law. The Prophets are divided into The Former Prophets, which include Joshua, Judges, Samuel, and Kings, The Latter Prophets, composed of Isaiah, Jeremiah, and Ezekiel, and those prophets called The Twelve, comprising Hosea, Joel, Amos, Obadiah, Jonah, Micah, Nahum, Habakkuk, Zephaniah, Haggai, Zechariah, and Malachi. The third and final section of the Hebrew Bible is called simply The Writings, and includes Psalms, Proverbs, Job, the Song of Songs, Ruth, Lamentations, Ecclesiastes, Esther, Daniel, Ezra, Nehemiah, and Chronicles. This authoritative listing is referred to as a canon and evolved between a.d. 70 and 135 into its present form by a process of rabbinical councils. When Jesus refers to the Scripture, and New Testament Jewish Christians speak of the Law and the Prophets, it is this Bible of which they speak.

When the early Christians, many of whom were Jewish, came to understand the Hebrew Bible as the necessary anticipation of their own Gospel, they reorganized the Hebrew Bible into four large categories: History, Poetry, the Major Prophets, and the Minor Prophets. Thus the elements of the Hebrew Bible were reconfigured into an "old" testament, which together with the authoritative Christian writings, the "new" testament, comprised the Christian Bible. The Christian scriptures were chosen from a wide range of early Christian writings, and the final product, the present canon, represents the consensus of usage and dignity confirmed by the earliest churches in a.d. 367. The New Testament is not arranged in chronological order. For example, all of the epistles of Saint Paul are older than any of the gospels. Recent scholarship places the Epistle of James as first by date, followed by I Thessalonians. To read the New Testament in chronological order is not necessarily superior to reading it in its canonical order, but it does allow us to follow the construction of the New Testament, and it reminds us once again that the New Testament is also the product of a self-conscious, human, and rational set of decisions. The canonical structure of the New Testament consists of History, which contains the four gospels and the Book of Acts; the Epistles of Paul, both those by him and those attributed to him; the General

Epistles; and in a category all by itself, the Apocalypse, or the Revelation of John.

The Apocrypha is a category of books that tends to confuse most Protestants unfamiliar with the construction of the Bible and the political implications of its various translations and editions. The books in the Apocrypha are those books and fragments that do not appear in the Hebrew Bible but which were placed into the Latin Vulgate as part of the Old Testament. These books were to be found in the Septuagint, the Greek version of the Hebrew Bible, but did not end up in the Hebrew canon. The Roman Catholic tradition regards these books as part of the canon, and since 1546, by decree of the Council of Trent, anathematizes anyone who says otherwise. Luther placed the Apocrypha between the two Testaments, and the English translations, while acknowledging that the apocryphal books were extra-canonical, found them to be useful and instructive. The Puritans decided that the Apocrypha was not inspired and thus removed it from their Bibles, and most modern editions of the King James Version, following the Puritan influence, exclude the Apocrypha, as do most of the newer English versions. The New English Bible, however, and of course versions approved for use by Roman Catholics, include it.

The place of the Bible in Christian theology is a subject of some complexity and goes back to the earliest debates of the forming Christian churches as to whether scripture or tradition took precedence in the determination of faith and practice. The dominance of the Bible in the Protestant traditions, particularly that part of Protestantism known as the Reformed Tradition, and in more modern times, the Evangelical branch of Protestantism, has generated what is generally known as a "high view" of scripture. This view has generated a number of slogans, which themselves are decidedly nonbiblical but which nevertheless convey certain doctrinal convictions by which the Bible is understood. The most famous of these is Luther's *sola scriptura*, which means "by scripture alone." Under this view, scripture itself is the sole sufficient rule of conduct and belief for the Christian. Another principle, which is derived from this one, is the "authority of scripture," and it is to that authority that the church and its members must submit. The scripture in this context is viewed very much like the federal Constitution of the United States, except, of course, that it cannot be amended.

Various other slogans designed to affirm the primacy of scripture actually in some cases make it harder to take scripture seriously. For example, in order to defend the integrity of scripture, some will say that either *all* is true, or *all* is false. This is meant to discourage picking and choosing from scripture the things that we like as opposed to the things that we dislike, but it strains credulity, and indeed the function of scripture, to argue that the Ten Commandments must be received in exactly the same fashion as the Song of Solomon, or that the Levitical Holiness Code is for Christians of the same order as the Beatitudes from Jesus' Sermon on the Mount. Critics of the Bible are quick to point to the implausible parts, the petty anthropology attributed to the Hebrew God, for example, or Jonah and the fish, or the dubious morality by modern standards of certain of the patriarchs and kings of Israel, and on this basis argue that the morality of the Bible and its claims to authority are either suspect or irrelevant. The "all true or all false" argument works both to defend scripture and to defame it, and as a principle of interpretation probably does more harm than good.

In the next chapter we will discuss in more detail the question of interpretation. What we suggest now, however, are some broad principles which the reader of the Bible ought to bear in mind in becoming more familiar with the shape and content of scripture. These have to do with the character of the Bible, which is public, dynamic, and inclusive.

A Public Book

When I say that the Bible is public, I mean to say that it is a treasure that is held in common, it belongs to the community of believers and not to any one individual or to any one part of the community of believers. The Bible may have its private uses, and it may be used privately and as a source of great strength in private devotion, but its fundamental identity is as a resource, a treasure for the people. In the sacramental sense which Christians recognize from the Communion Service, the Bible too is the "gift of God for the people of God." It is a very public record of the relationship between these people and their God, meant to be heard, understood, and remembered. When we realize the oral origins of scripture, and the fact that in the days before general literacy the only way that people became acquainted with the Bible was to hear it in the company of others, read aloud by one who could do so, then we realize that like the ancient tales of Homer and the histories of Greece and Rome, these were public stories that communicated public truths in the most public of ways. Even today in the churches of Christendom pride of place in the public liturgy is given to the public reading and hearing of the Bible.

The internal architecture of sacred space says it all. There is nearly always a splendid lectern upon which the book is placed, not simply for efficiency but for display as well. On the altar the gospel book is given a place of great honor, and in certain liturgical traditions the reading of the gospel is made all the more public and grand by a ceremonial procession of the book so that it can be read in the body of the church, and all turn toward it as it passes in procession. The pulpit itself is meant to be the place in which the public nature of the Bible is given its most explicit expression. A sermon that does not attempt to address the Bible is in fact not a sermon.

The public nature of the Bible is meant to have an impact upon public life. Again, it is not a secret of private vocation but a public proclamation of what can be discerned of God's intentions for the creation from the witness and testimony of scripture. People should not be surprised, therefore, that Christians always want to translate their understanding of scripture and its demands into the public lives that Christians lead. The Bible is meant to play a role in society, as are Christians. This public dimension of the Bible invariably produces conflict, even in allegedly homogeneous Christian societies, and certainly in secular and pluralistic societies. This, however, is a conflict responsible Christians cannot avoid, and the working out of the proper relationship between the public dimensions of one's biblical faith and one's citizenship in a community that does not necessarily share or appreciate that faith is part of the inevitable and uneasy burden that every responsible Christian must shoulder. The early Christian martyrs would have lived to ripe old ages had they not found it necessary to proclaim their biblical convictions in public. To try to create a "Christian society" where there is no risk to the public nature of the Bible and the faith that cherishes it is a form of arrogant escapism. The Bible is a public book, and as such will always give offense. Christians who take the Bible and themselves seriously have to be prepared for that.

A Living Text

The second thing to be remembered about the Bible, as we proceed in our thinking about it, is that it is dynamic, living, alive, lively. "For the word of God is living and active, sharper than a two-edged sword, piercing to the division of soul and spirit, or joint and marrow, and discerning the thoughts and intentions of the heart." (Hebrews 4:12) This means that behind the letter of the text is the spirit that animates it, the force that gave it and gives it life. Thus there is something always elusive about the Bible. This fixed text has a life of its own, which the reader cannot by some simple process of reading capture as his or her own. The dynamic quality of scripture has to do with the fact that while the text itself does not change, we who read that text do change; it is not that we adapt ourselves to the world of the Bible and play at re-creating it as in a pageant or tableau "long ago and far away." Rather, it is that the text actually adapts itself to our capacity to hear it. Thus we hear not as first-century Christians, nor even as eighteenth-century Christians, but as men and women alive here and now. We hear the same texts that our ancestors heard but we hear them not necessarily as they heard them, but as only we can. Thus the reading and the hearing of scripture are for Christians in each generation a Pentecostal experience. That experience is described in the Book of Acts as the great moment when the Holy Spirit descended upon the great and diverse crowd of believers in Jerusalem. The writer of Acts goes to great lengths to describe the diversity of that crowd, people from all over the known world who had little in common but Jerusalem as the object of the pilgrimage. They all were filled with the Holy Spirit, and began to speak in tongues.

Now often the emphasis here is placed on the ecstatic utterance, the Spirit-filled glossolalia, the exotic sounds of people under an extraordinary spell. Anyone who has ever experienced an outbreaking of speaking in tongues knows the exotic nature of that experience. What must be emphasized, however, and what is in fact the point of the writer of Acts, is that the people understood what was going on, and even more to the point, they understood in their own languages: not a paraphrase, not a delayed interpretation, not even a translation; they understood in their own languages. "We hear them telling in our own tongues," says the writer of Acts in Chapter 2, verse 11, "the mighty works of God."

The dynamic aspect of the Bible has to do with this quality of communication—not simply out of context or beyond context, but within our own singular and unique context—of the timeless and the timely message of the Bible. Christians believe that this dynamic quality is attributable directly to the power of the Holy Spirit, the agent of Pentecost. In other words, all our scholarship and research, our linguistic and philological skills, the tools of every form of criticism available to us, are merely means by which the living spirit of the text is taken from one context and appropriated totally into ours. The history of interpretation, perhaps the most useful field in which to study the dynamic dimension of scripture, bears witness to this in every age. In this sense, then, scripture is both transformed and transformative; that is to say, our understanding of what it says and means evolves, and so too do we as a result. This transformation does not always repudiate what was before, but it does always transcend it. The Buddhists say, "Seek not to follow in the footsteps of the men of old; rather, seek what they sought." To understand the dynamic aspect of scripture, we must appreciate the fact that "what they sought" seeks us, and in fact, "what they sought" is apprehendable to us in terms and times that we can best understand. So in the Bible we handle lively things, which means that we must be subtle, supple, and modest, all at the same time.

An Inclusive Word

The third and final landmark for those on this pilgrimage, in which we try to make sense of the Bible, is the fact that in addition to being both public and dynamic, the Bible is also inclusive. That is to say, it has the power to draw all people unto itself. Historically, we see the ever-widening circle of the Bible's appeal, and we can perhaps explain that by the cultural developments that moved out and beyond the provincial Mediterranean origins of the Bible into the Greco-Roman world, and then into the West, and then throughout the whole world. That, however, is simply a map maker's view of the matter. What is more significant to observe, and indeed more profound, is the fact that people and cultures foreign to the people and cultures of the Bible find themselves drawn to the Bible and understand it not as somebody else's book made available to them as an act of charity, conquest, or missionary endeavor, but as their own book, theirs legitimately and on their own terms. In the story of the Jewish patriarchs, non-Jews see themselves. In God's particular activity in Jesus Christ, people beyond the little world of primitive Jewish Christianity see themselves and their story included in God's activity. When in John's gospel (John 10:16) Jesus says, "And I have other sheep, that are not of this fold; I must bring them also, and they will heed my voice. So there shall be one flock, one shepherd," this is a great mandate for inclusivity which these "other sheep" recognize. As Jesus himself included among his own companions winebibbers, prostitutes, men and women of low degree, people who by who they were, by what they did, or from where they were excluded, so too does the Bible claim these very people as its own.

It is one of the unbecoming but unavoidable ironies of Christianity that Gentile Christians, who were excluded from the Jewish churches, and who in the times of the Roman persecution were themselves excluded from all hope in this life, should themselves become the arch practitioners of exclusion. Even centuries of Christian exclusivism, however, extending into our very own day, cannot diminish the inclusive mandate of the Bible, and the particular words of Jesus when he says, "Come unto me, all ye that labor and are heavy laden, and I will give you rest." What Roman Catholic social theory teaches as the church's "preferential option for the poor," to the annoyance of Christians rich in the things of this world, is the same principle that extends the hospitality of the Bible, indeed preferential hospitality, to those who have in fact been previously and deliberately excluded. So the Bible's inclusivity is claimed by the poor, the discriminated against, persons of color, homosexuals, women, and all persons beyond the conventional definitions of Western civilization.

The Bible is not inclusive simply in the abstract and in principle. It is inclusive in particular. Your story is written here, your sins and fears addressed, your hopes confirmed, your experiences validated, and your name known to God. The most reassuring conviction of the witness of scripture is that we are known by our own names. In Hebrew's 2:12, Jesus says, "I will proclaim thy name to my brethren," and the most telling moment of John's account of the resurrection is when the risen Christ addresses the distraught and confused Mary Magdalene by her own name, and in hearing her name called, she discovers who the risen one is.

One of the great paradoxes of race in America is the fact that the religion of the oppressor, Christianity, became the religion of the oppressed and the means of their liberation. Black Muslims ask incredulously how any black person in America could possibly be a Christian, given the legacy of white Christianity. The answer, of course, is that if Christianity in America depended upon white Christians, there would be no right-minded black Christians. What is the case is that Christianity, and the Bible in particular, did not depend upon Christians for its gospel of inclusion, but upon God. Thus black American Christians do not regard their Christianity as the hand-me-down religion of their masters, or an unnatural culture imposed upon them and thus a sign of their continuing servitude. No! They understand themselves to be Christians in their own right because the Gospel, the good news out of which the Bible comes, includes them and is in fact meant for them. We will find that when we look at the life of the Bible, and the life of the world in which it is to be found, we discover that the heart of its public dimension, and indeed the source of its dynamism, is this principle of inclusion by which all of the exclusive divisions of this world are transcended and transformed.

In thinking about the Bible—its public nature, its dynamic, living qualities, and its inclusivity—as we try to make sense of it with mind and heart, we would do well to remember these three principal characteristics. They serve as landmarks, points of departure and of return, and they will guide us even as we seek guidance in opening the Bible.

2

A MATTER OF INTERPRETATION

TO read is to interpret. When one is reading the Bible, interpretation is as risky as it is unavoidable, and it is not just trendy theologians or liberal Christian bishops who get into trouble over its interpretation. In a debate in the Israeli Parliament in December 1995, Foreign Minister Shimon Peres said that he disapproved of some of the practices of King David, particularly of his conquest of other peoples, and his seduction of a married woman, Bathsheba, whose husband, Uriah the Hittite, David sent to his death. In I Kings 15:5, it is written that David "did what was right in the sight of Yahweh and did not turn aside from anything that he commanded him all the days of his life, except in the matter of Uriah the Hittite." According to an account in *The New York Times* of December 15, 1995, outraged Orthodox rabbis screamed at the foreign minister to "shut up." Another shouted, "You will not give out grades to King David!" A third man flew into such a rage of apoplexy that he had to be treated for hypertension in the parliamentary infirmary, and a motion was introduced condemning the government for having besmirched the "sweet psalmist of Israel."

Earlier in the year the same rabbis had been outraged, and again over remarks about King David's sexual activity, but this time their fury was directed at a female member of Parliament, the daughter of the late Moshe Dayan, who read from II Samuel 1:26, in which David says of Jonathan, the son of Saul, "Very pleasant hast thou been unto me. Thy love to me was wonderful, passing the love of a woman." The homosexual implication was clear, and even more clearly denounced by the Orthodox parliamentarians. Despite what the Bible says, the rabbis have declared that King David was holy, "and," said one very prominent rabbi, head of the Education Ministry's Torah Culture Department, "whoever says that King David sinned does nothing but err."

To read is to interpret. This is neither an esoteric nor a subtle point, but when it comes to the reading and interpretation of the Bible it is a point that cannot be made too often or too clearly. A text may have a life of its own, but that life depends upon the author who gave it life, investing it with an intention, a purpose, and a meaning. The text therefore already participates in something other than itself; it participates in, and at least initially gives expression to, the intent of the author. To tease out the relationship of the text and its author is a responsible task, but that of course is not the only task of reading, for there is also whatever the reader brings to and finds in the text, and eventually takes from the text. This relationship among author, text, and reader is known in the literary trade as the "interpretive triangle," and since readers seldom read in isolation, and since texts, especially sacred or religious texts, are generally held in community, the interpretive triangle itself has a context, a set of circumstances that surround it and to which it responds. This context we call the "community of interpretation." Were we to visualize what we have just described, we would have a triangle within a circle within a square, a strange-looking device, which, like the symbols in mathematics, allows us to represent a process that itself is invisible and so fundamental as almost to be missed.

For most people, and despite centuries of sophisticated biblical scholarship, the precritical view of the Bible remains: a book in two parts, or testaments, old and new, which is meant to be, in the argot of the late twentieth century, "an owner's manual" for living the Christian life. It is of the same character as any of the other basic reference books available to us, and to be used in much the same way as we would use dictionaries, encyclopedias, telephone books, and other helpful compendia designed to get us through life. What *The Old Farmer's Almanack* was to nineteenth-century Yankee farmers, and *The Sears Roebuck Catalog* to their far-western cousins on the plains, the Bible was to the Christian. Often, in households where there were few books to be found, the Bible and one of these two would constitute the family's library. Many will say, "What's wrong with that?," and we can make for ourselves many arguments in favor of the simple virtues and values that issued forth from such households. These were the books, perhaps along with Bunyan's *The Pilgrim's Progress,* that made our country great. When the pastor of my boyhood church in Plymouth, Massachusetts, described himself as "preaching from the book that the Pilgrims brought" in the *Mayflower,* he didn't mean a commentary or a concordance or a volume of criticism, he meant the Bible, and in the Geneva translation. It is an interesting fact, and plentifully documented, that the Pilgrims brought many books with them in addition to the Bible, and many of these were in fact commentaries and books of biblical criticism and interpretation. As we shall see, the English Protestants loved their Bible, but they also loved books about their Bible, which tale we will defer to another place in this study.

Do We Really Need to Know All This?

Biblical criticism has a very bad name. The very term *criticism* implies a clinical disrespect and disregard for something of worth and value. Criticism means finding fault, taking apart, destroying. Whoever heard of a film critic who liked what he saw, or a book of criticism that edified anyone other than the critics? The critic sets himself up as an arbiter and expert, and from his lofty perch tells people either what they should think or that what they do think really isn't so. Criticism undermines our confidence in the thing criticized and, even more, our confidence in our own judgments and tastes.

Second only to lawyers we despise the critic, and our literature is filled with invective against them and their trade. Henry Fielding, the eighteenth-century novelist and author of the bawdy *Tom Jones,* must have got some bad reviews, for he said, "In reality, the world have played too great a compliment to critics, and have imagined them men of much greater profundity than they really are."

Alfred, Lord Tennyson, called the critic a "louse in the locks of literature"; Ernest Hemingway called them "eunuchs of literature."

The criticism of criticism and of critics is a rich field. Although critics could be left to do their worst in the pastures of high culture, when they applied their methods and opinions to that which by right belonged to the people, to the Bible, they invited a violent negative reaction which true popular piety made legitimate. When after years of study and research the Revised Standard Version of the Bible was issued in 1953—the product, as it was believed by many critical of it, of a century or more of the higher criticism—it was said by those who believed in an infallible text that fallible men, the revisers, were not competent to alter an infallible text: the King James Version.

Even an infallible text requires interpretation, however. One of the most helpful new books in the field of biblical interpretation is *Introduction to Biblical Interpretation,* written in 1993 by

William Klein, Craig Blomberg, and Robert Hubbard, all three of whom are professors in Denver Seminary and from an evangelical tradition. They believe the "Bible to be God's written revelation to his people," and that "it records in human words what God desires." Their work is endorsed by an impressive list of scholars who share many of their theological and interpretive presuppositions about the role of the Bible in the life of the church. One of these says, "Discovering what God really means is a matter of life and death. Understanding what the Bible says to us at the end of the twentieth century will be easier because of their work."

The authors acknowledge the difficulty of the task before them. How can one interpret a Bible "full of alien genealogies, barbaric practices, strange prophecies, and eccentric epistles"? While we might like a Bible that is simpler to deal with, perhaps a list of principles, or a straightforward narrative, or a collection of aphorisms, we are stuck—my word, not theirs—with the Bible as it is.

"As it is," however, presents some significant tensions, if not out and out problems, in reading and interpretation. Citing Moises Silva's *Has the Church Misread the Bible?*, they face the problem:

> The Bible is divine, yet it has come to us in human form. The commands of God are absolute, yet the historic context of the writings appears to relativize certain elements. The divine message must be clear, yet many

passages seem ambiguous. We are dependent only on the Spirit for instruction, yet scholarship is surely necessary. The Scriptures seem to presuppose a literal and historical reading, yet we are also confronted by the figurative and nonhistorical, e.g., parables. Proper interpretation requires the interpreter's personal freedom, yet some degree of external, corporate authority appears imperative. The objectivity of the biblical message is essential, yet our presuppositions seem to inject a degree of subjectivity into the interpretive process.

These issues reflect the history of the interpretation of the Bible. *Hermeneutics* is the technical term for the discipline of interpretation, and the history of interpretation is how people in various ages and from various traditions have come to terms with the complexities that these assumptions and concerns represent. If we are going to attempt to understand the Bible "as it is," we are going to have to make the effort to understand how it came to be "as it is."

Who Needs Interpretation?

We do. It is impossible to avoid. The earliest Christians were forced to engage in an act of interpretation of colossal importance when they had to figure out how to reconcile their scriptures, the Hebrew Bible, with the most significant event that had happened to them, the resurrection of Jesus. For orthodox Jews, the resurrection of Jesus was an event outside of scripture and impossible to reconcile with scripture as they read it. Those who followed Jesus and believed him to be resurrected from the dead were regarded as discontinuous with scripture, and indeed as blasphemers and heretics. The debate in Paul's letter to the Romans is not so much about whether the Jews can be saved under the cross, but about whether Jews who believed in Jesus were Jews at all, and heirs of the promises to Abraham. Thus, when in the writings of the early Christians scripture is mentioned, that scripture is of course the Hebrew scripture, the only Bible that Jesus, Paul, and the earliest disciples and apostles would have known. The first hermeneutical task, therefore, was to reconcile the transforming event of Jesus' resurrection with the body of scripture and with those who interpreted it.

There were two options available. One was to regard Jesus and his teaching, now seen through the experience of the resurrection, as discontinuous with the Hebrew scripture. A new order of reality had been created which was out of harmony with, and therefore superior to, the old. To be a follower of Jesus was to repudiate Moses. The other option was to see in Jesus the fulfillment of all that had been promised and expected in Hebrew scripture and Jewish prophecy. Thus Jesus is not antithetical to Moses; he is the successor to Moses and to all of the prophets, and it is therefore through the apparent discontinuity of the experience of Jesus that we are able to make sense both of Jesus and of

Hebrew scripture. The "formed" or "formal" scripture, as we can at this time call Hebrew scripture, is reconciled to the new experience of Jesus in the minds of those for whom that experience has become definitive, and their writings on this subject, what we may begin to call the "forming" scriptures, become the New Testament. To make this point more clear, it is fair to describe the New Testament as a Christian commentary on the Old Testament, a commentary that does not simply reconcile one to the other but appropriates the Old as its own. Thus, to the question about that body of scripture known as the Hebrew Bible—"Whose Bible is it, anyway?"—the Christian answer becomes an emphatic "Ours!" It is Augustine who puts it most succinctly: "What was concealed in the Old is revealed in the New." The New Testament itself is the product of an early and radical hermeneutic.

This may sound too technical and too polemical at first blush, but most Christians have for so long adapted to this phenomenon of the appropriation of Hebrew scripture as our own that only when the liturgical fashion of just a few years began to refer to the Old Testament as Hebrew scripture, or the Hebrew Bible, did we begin to ask if it was theirs or ours, and how it could be both. When I asked my students this question—"Whose book is it, anyway?"—referring to the Old Testament, I got blank stares; and then I asked the class to listen to excerpts from perhaps the most famous piece of choral music in the world, the *Messiah* of George Frideric Handel. Immediately they got a very clear picture of prophecy and fulfillment, which is what Handel's librettist, Charles Jennens, intended. It is virtually impossible to dislodge the prophecies of Isaiah from the fulfillments of the Gospel, and for some, even the notion is heretical that one could consider such a possibility. Yet that fusion, that construction, if you will, is indeed a matter of interpretation.

There are many devout and sincere Christians for whom the notion of interpretation in scripture is anathema. They argue that scripture has a clear and plain meaning. To interpret is either to intrude upon that meaning with a view of one's own, or to otherwise confuse or confound. Interpretation is either to add or to subtract from what is already there; it amounts to a form of vandalism, and it is to be prevented at all costs. Those who hold to this view are fond of the aphorism "The Bible says what it means and means what it says." For example, in Matthew 8:12, the outer darkness into which the wicked are cast is described as a place where "men will weep and gnash their teeth." A toothless reprobate asked his hellfire-preaching pastor what would happen to those who had no teeth to gnash: "Teeth will be provided" was his answer.

As far as scripture is concerned, interpretation almost always implies that human meanings are being imposed upon divine words. That point of view, however, I wish to argue, is itself unscriptural. Scripture is filled with an attempt

43

to interpret, to make sense of the things of which it speaks. In fact, Jesus' first sermon, in his hometown, was a reading from the prophet Isaiah upon which he expounded in good rabbinic fashion. For an account of this, see Luke 4:16–30. This is what teachers did: They took a text and drew their listeners into the interpretive triangle. Sometimes the interpretation was pleasing to the people, and sometimes, as in the case of Jesus' debut, the people were not at all pleased with the interpretation. Jesus' congregation sought to kill him, an extreme reaction. Today the congregation would simply fire the preacher.

Jesus himself is not always the clearest teacher, if his audience of disciples is to be believed. His parables were meant to amplify points or to make clearer points of moral teaching, but his closest listeners, the apostles, never seemed to get it. The parables, however, and indeed, the miracles and the healings, are all teaching devices, exercises in interpreting the larger principles of scripture that Jesus was intending to convey. The Sermon on the Mount, beginning in Matthew 5, is one extended interpretive discourse on what it means to live in the kingdom of God, to be a full human being under the divine plan for society. The Sermon on the Mount is the sermon Jesus might have given in his hometown, for it is a consummate commentary and interpretation on what the Jews would call "all the law and the prophets."

One of the most vivid instances of the function of interpretation with regard to the interpretation of scripture is recorded in Acts 8:26–40, where the Apostle Philip encounters an Ethiopian eunuch on the road from Jerusalem to Gaza. The eunuch, a minister of state of the queen of the Ethiopians, and her treasurer, is, we are meant to understand, a man of parts. He had come to Jerusalem to worship and was on his way home; and seated in his chariot, he was reading a scroll from the prophet Isaiah. The writer of Acts tells us that the spirit moved Philip to run up to the Ethiopian, and when he heard him reading aloud from the prophet, he asked, "Do you understand what you are reading?" The Ethiopian replied, "How can I, unless someone guides me?" He invited Philip into his chariot, and then, "Philip opened his mouth and beginning with this scripture he told him the good news of Jesus." The Ethiopian was so impressed that he asked to be baptized, and Philip baptized him on the spot.

"Do you understand what you are reading?"
"How can I, unless someone guides me?"

Philip asks the right question of the reader of scripture, and the Ethiopian gives the right answer as the reader who begins with the premise that help is needed. Full credit is due the Ethiopian, but credit must also be given to Philip, who used his proximity and his gift of interpretation to such good effect. He was, we learn from Acts, sent by the Spirit to accomplish this purpose. This is an example of what Paul means when in Romans he asks, "But

45

how are men to call upon him in whom they have not believed? And how are they to believe in him of whom they have never heard? And how are they to hear without a preacher? And how can men preach unless they be sent?" He answers his own questions: "So faith comes from what is heard, and what is heard comes by the preaching of Christ." (Romans 10:14–17)

Interpretation is the fuel that drives understanding. The making of meaning is what scripture is all about, the effort by every possible device to make sense of the divine in search of the human, and the human in search of the divine, the joy of discovery, the sorrow of loss. If scripture is about anything in all of its splendid diversity, it is about this, and so it is not really about whether there is or is not interpretation in the reading of scripture. Of course there is interpretation. The question is, what kind of interpretation? What do we bring to the text to discern what the text intends for us to find? For some it may well be a matter of technique, those technical skills that one must bring to get the most possible from the reading. All of us are not skilled linguists, however, able to read the Old Testament in Hebrew, the New Testament in Greek, and to supplement those linguistic skills with an array of theological, historical, philosophical, philological, and analytical skills such as will make us masters of the fields of translation and interpretation. Few clergy, and, alas, even fewer laity, now possess sufficient of these skills to be reliant upon themselves alone.

If not technique, perhaps chance is the best

way to take the measure of the scriptures. There are many who still practice the random reading of verses once popular in certain Bible-minded communities. The theory is this: In that all of scripture is equally inspired and is therefore equally instructive in all matters, any verse, and any sequence of verses, is sufficient for guidance provided you are guided to them not by chance but by the Spirit. Theologian Robert McAfee Brown tells us of the devout practitioner of this method, who, in search of guidance, opened the Bible and put his finger at random on a verse. It was "And Judas went out and hanged himself." (Matthew 27:5) Trying again, this time he happened upon Luke 10:37, "Go and do likewise." To read the Bible as one would a Chinese fortune cookie or some book of chance is to fail to understand what scripture is or what it demands or how one ought to seek its message. Scripture is not passive, and neither should those who read it be passive. As we read in Proverbs 4:7, "The beginning of wisdom is this: get wisdom, and whatever you get, get under-standing."

If interpretation is not simply a matter of technique, and is too important to be left merely to chance, perhaps, at least at the beginning, it is a matter of trust. In the teaching of preaching I try to communicate this aspect of trust and interpretation to my students. I do this by asking them to do four things: Trust the text. Trust themselves. Trust the people. Trust the Spirit. The idea here is that the text has some-thing to say and that we may in fact be able to hear what that is in terms that we can understand and appropriate. Our listeners trust that we will help them in their process of discovery and discernment, and both preacher and listener are guided by the Spirit into a lively encounter with the text.

The element of trust enters into the art of interpretation of scripture when we understand that the Bible comes to us as a trust both from God and from the people of God. It is the record of holy encounters between people and God, encounters that have been reckoned to be decisive and compelling, and that have been preserved from generation to generation because they remind each generation of the presence of God in their lives and the search for God when the divine absence is felt. When we consider the sweeping themes with which the Bible is concerned, the fundamental questions that its protagonists ask, the portraits of God and of men and women that it paints, the dilemmas that it describes and the hope that it offers, we can trust the Bible to be a window into the complexity of the human and of the divine. These words are trustworthy and true not because they correspond to verifiable fact and scientific data, but because they speak with a perceptive, truthful accuracy of the hearts and minds of men and women very much like ourselves. We trust the text not because it is "true" in the sense of fact, but because in its infinite variety it points to the truth and communicates truth because it comes from the truth which we call God.

One of the greatest ironies available to people who take the Bible seriously is that they may be tempted to take it, and themselves, so seriously that God and the truths of God to which the Bible points may be obscured, perverted, or lost entirely. The temptation to see in the Bible only the Bible, and to see no further than our own understanding of what we see, has frequently led to an idolatry of scripture as dangerous and perverse as any blandishment of Satan in the Garden or in the wilderness. This dangerous perversion of scripture is as old as scripture itself, and it is a result of temptation so subtle that we may not even recognize that we are being tempted. Such temptation flourishes at the point where the Bible is most relevant to us and where we feel the strongest in our understanding of it. We acknowledge the power of the Bible, which we understand as the word of God, and at the same time we want that power for ourselves, to order our lives by it and to make sense of the world in which we find ourselves. So we seek to possess what the church calls the "true and lively word," and to invest God's word with our meaning. The results have often been disastrous, and the problem is as old as the effort to interpret scripture.

The temptations of interpretation take three forms, all related and equally dangerous. These temptations are a form of idolatry. They violate the first commandment, and they violate the believer just as Adam and Eve were violated, and just as Satan would have violated Jesus in the wilderness if he could have. When we read the Bible, and by doing so interpret it, we should be mindful of these three temptations:

1. The worship of the Bible, making of it an object of veneration and ascribing to it the glory due to God
2. The worship of the text, in which the letter is given an inappropriate superiority over the spirit
3. The worship of the culture, in which the Bible is forced to conform to the norms of the prevailing culture

We may call these three temptations *bibliolatry, literalism,* and *culturism*: Each plays its subtle part in interpreting the Bible.

Bibliolatry

Years ago, in the days of compulsory attendance at chapel in the colleges across America, a preacher would have to go very far indeed to capture the attention of a jaded congregation worshiping under compulsion and the watchful eyes of monitors taking attendance. I recall one of my own experiences in the chapel of Bates College, when, to the consternation of the congregation, one morning the preacher of the day, a young and somewhat iconoclastic assistant professor of religion, took from beneath the folds of his gown a carved wooden African idol of some fertility deity, took it to the altar, and placed it square in front of the cross. He then told us that this was his god, and that there were lots more where this came from, and that as far as he knew they worked just as well, and perhaps even better, than the one in whose name the chapel had been built. Well, this was strong stuff even for the pew-hardened undergraduates of nearly forty years ago. The dean and the president, both pious Baptists, were lost for words but their faces spoke volumes. Our young professor had wanted to get our attention and he had got it; and for days afterward we talked of what we had seen and heard in the chapel. One had to work hard to remember that his text, forgotten in the excitement of his heresy, was Exodus 20:3, "Thou shalt have no other god before me."

A colleague who went to a small Christian college in the South told me of a similar incident, this one, however, even more vivid. The preacher of her experience stood up and read his lesson from his Bible. He then closed the book and threw it out of the nearby open chancel window, and said, "Well, there goes your god." He was of course making a point about idolatry, and he was illustrating it with an attack upon bibliolatry, or the worship of the Bible.

In the absence of a visible God, the temptation is always near to make a god of whatever is visible and related in some proximate way to the real thing. At its best we call this symbolism, the appropriation of qualities and signs that we can and do see and assigning them a function in behalf of the ultimate thing that we cannot see. In the state we do this through, for example, the symbol of the flag, which represents for us the substance of the state. In Christianity we do this with the cross. Liturgically, we recognize this process in what we call "sacraments," which are, in the language of the English catechism, "the outward and visible sign of an inward and spiritual grace." Statues of saints and martyrs, holy relics, even the architecture of buildings devoted to holy purposes, such as cathedrals, are all part of our human need to "see" the invisible, to vest what we cannot see but what we truly believe in something that represents that belief to the naked eye. Such signs and symbols are means to direct our senses and our spirits to the realm of invisible spiritual realities.

This symbolism has always been a difficult concept for people of faith, for faith ought not to depend for its veracity upon what people can see. The inherent risk in symbolism is that the symbol becomes a substitute for what it is meant to represent. The means becomes an end in itself, and the worship and devotion which the end requires, when devoted merely to the means, become a form of idolatry and an exercise in fraud. The history of belief is, in the West, replete with instances of this conflict. Early on in the Bible, the golden calf discussed in Exodus 32 is an instance of this dangerous substitution. Moses had gone up to Mount Sinai to receive the tablets of the law from God, and while he was away his brother, Aaron, was left to contend with a people restless for some tangible sign of God's favor, and for a deity who could compete with the Egyptian fertility gods whom they had known in their slavery. Aaron thereupon fashioned a golden calf from the gathered-up earrings of the Israelites, which they proceeded to worship.

The creation of the calf can be read as a longing after God, and the calf as a surrogate for the distant Moses whose absence distressed the people. Neither Moses nor God, however, took a benign view of what the people had done, and the golden calf and the worship and sacrifice that went with it were denounced as rank idolatry. God called the people a "stiff-necked people," and intended to destroy them for their ingratitude, but they were spared by the intercessions of Moses, who himself was furious at their behavior. Upon his return to the people he smashed the tablets of the law, and destroyed the calf. Idolatry was not to be tolerated. Throughout Hebrew scripture one of the corporate besetting sins is cultic idolatry, which we may take to represent in part a moral impatience and a desire to possess as one's very own the word and works of God.

What we see, and what we taste, and what we touch all have the illusion of reality, and thus does an image or a statue or a token or a book appear to be much more real than what the image, statue, token, or book represents. A picture *is* worth a thousand words both in advertising and in religion, even when in religion those words are the words of God, but the appearance of reality, which the image is meant to represent, is illusory. Plato's famous dialogue on the shadows on the walls of the cave, and whether they were or were not reality, is an ancient formulation of the problem. The question of image and reality is one to which Saint Paul turned in one of his most famous passages when in II Corinthians 4:17–18 he writes, "For this slight momentary affliction is preparing for us an eternal weight of glory beyond all comparison, because we look not to the things that are seen but to the things that are unseen; for the things that are seen are transient, but the things that are unseen are eternal."

In Christian culture the idolatry debate has usually associated itself with the notion of graven images. The early church was concerned with the question of whether or not the icons used in devotion, particularly in the Eastern Church, were a violation of the prohibition against graven images as set out in Exodus 20. Those people against idols—the iconoclasts—saw the reverence paid them as idolatry; those in favor argued for the pedagogical benefits for the faithful. The controversy was settled by the Council of Nicaea in 787, which permitted the placement of icons in churches as aids to devotion but made the useful distinction between authentic worship, which belonged only to God, and the reverence that could be accorded images, noting that the reverence paid to images was really reverence to that which the image represented.

Protestantism, with its Calvinist and Puritan inheritance, has always been nervous about representational figures, and the accounts of Oliver Cromwell's army and its desecration of statuary in English cathedrals and parish churches are all too familiar instances of Protestant iconoclasm. Calvin, we know, was much against the use of graven images, as he felt that such use encouraged the unlettered in superstition and the temptations of idolatry. He took consolation in the hope that Christians, as a result of the reforms of his day, would be able to read the scriptures for themselves, and therefore would not have to depend upon images and representation for the word of God. It never occurred to him that the Bible, now available to all who could read, could easily itself become an object of veneration, an idol as dangerous as any statue or mural.

It was Martin Luther, however, whose reformation slogan, *sola scriptura*, "by scripture alone," gave rise to the greatest temptation yet, which was to make of the Bible a domesticated substitute for the authority of God. Luther challenged the authority of the pope. The teaching tradition of the Roman Church, with the authority it conferred upon its bishops and priests, and most especially upon the pope, made the Bible a book that could not be understood outside the teachings of the Roman Church. The Bible, in a tongue foreign to the people, and mediated by a church whose clergy had a monopoly upon the interpretation of scripture, was thus an inaccessible book, its truths and riches unavailable to the average Christian. Through Luther's challenge, the authority of the Bible was substituted for the authority of the pope and the Roman Church, and by this, for Martin Luther, both Bible and people were liberated. Nothing was to be interposed between the people of God and the word of God in the Bible.

Historically, the Roman Catholic Church has seen this quite differently, and has been fearful of what it called "the shifting sands of private judgment." A popular Roman Catholic commentary on scripture has this view of the Reformation and the doctrine of *sola scriptura*:

> Through Luther, although Calvin seems to have been the first to announce Monobiblicism clearly, the Bible became the arm of the Protestant revolt. A dumb and difficult book was substituted for the living voice of the Church, in order that each one should be able to make for himself a religion which suited his feelings. And the Bible, open before every literate man and woman to interpret for themselves, was the attractive bait used to win adherents. Not the solid rock of truth but the shifting sand of private judgment is the foundation upon which Protestantism was built.

Such a harsh judgment is not a completely just representation of the situation, but there is within this characterization of Protestantism a painfully familiar glimmer of truth. When the Catholic critics speak of the Bible as a "dumb and difficult book," they are, of course, not

56

calling the Bible stupid, nor are they debasing it in any way. They speak of it as "dumb" in the sense of silent, that is to say, not in itself capable of explaining itself; and "difficult" because it is not, contrary to popular Protestant piety, clear and revelatory to anyone who chooses to read it. To give such a book the reverence due God, and to submit the Bible to the sovereignty of one's own reading of it, is to come dangerously close to the kind of idolatry that caused God to despair and Moses to lose his temper in a fit of tablet smashing. The Bible is not God, nor is it a substitute for God, and to treat it as if it were God or a surrogate of God is to treat it in the very way that it itself condemns over and over again. This first danger, giving to the Bible what belongs to God, while an understandable temptation on the part of the faithful, is nevertheless profoundly dangerous. In the name of God, and in the pursuit of good, this danger will cause many to do much harm. We will see just how much harm in the other dangers and temptations associated with the interpretation of scripture: literalism and culturism.

Literalism

"The Bible says what it means and means what it says." This is a popular defense of the authority of scripture, and it is as dangerous and wrong as it is simple and memorable. We should always be suspicious when a proposition that involves anything as complex as the scriptures is reduced to a mere bumper sticker. We can certainly say that the Bible says what it means, but that presupposes that we know what it says, and, as well, that we understand what it means when it says it. But we must remember, in English-speaking Christendom, that the Bible was written not in English nor by a single literary hand but in an ancient form of Hebrew, in which the Jewish scriptures speak, and in a corrupted form of Greek, in which much of the New Testament is found. Moreover, these languages themselves were translated first into Latin, and then back again, and only thereafter into now very archaic forms of English from which our contemporary translations are descended. So we must approach this question of what the Bible says and what it means with a certain amount of modesty unfamiliar and uncongenial to most Christians who describe themselves as "Bible-believing."

At the time of the Protestant Reformation it was politically incorrect to suggest that the Bible was too complex and difficult for the average untutored believer to interpret at will. In order to break the interpretive monopoly of the Roman Catholic Church with its doctrines of the papacy, councils, and the exalted role of tradition as the context for understanding the Bible, the reformers had to argue that meaning was accessible and democratic, that anyone who could read could interpret. To place the Bible in the hands of the people was to place the people in charge of the Bible, or so they thought. True, the Holy Spirit was to mediate meaning to the individual reader, but authority was now removed from the community of the church to the conscience and mind of the reader. Since experts were no longer needed, every reader became an expert.

What then would prevent spiritual anarchy and as many readings of scriptural truth as there were readers to read them? A new authority had to be created in the place of the deposed papal authority and the discredited reign of experts. That authority, a phenomenon of a Protestantism carried to its logical conclusion, was not the authority of the individual reader but rather the authority of the literal text to which the reader submitted himself. Literalism offered to the reader the security that numbers offer to the numerate: a reliable and fixed content and meaning. One does not have to be a nuclear physicist to know that $2+2=4$. That fact is democratically available to all who know it, and it is always so. Thus, if we can find out what words say, and hence what they mean, we as readers will be able once and for all, aided by the Holy Spirit but on our own, to know what scripture says and means. The words are absolute and fixed. Literalism thus becomes a means of liberation from the tyranny of a churchly and intellectual elite.

By the eighteenth century this power of the ordinary believer to read and understand the scriptures at their only significant level of meaning, the literal sense, would be called "common sense," and would appeal to the humanistic ambitions of Protestant believers unavoidably influenced by the principles of the Enlightenment. The great irony of the Enlightenment, now so much disparaged by the cultural revisionists of our own age, is that while it did celebrate secular culture and appear to dethrone piety in favor of reason, it, at the same time, made it possible for the pious to be liberated from the tyranny of their intellectual and spiritual overlords. Indeed, common sense was the coin of the realm for the common man. The secular principles of the Enlightenment enfranchised the pious and gave them the ultimate sense of self-confidence that made that "dumb and difficult book" available to the most ordinary of them. Literalism was the key to this newfound freedom; the sovereignty of words now replaced the sovereignty of the church's interpretation of scripture.

In late-twentieth-century America the vast majority of those Christians who would define themselves as Bible-believing, largely drawn from the evangelical and fundamentalist movements of Protestantism, actually believe that they believe in a literal reading of the Bible. In fact, they are not literalist, at least not wholly or consistently literalists, but they espouse literalism because they believe that it liberates them and the text from obscurantism and secret knowledge not readily accessible to any believer, by the use of common sense. Why the literalists are not really literalists I will address later on, but the appeal of literalism and its contention with other means of interpretation are as old as scripture itself.

Literalism is not meant to be a source of license or of liberty. Paradoxically, it is meant to be a source of authority to safeguard both the text and the reader from error, and even modern literalists believe that they are protecting scripture from the ruination of false interpretation and the individual reader from error. For the literalist, what counts is not what the reader brings to the text but rather what the reader discovers that the author brought to the text. Americans will recognize this intellectual principle in the doctrine of original intent, as it applies to the federal Constitution. The issue, framed in American constitutional discourse, is not what you and I might think the Constitution means; nor is it what the Supreme Court, at any given point, thinks it means. The only valid line of inquiry, according to the doctrine of original intent, is what the authors, the framers, had in their minds when they wrote what they wrote. It is the business of the courts to interpret the Constitution on that basis, and the business of the legislature to legislate with that intent clearly in mind. It is no small point of cultural coincidence in contemporary America that those who find security in the authority of the text and its authors' intent in scripture, will be equally anxious to submit themselves and others to the same authority in constitutional discourse.

The fact that the Constitution of the United States was written in English a mere two hundred years ago by men of whom we know a great deal and whose political philosophy and worldviews are familiar to us, does not mean, despite that proximity, that our constitutional process has been any easier to understand. We know, for example and fact, that the framers took no constitutional cognizance of women despite Abigail Adams's plea to John to "remember the ladies." We also know full well their view concerning the African-American slaves. Most of us would not want to reconform our country's civilization to these original intents, even though we know what they are.

In biblical interpretation, however, it is the combined fear of errors and experts that gives literalism its claim to legitimate authority on the part of those who would take the scriptures seriously. "We don't need experts to tell us what God wants us to hear" is a familiar and impassioned cry in favor of the accessibility of the scriptures, yet there is an equally passionate desire to make sure that what we hear, or read, is in fact what God intends. If we cannot be certain of the fact, then not only is there an intellectual problem, but of even greater significance, there is a moral problem, for how can we do God's will if we are not certain what it is?

Among the most public and bitter moral debates of our time is the debate over abortion. The Bible is silent about abortion, but the religious zeal of the protestors at abortion clinics is based upon what they believe to be the plain and clear meaning of Exodus 20:13, where in many English translations the familiar commandment says, "Thou shalt not kill." The moral energy of the anti-abortion movement is fueled in large part by this clear and unambiguous commandment, which it claims is violated with impunity every time an abortion is performed. One has only to listen to the chilling justification of his action by Paul Hill, the minister convicted of first-degree murder at a Pensacola abortion clinic, to sense the depth of conviction based upon the moral force of this commandment. The English is clear and unmistakable, but what the English says is not precisely what the Hebrew says or means. The older translators got it better when they translated the Hebrew *ratsach* in Exodus 20:13 as "Thou shalt do no murder," and the distinction between murder and killing is not a small one. Murder, in the Hebrew language and culture, refers to the premeditated taking of a life outside the womb; killing had to do with the ritual slaughter of animals for sacrifice. The words are not interchangeable because the concepts to which they refer are quite distinct. Not only is the Bible therefore silent on the question of abortion, but the one text used to justify opposition to it is wrongly construed in English. There are strongly held moral opinions on abortion, and there are many valid and moral extra-biblical grounds for an opposition to abortion, but the literal, and commonsense, reading of Exodus 20:13 renders a weak and inadequate proof text against it.

Literalism is dangerous for two reasons. First, it indulges the reader in the fanciful notion that by virtue of natural intelligence the text is apprehensible and therefore sensible. Despite genuflections to the notion of original or authorial intent, meaning is determined by what the reader takes out of the text, and this meaning the reader attributes to the author. Thus, what the reader thinks is there becomes not merely the reader's opinion, but the will of God, with all the moral consequences and authority that that implies. When Paul Hill and other zealots murder in the name of God, this terrible danger becomes incarnate.

The second danger of literalism is that the power of private judgment may well obscure the meaning of a text by paying attention only to what it says. Literalism thinks that it is freeing the text from layers of early Christian antiquity and medieval exegesis. Allegories, typologies, and symbolic interpretations are to be avoided in favor of the pure and uncorrupted word. Literalism does not want the text held hostage to these devices, but literalism itself is hostage to the eighteenth-century illusion that truth and meaning are the same thing, and that they are fixed and discernible by the application of the faculties of reason and common sense.

The debate between what words mean and what we think they mean is as old as language itself. The positions are clearly depicted in the colloquy between Humpty-Dumpty and Alice, in *Through the Looking-Glass*:

"I don't know what you mean by 'glory,'" Alice said.

Humpty-Dumpty smiled contemptuously.

"Of course you don't—'til I tell you."

"I meant 'There's a nice knock-down argument,'" Alice objected.

"When I use a word," Humpty-Dumpty said in a rather scornful tone, "it means just what I choose it to mean—neither more nor less."

"The question is," said Alice, "whether you *can* make words mean so many different things."

"The question is," said Humpty-Dumpty, "which is to be master—that's all."

They argue on, although each confesses to much confusion. Humpty uses the word *impenetrability,* and Alice, no longer sure of English, asks him what it means, and really what does *he* mean when he uses it. Humpty gives such an impossible answer that Alice replies, "That's a great deal to make one word mean," and Humpty-Dumpty says, "When I make a word do a lot of work like that, I always pay it extra."

Language is not an end but a means, and the end is communication with meaning and significance. The language of the Bible is meant always to point us to a truth beyond the text, a meaning that transcends the particular and imperfectly understood context of the original writers, and our own prejudices and parochialisms that we bring to the text. Literalism is not part of the solution to this problem—literalism *is* the problem.

How can one not live in one's own time? How can one not be a part of the culture that frames one's experience? It is almost impossible to transcend one's own particular place in the world and in time, for we are who we are and where we are. Culture is the world in which we find ourselves, and out of which we make meaning for ourselves. Christians have an inherited culture problem, however, for we are called to transcend this culture in which we live for one to which we belong by virtue of our baptism and our faith, but which has not yet established itself among us. Jesus is understood as the one who was to introduce the new age, a new and radically different culture from the one in which he lived and died, and his resurrection was the unambiguous sign that the new age had begun. All who followed him were citizens of that new culture. Saint Paul tells us as much, when in Romans 12 he writes that we are not to be conformed to this world, but "be ye transformed by the renewal of your mind." Earlier, we have cited Paul's invocation of the superiority of things that are unseen over things that are seen, for "the things that are seen are temporary, but the things that are unseen are eternal." Saint Augustine's enormous classic, *The City of God*, is an account of how the Christian is to live in two worlds at the same time, the visible and the invisible, coping with the one while hoping for the other. That tension between what is and what is to be is an unavoidable one in a

Christian faith that takes seriously Old Testament prophecy and New Testament experience.

This is a problem, but it is not the problem of culturism, and it is to that problem and its relationship to scripture to which we now turn. Culturism—I confess to its coinage for purposes of this discussion—is the notion, more often unacknowledged than not, that we read scripture not only in the light of our own culture but as a means of defining and defending that very culture over and against which scripture by its very nature is meant to stand. In other words, scripture is invariably used to support the status quo, no matter what the status quo, and despite the revolutionary origins and implications of scripture itself. Under the rubric of culturism, scripture, rather than a critique of culture or a vision of another way and day, is chiefly understood as the justification for what has been and what is, a divinely inspired apologist for whatever presently obtains. An early twentieth-century African proverb puts it well: "When the missionaries came," it says, "they had the Bible and we had the land. Now we have the Bible and they have the land."

In reading and interpreting the Bible, the great temptation is to use it as the moral sanction for our own culture. In making an idol of the culture we seduce the Bible into its service, and reduce the will and word of God to a mere artifact of things as we know them. American Christians for most of the twentieth century were pleased to describe the Soviet Union as an oppressive system because it was ruled by godless atheists. These same Christians, however, were not so quick to point out that one of the most conspicuously Christian countries on earth, South Africa, justified its oppressive regime of apartheid, and the brutality necessary to sustain it, as the work of the Bible-believing Christians who were simply fulfilling God's will.

This understanding of scripture as a force for the preservation of the existing culture is not foreign to the United States; indeed, we might say that such a hermeneutical principle is as American as apple pie. It does not take any effort to find at nearly every instance of our national history scriptural justification for whatever it was we wished to do. When the Pilgrims landed at Plymouth in the winter of 1620 and found both cleared cornfields and the local Native Americans enfeebled by sickness and plague, they saw all of this as an act of divine providence, likening themselves to the children of Israel entering into the Promised Land, which inconveniently had been previously occupied. The Indian wars of the next two centuries were sanctioned on not much more exegesis of scripture than this. The doctrine of Manifest Destiny, the notion that it was the will of God that America should civilize the continent from sea to shining sea, is a reading both of scripture and of history in overwhelming favor of the nationalist appetite for territory.

The most vivid instance of the appeal to scripture in support of the culture, however, is in America's racial policies and its struggle, not yet by any means ended, between rights and right. Both slavery, and then segregation, were supported on the moral grounds of the Bible. Slavery, and then segregation, were not inadvertent in America; they were part of the divine plan. Many have wondered how southern Christians, far more fervent in the faith and visible in their Christian civility than others, could reconcile the apparent contradiction between their ardent profession of faith and their vigorous support of slavery and segregation. One must understand that southern Christians, by and large, saw no such contradiction at all, for it was all in the Bible. The southern way of life, and the "peculiar institution" of slavery, were divinely approved. More, perhaps, than any other charge laid against them, southern whites resented the charge that they were un-Christian and hypocritical because of their treatment of African Americans.

They knew their Bible, and they knew that the basis of the subjugation of the African was to be found in Genesis 9:18–27. This is the account of the debauchery of Noah, and the indiscreet discovery of his naked drunkenness by his son Ham. Ham told his brothers of their father's condition, but they, averting their eyes from the humiliating sight, did not see what Ham had seen, and were therefore spared the curse that Noah laid upon Ham and his descendants. The curse on Canaan, Ham's son, found in Genesis 9:25, was this: "Cursed be Canaan: a slave of slaves shall he be to his brothers." The Talmudic scholars from ancient times have wondered what it was that Ham had done to provoke so vicious a curse upon his posterity, and there are many speculations: that Ham had engaged in immoral sexual conduct on the Ark; that he had sodomized his drunken father; even that he had castrated Noah so that there could be no more heirs from his father's loins. In various literatures Ham's son Canaan is the father of the Philistines, the progenitor of cultic bestial and fertility rites, and the ancestor of all Africa. For the sin of his father, Canaan and his descendants are cursed to serve other races, are themselves to be regarded as suspect, and in sexual matters are to be restrained, as they are by nature potent and lascivious.

In the American South, as in South Africa, the two greatest fears of the white Christian population had to do with rebellion and the uprising of the sons of Canaan fueled by a long-standing thirst for revenge, and a sexual revolution in which the fabled potency of the black male would be used to seduce and overcome sexually unsatisfied white womanhood. These two fears, cultural phobias, we might well call them, were sufficient to keep the white Christian civilizations who shared them in a state of perpetual and militant vigilance against the black populations in their midst. It is only when we understand these phobias and their biblical basis that we can begin to understand the brutality to which the whites subjected the blacks, and to which they subjected themselves. The sanctions of scripture made it all bearable, and thus they need not wonder about their own morality or humanity, or about the values of the culture that they regarded as steadfastly Christian. In the American South in particular, it was Bible-reading, churchgoing Christians, chiefly Protestants and largely Baptist, who could and would lynch, castrate, and horribly mutilate errant black men on Saturday night, and pray and praise all day in church on Sunday, without a hint of schizophrenia or even of guilt. How could they sustain such a culture for so long? The Bible told them so.

The African-American theologian Howard Thurman wrote about his grandmother, who in her girlhood had been a slave, in his autobiography. She had been taught to read and write, and she had been taught the Bible, and she knew most of it by heart. It was she who had taught her grandson the scriptures. When he got to theological school he noted that his grandmother had never mentioned anything about Saint Paul. He asked her why. She replied that when she was a girl the black slave preacher always preached about Moses and Jesus, but that when the white preacher came once a month to preach, he always preached from Ephesians 6:5, where Saint Paul says, "Slaves, be obedient to those who are your earthly masters, with fear and trembling, in singleness of heart, as to Christ." When she learned to read the scriptures for herself she took her scissors and cut out all of Paul's writings from the New Testament, on the grounds that they were inconsistent with what Jesus taught, and that they therefore had no place in the Bible.

71

Farther on in this book we will examine in some detail case studies of America's use and abuse of scripture, and the relationship between the Bible, which remains the same yesterday, today, and forever, and a culture that is forever changing and evolving. There we will see the dangerous consequences, both to culture and to the integrity of the Bible, of culturism as a means, however inadvertent, of sustaining and validating in the name of God the prejudices of a parochial human community. Of the three dangers and temptations to which I have referred in this chapter, this one is by far the greatest. Why it is so can be explained through an old aphorism that I learned from a friend who had first heard it many years ago, and could not remember its source.

"A surplus of virtue," it says, "is more dangerous than a surplus of vice."

"Why?" we ask naturally.

"Because a surplus of virtue is not subject to the constraints of conscience."

That is the powerful danger of culturism. In the American South of slavery and segregation, at least until the time of Martin Luther King, Jr., most people could not be appealed to on the basis of the constraints of conscience because they understood themselves to be good and faithful people who were simply doing God's will. They read the Bible, they heard their preachers, they said their prayers, and they knew in their hearts that they were right and justified by the Bible in the cause that they sought to uphold by any and every means necessary.

Yet the very gospel they used to maintain the status quo would eventually destroy that status quo, and that is the story that remains to be told.

Modesty, Fear, and Trembling

When we read the Bible we are looking at the result of a set of assumptions and ambitions which themselves are not necessarily made explicit or systematic, but which contribute to the construction of the Bible "as it is." In fact, what makes the Bible "run," or "tick," if you will, are these assumptions and expectations with which it is constructed. We do not know all that we need to know. We do not know all that "they" knew. We do know, however, that what we have is what they have left to us, and that translating that treasure from their time into ours and back again is an enterprise that calls for patience, endurance, diligence, skill, and perhaps above all, humility. Arrogance in reading these texts is perhaps an even greater sin than unbelief, and for that arrogance that crowds out the spirit of God, Christians will be held to a strict account at the final judgment. Since discerning what God, in the Bible, means for us to hear and to do is a matter of life and death, we must approach the interpretation of scripture as we do our own salvation, working it out in fear and trembling.

CHAPTER 3

THE BIBLE IN AMERICA

JESSE Jackson and Patrick Buchanan would appear to have very little in common except for a delight in addressing audiences. Their visions for America could not be farther apart, and yet both appeal to the vision of the Bible to sustain their own vision, and both regard the Bible as the moral platform upon which the well-being of the republic ought to be reconstructed. Buchanan argues that we once had that biblical basis for a civil society and have since lost it; and his goal is to revive a lost ideal. Jackson agrees that biblical ideals make for the best of civil society, arguing that we have not yet achieved those ideals, however, and that change, not revival, ought to be the order of the day.

Conflicting visions for America arising from differing interpretations of the Bible are nothing new; that conflict is inherent in the very nature of America and its historic intimacy with the Bible as America's own book. Indeed, the first book printed in New England on the seventeenth-century press of Harvard College was the Bible. Our presidents are sworn into office on the Bible, and oaths in court are taken on them. In the culture wars we argue about the place of the Bible in our civic society, and politicians quote from the Bible in justification of their policy positions on moral questions. The ubiquity of the Bible in American public life has long been an object of comment on the part of observers of the American scene.

The City Set on a Hill

The process began early. The English Puritans who settled the eastern seaboard did not suffer from modesty but saw themselves as the New Israel, heirs of God's promises to the Jews of the Old Testament, and their leaders as reincarnations of the biblical patriarchs and prophets. They saw the New World as their own New Canaan into which they would enter from slavery in England, or "Egypt," by means of the "Red Sea," otherwise known as the Atlantic Ocean. Armed with these self-enabling metaphors, these English Puritans entered upon their destinies. The native inhabitants of the land also fit well into the biblical metaphor. They were the equivalent of the Philistines and the Canaanites, whose destruction at the hands of the Israelites is the substance of the early books of the biblical narrative.

When in 1630 the Puritan armada reached the outer waters of Boston Harbor, John Winthrop, leader of the colony and a lay preacher, delivered a sermon aboard the lead ship *Arbella,* which he titled "A New Modell for Christian Charity." The ambition of the sermon was to establish the Christian basis for

75

the new civilization to be established in what was then thought to be the "howling wilderness." The basis of this society was to be Christian charity, where, on the basis of those principles enunciated in the Bible, particularly in the Sermon on the Mount, the strong would bear with the weak, the rich would relieve the necessities of the poor, and all would strive to construct an exemplary society that would be like a city set upon a hill. This was not meant to be only for the comfort and consolation of the inhabitants but a beacon to the whole world, to prove to the old and tottering kingdoms of Europe that it was possible to construct a Christian society that would work. New England was not to be a retreat from the world, it was to be an example to the world; and of the three hills upon which the city of Boston was built, the principal one was named Beacon Hill, for not only would the light on its summit guide ships into the harbor, but that light would illumine the Christian world. "The eyes of the world will be upon us," Winthrop said. If the colony succeeded, the credit and glory would go, of course, to God. If, however, the colony and its Christian mandate failed, "Then," said Winthrop, "we shall be a by-word among the nations," a laughing-stock, another failed utopia.

The vivid and explicitly religious sensibility in this founding metaphor has incorporated itself into the American sense of itself, and in various forms and transformations it has been at the heart of much of our psychic identity ever since.

Our wars, including the Indian Wars, the Revolutionary War, most certainly the Civil War, and the two World Wars of the twentieth century, are all in some sense Holy Wars, fought with God on our side, and in behalf of a divine mission. Our physical expansion across the continent in the nineteenth century, from sea to shining sea, was described as our Manifest Destiny, a mandate from heaven. America believes in God at a higher proportion of the population than does any other country in the West, and what is even more striking is that Americans believe that God believes in them! The literary critic Harold Bloom has written, "The United States is a religion-mad country. It has been inflamed in this regard for about two centuries now," and he calls America's intoxication with religion "the poetry, not the opiate, of the masses."

An American Book?

Is the Bible, then, an American book? Does it "belong" to us in the same way that *The Scarlet Letter, Huckleberry Finn, Gone With the Wind,* and *The Great Gatsby* belong to us? If the Bible does belong to the American experience and defines and is defined by that experience, is there then an American way of reading the Bible? These are interrelated questions. One can argue that the Bible is an American book because it defines the American experience, and one can also argue that the American experience is biblical because only an understanding of the place of the Bible in the American culture will help in trying to understand that culture.

To fail to understand or to appreciate the religious dimension of the American culture is to be unable to read that culture or its nuances in any effective way. Religion in America is not a hobby or merely a private pursuit—it never has been—and the religious dimensions of our culture are not likely to diminish in the foreseeable future. To imagine that as our American culture matures and grows old and sophisticated, diverse and pluralistic, we will grow "out of—" or "away from" religion, as, for example, France did after the Enlightenment and its revolution, or as we imagined that Russia did after its revolution and embrace of communism, is to be as wrong as wrong can be.

Seventy years ago, after the public relations disaster of the Scopes trial for conservative Christian religion in America, the considered opinion of the pundits was that fundamentalism was dead or was living in exile in the hill country of the Bible Belt. Fewer than forty years ago, at the high noon of the countercultural revolution of the 1960s, these same pundits opined that the secular age was upon us and was here to stay. The "God Is Dead" theologians spoke of an age after God, *Time* magazine had as its 1967 Good Friday cover story "The Death of God," and the Beatles announced that they were more popular than Jesus Christ.

Now, in the twilight of this century and millennium, these predictions seem rather out-of-date. We find ourselves in a social, political, and cultural environment where religion is not only an issue, but it is *the* issue; and our struggles, which used to be defined in America as battles for the "minds and hearts" of the people are today culture wars fought for the "soul" of America, and for the souls of Americans. This is not simply a shift in vocabulary, an appropriation of a new metaphor; it is a struggle for the reformation of our national character, a reformation as complex, ambitious, and destabilizing as any of those reformations that traumatized sixteenth-century Germany and seventeenth-century England. Marx thought that religion was the opiate of the masses: Harold Bloom sees religion as the poetry rather than the opiate of the American people. For so many Americans who feel dispossessed, disempowered, and victimized by the forces of change that intimidate them and seem beyond their control, religion is neither opiate nor poetry, it is fuel, a form of cultural adrenaline that gives would-be victims the courage to fight back, to reclaim what they believe to be a lost religious inheritance, and to insist upon much more than mere toleration. They want affirmation, recognition, and indeed restoration of what they believe was once their place in the cultural sun.

Change and Continuity

It is into this wellspring of frustrated, spiritually denied Christians that Pat Buchanan tapped in both his 1992 Republican Culture Wars address, and in his 1996 presidential campaign. The secular establishment, with its values-neutral morality, its distrust of religion as fundamentally divisive, and in consequence, its segregation of religion into the private sphere, has managed to do what a generation of revivalist preachers and evangelists could not do. It has fired up Christian America and sent it marching into the voting booths of the nation. First the Moral Majority, and now the Christian Coalition, command the allegiance of millions of frustrated American Christians who feel that not only their religion, but the country which their religion built and sustained, have been taken away from them. With nowhere to go they have determined to fight to retrieve what is for them the lost ideal of a Christian state, an ideal that is decidedly "conservative." What we might call nostalgia with an attitude.

For many of the Christians who enlist in the current culture war, the struggle began with what they believe to be the secularists' sustained attack upon prayer and Bible reading in the public schools. The separation of Church and State, they rightly point out, historically was designed to protect the vitality and integrity of the churches from either the favoritism or the hostility of the state. A nation whose chief legislature and highest court are opened with prayer, where the president is sworn into office on a Bible, and whose currency bears the motto In God We Trust can hardly be described as a secular state. Thus, to remove the symbols of public piety, and, we might add, the historic Protestant hegemony, from the civic culture of the schools was to betray an inheritance and offer an affront not only to God but to millions of believers in God and in God's special relationship with the United States.

The symbolic potency of the Bible as an "American book," that is to say, a book upon which Americans had a special claim and which had a special claim for America, cannot be overestimated. The present religious activism in America on the part of those who feel themselves estranged from their own culture is essentially the response, at a distance of three decades, to that cultural wound inflicted by the removal of prayer and Bible reading from the public schools. Just as historians now think of World Wars I and II as but two episodes of one great twentieth-century conflict with a brief interlude of an illusory peace, so may we regard the current culture war as a continuation of that post-1945 American domestic struggle to redefine the culture.

For those who hold to the intimate relationship between the Bible and the culture, the Bible often becomes an icon of that culture. The culture sees itself mirrored in the Bible, the Bible is understood to be the norm by which the culture is defined, and this often results in the Bible's use as a textbook for the status quo. Nearly every motion for social change in America has been resisted on biblical grounds— to change is to go against the Bible. What is, is what is mandated by the Bible. What is not, is not because the Bible either forbids it or does not endorse or require it. Thus, change is not simply tinkering with the culture, it is tinkering with the Bible, and therefore tinkering with God. This sort of view was expressed by the middle-aged Englishwoman of a generation ago, who said, "If God had intended man to fly, He would not have given us the railroads." Every reform movement in America, every movement for social or political or cultural change, has had to encounter an argument of this sort, and the ultimate resistance of appeals to fidelity to scripture. The example was set by John Winthrop in 1630, and we have not departed from it.

This appeal to scripture has ironically also been made in behalf of wide-ranging and comprehensive change in American life. The Bible that to many seems an icon of the cultural status quo is seen by many others as an agent for social change, much of it radical. The arguments from scripture for and against slavery, for example, come to mind, and we shall examine these and other hard texts and changing times in the second portion of this book. Here, however, we should look at a powerful movement of our own time, itself a part of the renovation of the American cultural household after World War II: the movement for civil rights.

Many will argue that the history of civil rights in twentieth-century America is a history of the law and public policy. Others will argue that the achievement of civil rights for African Americans was one of the great social inevitabilities of our nation, an idea whose time had to come. Still others will see it as merely the last battle of the Civil War. It may be any or all of these, but I think that it is important for us to understand the civil rights movement as a religious movement based upon a particular reading not only of the national documents of the Declaration of Independence and the Constitution, but of the Bible. The civil rights movement was a moral crusade, and the content of that morality was determined by a sense of biblical justice and equity before God.

It is the fashion to remember Martin Luther King, Jr., as the master orator and strategist of the movement, and its ultimate martyr; he was, for many, the conscience of twentieth-century America. It is also a part of the fashion, however, to forget that he was first and foremost a Christian minister whose thought and cadence were framed by an understanding of the Bible as a way of understanding God's design for human beings. He was a Christian preacher before he was anything else. Revisionist historians who minimize this dimension of Dr. King and the movement he led diminish that movement and are incapable of seeing it whole, or of understanding its motivation or its impact.

The trouble with Martin Luther King, Jr., is that he believed more in America and in America's God than America did. He actually believed that the nation wished to be a nation under God, that it wished to live up to the moral ambition of its founding documents, that it wished to find a way to do right and to be right. Historians of the movement and biographers of King all emphasize his reliance upon the strategy of Gandhi and the principles of passive resistance, and that that strategy was only part of a much larger one, which was to shame America into being what it pretended to be. He did not invite America to revolution or to fundamental change, much to the annoyance of his more radical critics both white and black; his case was to urge America, and to shame it if he had to, into upholding its own first principles, to affirming its own myths and metaphors, to becoming the very "city set upon a hill" that the very white John Winthrop had so long before invoked as a vision of the New World.

For King, the Bible hardly read as a textbook of the status quo, for it was full of change from Genesis to Revelation. Adam and Eve are not permitted to abide in eternal felicity in the Garden of Eden. They must move on. Moses leads his people, often against their will, out of the stability of slavery in Egypt and into the vividly vague uncertainties of the promised land. The prophets of Israel are always warning the powers-that-be against complacency and against taking too much for granted. King would have known with delight and urgency the words of the prophet Amos, "Woe to those who are at ease in Zion, and to those who feel secure on the mountain of Samaria, the notable men of the first of the nations, to whom the house of Israel come!" (Amos 6:1)

In the Bible, kings are upended, kingdoms totter and fall, those who have power lose it, those who have none gain it. The New Testament is no easier: Jesus' very existence is a threat to any and every status quo, and his resurrection even overturns the rule of nature. The Christians of Paul's era reject the blandishments and power of this world; the Book of Hebrews celebrates a kingdom unlike those of this world, one that cannot be shaken; Paul seeks a peace that this world can neither give nor take away, that passeth understanding; and the Revelation of John is as radical a vision of the future in triumph over the present as the mind of man has yet devised. No, for Martin Luther King, Jr., the proof text for the movement, for himself, and for America was not one of the prophetic paeans to social justice from the Old Testament, but rather I Corinthians 15:52: "The trumpet shall sound and we shall all be changed."

Our Current Discontents

Today, both social conservatives and social activists are unhappy with the status quo. Each feels that the culture has reneged on a moral commitment in which each has invested heavily. To listen to the Christians who support Pat Robertson's 700 Club is to hear a litany of betrayal and disenfranchisement and profound dissatisfaction with the direction of the country. "Moral drift" is what they call it. They recognize it in changing social mores that are tolerant on such matters as abortion and homosexuality, and in a climate that seems to be driven by anti-family values, social violence, and the corrosive effects of an ever-present pornography.

If the social conservatives are unhappy one would suspect in this win-lose culture that the social activists should be happy, but they too pine for the days of yore and the days that are yet to be. There is nothing more depressing than to hear recited the litany of lost ground and lost opportunity which so often is at the center of today's Martin Luther King, Jr., Day celebrations. As veterans of the movement age and their glory days grow more distant, they compare the moral energy of that generation with the apparent moral indifference of today. The backlash against affirmative action, the cut in social-service budgets, the hardening of attitudes toward minorities and the poor, particularly toward the urban poor, the seemingly intractable problems of black crime, the decline of the black family, and the economic instability of the black middle class—all of these cause social activists, in flights of rhetorical fancy not too far removed from fact, to declare that "we are worse off now than we were before the Civil Rights Act of 1964." The wholesale burning of black churches across the American South in the summer of 1996 is a hideous flashback to those long hot summers not so long ago, when in the South, instead of burning churches, they lynched the black people who went to them.

Two things hold these apparently polar constituencies of social conservatives and social activists together in what ought to be a creative tension: their anger and their expectation that things ought to be better. Of this visceral cultural anger that cuts across all conventional divisions in our society, Russell Baker has written, under the heading "God's Angry Land,"

America is angry at Washington, angry at the press, angry at immigrants, angry at television, angry at traffic, angry at people who are well off, angry at people who are poor, angry at blacks and angry at whites. The old are angry at the young, the young angry at the old. Suburbs are angry at cities, cities are angry at suburbs, and rustic America is angry at both whenever urban and suburban intruders threaten the peaceful rustic sense of having escaped from God's angry land.

Baker calls anger in America "a new national habit." Angry white Christians and angry black social activists both feel cheated. The things that have always worked for them no longer do so, and their anger stems from a disappointed conviction that somehow progress was inevitable and things and people would get better. As a British critic of the Welfare State once noted, however, "Things have got better; it's people who have got bloody worse."

Sir Isaiah Berlin once observed that "the ideas that liberate one generation become the shackles of the next," and in these tendentious times in America we are coming to a painful realization of that truth. We have always celebrated the notion of freedom, and by it we have usually meant freedom from restraint or constraint, and liberation from various forms of bondage and tyrannies political, social, economic, and ideological. The history of our social experiment may well be the extension of that premise to its logical conclusion—the ultimate, nearly autonomous freedom of the solitary individual from all restraints, constraints, obligations, and relationships. In these celebrations of "freedom from" as a uniquely American form of self-indulgence, the middle-aged Freemen of Justus Township, Montana, are the 1990s descendants of the flower children of the 1960s Haight-Ashbury District, a comparison neither would find flattering.

That rugged individualism that is the personification of our American sense of freedom, and which we celebrate on the Fourth of July and in our popular myths and heroes, also contributes to the breakdown of the social fabric that has always provided a secure context for our freedoms. Freedom "from" has not yielded to an appropriate freedom "for," and the national culture is much the poorer for it. We are perhaps further now from Winthrop's ideal of a city set upon a hill than at any point in our national history.

Back to the Bible?

In times like these in America, historically we have been invited "back to the Bible," and there are many who issue that call today. So-called Bible churches are filled on Sundays with people seeking a way into the good life, people who are literally hungering and thirsting after righteousness. We will discuss that search in more detail in the final section of this book. "Back to the Bible!" is the cry of many sincere Christians, and as we draw nearer to the millennium, and as our troubles and problems develop new immunities to our quick-fix vaccines, that cry will grow in volume and in intensity. If the concept of "back to the Bible" means an effort to find a time and a place in which we will not be disturbed by the world in which we find ourselves, and an effort to find a secure, user-friendly, no-risk place to conserve ourselves and our worldly goods from threat and danger—much like those 1950s Cold War backyard bomb shelters—then we are doomed to disappointment, for the Bible makes no such promises to Americans or to anyone else in this life.

If we accept the call to go back to the Bible, we will have to do so with an unnatural cultural modesty that makes it clear that we are seeking what we have not yet enjoyed—the effort to conform our will and our work to the will and the work of God. The land we seek is not behind us, it is before us, and that is the secret the Bible has always been willing to impart to those who would seek it. The Bible opens with an account of creation in the Book of Genesis; it closes with a revelation of a time superior to this one, a time that is yet to be. Reading the Bible to find ways of justifying the status quo, then, is an enterprise that is bound for frustration and failure.

The temptations to misread the Bible on our

own behalf and to domesticate it for our own purposes are many and dangerous, and in America, devoted as we are to the Bible, we have tried them all. Bibliolatry, the worship of the Bible and the making of it an object of veneration, of ascribing to it the glory due to God, is one of those temptations that we ought to avoid. Literalism, which worships the text and gives it an inappropriate superiority over the spirit that animates it, is another temptation to be eschewed. And the worst of these, what I call culturism, is the worship of a culture in which the Bible is forced to conform to the spirit of the age. In our discussions of interpretation we have addressed those temptations, which in the context of the religious culture of the United States have not served us very well.

The Bible is a book for the future, about the future, and written with confidence in the future. It embraces the future not out of disgust with the present or with the past but out of the conviction that God is in the future, and to be where God is, is to know fulfillment, purpose, and bliss. Who should be satisfied with anything less than that? Recovering the lost vision for America may mean recovering God's vision for a future society of equity, love, and peace, a society rich with change and destined for a world we have not yet known. Making sense of the Bible has been an American cultural preoccupation now for nearly four hundred years. We are neither righteous Israel nor decadent Rome. We are, however, a needy nation, as needy of God and of one another as we have ever been.

Perhaps this bottoming out of our experience will make us less arrogant, less certain of our Manifest Destiny, more desirous of being transformed, and less willing to conform. The Bible is not a therapy program nor is it a human success story, a moral tale with an inevitably happy ending. It is the account of a faithless people and a faithful God who seek constantly to renew their relationship each with the other. Perhaps we are prepared to hear that story for the first time.

PART TWO

THE USE AND ABUSE OF THE BIBLE

"Either this is not the gospel,
or we are not Christians."

—Thomas Linacre (1460–1524),
upon reading the gospels
late in life for the first time

CHAPTER 4

HARD TEXTS AND CHANGING TIMES

THE Bible would be a difficult enough book to read were it used simply as an aid to private devotion and inspiration, and even in reading for that purpose one would usually read with some selectivity. Pocket versions of the Bible often contain the Psalms and the gospels. Within the Psalms alone one is likely to encounter powerfully disturbing passages that are not all soothing and "spiritual." How, for example, does one apply to one's devotions Psalm 137:9, which reads, "Happy shall he be who takes your little ones and dashes them against the rock"?

More Than a Private Book?

The Bible has always been more than a private book. It is, in fact, and always has been, a very public book; public in the sense that it is to be read and commented upon in public. We see this in the account of Jesus' visit to his home synagogue at the start of his public ministry, when his first act was to read the scroll of the prophet Isaiah, to do so in public, and then to comment on it. The implication is that the Bible is meant to have an effect upon the way in which people and their communities go about the business of life.

When we read in Exodus and Deuteronomy of the delivery to Moses of the law, in the form of the commandments from God on Mount Sinai, we are meant to understand that this is not simply a public occasion, but the establishment of what we would today call public policy. The Bible is for people, but more than that, it is understood to be for the ordering of the private and the public, the individual and the corporate affairs of a community of people. In Jewish history, the community is formed when it is given the law: Whereas before the delivery of the law the people are a rowdy assortment of individuals with private and personal agendas, they become something other than that when the law is given to them; they become the people of God. I Peter 2:9–10 alludes to this transformation:

> But you are a chosen race, a royal priesthood, a holy nation, God's own people, that you may declare the wonderful deeds of him who called you out of darkness into his marvelous light. Once you were no people but now you are God's people; once you had not received mercy but now you have received mercy.

The Bible, then, does not simply have a public dimension; it is a public book, and those to whom it is given and who take it seriously are meant to order their affairs from it.

This public dimension of the Bible has a long history, and some of that history is heroic and dramatic. We have a clear image of Daniel in the lion's den—the brave Jew and the menacing lions ready to tear him apart—but we ought to remember that Daniel was thrown into the lion's den because he practiced his Jewish religion in public and at great consequence in the face of the Babylonians who had captured Jerusalem. We know what happened: God stopped the mouths of the lions and Daniel was spared.

Hebrew scripture is filled with accounts of public fidelity to God's law against powerful opposition. It was public fidelity to the law as found in the Bible that distinguished the Jewish people from every other people on the earth, when in their minority status and in exile this public fidelity preserved them as well as distinguished them. Christians also became people of the Book. In the days when they too were a persecuted and then barely tolerated minority within the Roman Empire, they and their Book were considered to be subversive. The Christian loyalty to its own system, to its one Book and its one God, was held to contribute directly to the fall of Rome to the Vandals: The Roman gods, in the city's hour of need, felt unappeased and thereby failed to protect the Romans from their fate. It was to counter this charge that Augustine wrote *The City of God*.

When Christian culture succeeded to the place once held by that of Rome, the Christian biblical worldview, now no longer a private or minority sectarian point of view, became the basis of Christian society. Until the world should come to its appointed end and Jesus return to rule it himself in glory, the best that Christians could do with their unexpected inheritance of temporal power was to order that society according to biblical principles. That goal is perhaps best expressed in the phrase from the Lord's Prayer of the Sermon on the Mount, which both anticipates the establishment of the kingdom of God on earth and also proposes how to manage until it comes. When Christians pray "...Thy kingdom come, Thy will be done on earth, as it is in heaven..." they mean to keep their anticipation of the future high, but rather than wait for the society of heaven and the rule of God, they seek to establish here on earth as much of that divine society as possible, so that, in Augustine's revealing phrase, earth becomes but a "colony of heaven."

It is thus from an unexpected and extended possession of temporal power that Christians adapt their vision of heaven and rule of God to a vision of earthly society; and in that heavenly vision transferred to earthly geography, the Bible, for Christians, plays an enormous role, for it contains the powerful examples of ancient societies that professed to follow the Lord and then did not. The historical books of the Old Testament, with their accounts of the flawed kings and kingdoms of Israel, were a vivid lesson in civics. God would dwell among and bless his people, but only if they followed his commandments and respected his demands. Indeed, the notion of a Messiah, one who would come in glory to reign in equity forever, was increasingly thought to be dependent upon the moral and spiritual perfection of the people to whom he was to come. The Messiah would come when the world was fit to receive him. The delay in his coming was therefore not an arbitrary capriciousness, but a sign that the work of human improvement, the colonization of earth after the heavenly model, still remained to be done. In this spiritual ambition with its enormous social, political, and cultural consequences, the Bible comes to play a very significant role, and thus its interpretation and application become ever more important.

The image and ideal of Christian society, a heavenly vision mediated by the priests, sacraments, and traditions of the Roman Catholic Church, was at the center of medieval Western civilization. When they were once taught to us all, courses in Western civilization were essentially courses in the integrating force of Christian theology upon civil society: Gothic architecture, the writings of Dante, and the theology of Thomas Aquinas were all saying and doing and meaning the same thing, as part of the same plan.

Protestantism was by no means a repudiation of that plan; in fact, it regarded itself as restoring the purity of the vision by recovering the place of the Bible in defining and ordering it. Those who credit the Protestant Reformation less to Luther's piety and German nationalism and more to the mechanics of Gutenberg's printing press are nearer the truth than we might wish. It was the invention of printing that enabled the results of biblical scholarship, and generations of furtive translations of the sacred text into popular language, to be placed into the hands of people other than theologians and textual experts. Thus, William Tyndale, who has been called the father of the English Bible, could, before his death in 1536, say in his *Remarks to a Learned Man,* "If God spare my life, ere many years, I will cause a boy that driveth the plough shall know more of scripture than thou doest."

For Protestants, what the priests and the sacraments and the magisterium of the Roman Church had not yet achieved, and could never achieve—the kingdom of God on earth and hence the coming to earth of the kingdom of heaven—the Bible, when rightly understood and applied, could. Interest in the Bible and in its translation was not academic, an enterprise of pure scholarship; it was the potent union of piety and politics designed to hasten the day when, as is written in Revelation 11:15, "The kingdom of the world has become the kingdom of our Lord and of his Christ, and he shall reign forever and ever." This phrase is recognizable from the "Hallelujah Chorus," centerpiece of Handel's *Messiah*.

Thus, the private and subversive book moves to the center of the public stage, its meaning, if not clearer, then certainly more accessible by the translation of the text into the language of the reader. Readers of the English Bible continue to have a difficult time with the notion that they are reading a book not written by or for them nor in their own language, and so, conveniently, they forget that inconvenient fact. The task of reading scripture has always been to attempt a reconciliation between what is particular and peculiar to the time and place of its writing and what is universally applicable beyond the bounds of time and place, and beyond circumstance and culture. This task, always difficult, is made even more so when the biblical culture and the culture in which the Bible finds itself are far removed from one another. One can appeal, as Christians often do, to the unchangeable character of God, and the fundamental human condition, as two fixed realities. That is a convincing argument, and yet it has to be qualified by the fact that the apprehension of that unchangeable character of God and the understanding of that fundamental human condition invariably change and are subject to change. Human beings may be universally and always flawed; and yet the expression and the context of those flaws are subject to the changing circumstances of our history and culture.

In trying to make sense of scripture, as we have said before, it is difficult enough to understand what the text meant "then," in the period in which it was first written, to say nothing of what it means "now." The meaning is naturally tied up with the writer's intention, and with what the listener could reasonably be expected to understand. That interpretation itself is no easy task, and all of the linguistic tricks in the repertoire of the scholars will not make it any easier; and then to that task comes the additional responsibility of questioning whether we hear it or read it in the same way, and if, in fact, we are meant to.

Beyond "Original Intent"

Some schools of thought argue that the only important thing to know is what scripture meant then—the school of "original intent," with which the confederates of Edwin Meese approached the United States Constitution. Find out what they meant, and do it or follow it. Anything else is tampering with the text and its intention. Other schools argue that while it may be interesting to know what scripture meant and what was intended and what was heard, it is far more critical to ask, in light of that knowledge, what it can and does mean now. If scripture is a living and not a static text, we must determine in what ways it can, and possibly cannot, speak to its present hearers and readers. Interestingly enough, while these positions would appear to be quite opposite, what they have in common is a reverence for the Bible that requires them to find a way to respond to it, for the sanction of the Bible is essential to the legitimacy of both schools of thought. Where the Bible is taken most seriously, the struggles for the rights to its interpretation will be the keenest. Thus it is no accident that in America, where the Bible remains at the center of cultural discourse after nearly four hundred years of Christian civilization, the battles for the Bible and the culture of which it is so significant a part remain so intense, so unforgiving, and as relevant as the next election.

The Bible does not make this appropriation of itself an easy thing. It is full of hard texts that either do not easily translate themselves into the contemporary view of the world, or if they do, and in fact are too clear, create a form of cultural dissonance that is in itself problematic, and even destructive. Some of the hard texts are hard because they are difficult to understand, others are hard because they might represent points of view at odds with our conventional wisdom or with other parts of scripture, and still others are hard because they may demand too much of us. The hardest part of any exercise in applied scripture is to determine the relationship between what we can see developing as biblical principles, and what are clearly biblical practices, some of which in fact may be at odds with those principles. When we are tempted in frustration to argue that the Bible isn't consistent, we must of course remember that the Bible wasn't set out to be a textbook of morals and philosophy and political economy. That is a burden we have placed on it, quite foreign to its nature; and while it is true that, as Emerson says, "a foolish consistency is the hobgoblin of little minds," we all know that inconsistency is a flaw only in the constrained world of logic, and that we nevertheless, as perhaps too tidy-minded men and women, want to find some larger light by which to read and appropriate scripture to our own circumstances.

In this section of the book I will look at some hard texts that embrace many of the issues I have just discussed, and look at them in what I would call their public or civil context, the degree to which the readings of scripture either lead to or reflect policies that have an enormous significance for the public life we share together, and, as well, for the public repute of the Bible itself. Let me begin with a relatively benign, though by no means irrelevant, case of hard texts and changing times, from which I hope to derive a principle that will allow us to look more closely at more pressing and contemporary issues. Let us look now at the hard texts and changing times concerning the issue of temperance.

The Case of Drink

"Wine is a mocker, strong drink a brawler; and whoever is led astray by it is not wise." (Proverbs 20:1) This was the text used by the man from the Temperance League when he visited my Sunday school class of prepubescent boys nearly fifty years ago. Prohibition as a national policy had been dead twenty years, but with the Baptists among whom I was brought up, drink was still irrigation for the fields of sin. We were encouraged to "vote dry" in the annual referendum on the sale of alcoholic beverages in our town, grape juice was still the drink of choice in the celebration of the Holy Communion, and the young, especially the boys, were given early and routine lectures on the evils of drink. It was for just such a purpose, to terrify us, that we boys were treated to a demonstration by the temperance lecturer. On the platform he had put a jar of what he said was alcohol, and into the jar he dropped a large beefsteak. Instantly the alcohol stripped the flesh from the bone, and while we stood there amazed, the lecturer told us that this was what drink would do to our bodies and sin to our souls. He then cited Saint Paul: "Know ye not that ye are the temple of God, and that the Spirit of God dwelleth in you? If any man defile the temple of God, him shall God destroy; for the temple of God is holy, which temple ye are." (I Corinthians 3:16–17)

Allowing this to sink in, he then passed out cards with these verses printed on them, and we were invited to "take the pledge" against drinking by signing the card and pledging abstinence, and to pray for those who drank. There was no doubt in our minds that the Bible was against drink. There was even a section on temperance among the Responsive Readings from Scripture in the back of the *New Baptist Hym-*

nal; and in the Baptist Church covenants, in which members pledged their Christian duty to one another, among the promises made was this one: "...To abstain from the sale and use of intoxicating drinks as a beverage."

This appeal to the young to take the pledge was an old and approved tactic in the American crusade for temperance, and it was based upon the sound, but decidedly un-American, Jesuit principle that the moral foundation inculcated in the young before the age of ten would form the principles of the adult for life. It did not matter that they were abstaining from something that they had not yet had. The pledge was part of the moral armor with which the evil darts of Satan could be withstood. The text for this endeavor came from Proverbs 22:6: "Train up a child in the way he should go, and when he is old he will not depart from it." From the first third of the nineteenth century, young American Christians, mostly Protestants, were invited to join the growing temperance movement by "enlisting" in what its founder, a Presbyterian minister, Thomas Hunt, called the Cold Water Army. Thousands sang the army's anthem:

> *I do not think*
> *I'll ever drink*
> *Whiskey or gin,*
> *Brandy or rum,*
> *Or anything that*
> *Will make drunk come.*

Girls as well were encouraged to stave off drink and to reform their male friends with the line "Lips that touch wine will never touch mine." By the close of the nineteenth century most people of Protestant America's churches, with the notable exception of the Episcopalians, who were referred to by their abstemious critics as the "Whiskey-palians," had substituted the unfermented juice of the grape in their sacramental usage. Indeed, the considerable fortunes of the Welch grape juice empire were founded in part upon the successful production and marketing of a cheap and nonalcoholic grape-juice substitute for the Lord's Table, first in Methodism, which embraced total abstinence with enthusiasm, and then throughout American Protestantism.

Temperance also played an ugly role in America's rising anti-Catholicism and chauvinism in the closing days of the nineteenth century. The fact that the Roman Catholic mass featured wine, although the people as yet communicated only in one kind, the wafer, fueled the perception that the Church of Rome and its growing immigrant constituency was fundamentally alien and dangerous to the American way. Few arguments against Catholic immigrants, and against the Irish in particular, were more repeated than were the claims that they were habitual drunkards who would live at the charge of the general welfare, and because of their enormous capacity to reproduce would forever be a burden upon the pure and reformed native stock. When James G. Blaine of Maine, in a remark that cost him the presidency, called the Democrats the party of "Rum, Romanism, and Rebellion," prejudice and morality were efficiently combined.

What Does the Bible Say About Drink?

Paradoxically, the Bible proved to be a rather shaky platform upon which to base a campaign against drink. Despite the unfortunate and vivid instance of Noah's drunkenness in Genesis 9:20–27, and the terrible consequences that befell his second son, the cursed Ham, no doctrine against drink can be found by precept or example among the writers of the Old Testament. It is difficult to reconcile a biblical argument against drink with the hospitable sentiments, for example, of Psalm 104, which praises God who "...dost cause the grass to grow for the cattle, and plants for man to cultivate, that he may bring forth food from the earth, and wine to gladden the heart of man..."

The New Testament is no more helpful. The first miracle attributed to Jesus is the one he performed at the wedding at Cana, as recorded in John. There he turns water into wine, and a very good wine at that, to replenish that which had run out. The miracle is one of blessing and abundance, the sign of which is wine, which in the formula used in the Christian Eucharist must now be understood as the gift of God for the people of God.

Jesus ends his earthly life at a Passover seder, which Christians refer to as the Last Supper.

It is impossible to imagine that so fundamentally Jewish a celebration of hospitality and the providence of God would be celebrated with anything less than the best wine available. Saint Paul, in giving practical advice to his young apprentice Timothy, tells him, "No longer drink only water, but use a little wine for the sake of your stomach and your frequent ailments." (I Timothy 5:23) His pastoral advice to Titus is to bid the older women of the Christian community "to be reverent in behavior, not to be slanderers or slaves to drink...." (Titus 2:3)

The ambiguous witness of the Bible created a problem for the temperance movement, which required the sanction of the Bible for its moral position on alcohol. The temperance advocates were thus forced to a series of ingenious interpretive or exegetical devices if they were to maintain the authority of scripture together with their reformist principles, chief of which was what we would call today "contextuality," or "situationalism," which is that the context or situation in which the Bible appears to permit the social use of alcohol must be understood, and indeed understood as significantly different from our own time. We know more about the dangers of drink than did our biblical predecessors, and thus if they knew then what we know now their position would agree with ours. If Jesus had known of the evils of drink as manifested in industrial Western society, he would not have been so free with his transformation of water into wine. Everything that the Bible describes is not necessarily to be permitted or approved of. The patriarchs, for instance, practiced polygamy and required circumcision. Christians no longer approve of the one nor require the other, but the authority of scripture is not compromised. So goes this argument.

Another argument was an ingenious, albeit tedious and ultimately unconvincing one, that there were in fact two kinds of wine of which the Bible spoke: an intoxicating one that was generally condemned and presumably was that which Noah drank, and an innocuous one not unlike Welch's formula, which taken in moderation was that which Jesus himself used and which was familiar to the early Christians. Nineteenth-century biblical scholars who were also devoted to the cause of temperance found the two-wine theory necessary not only to advance the social reform cause of temperance but to preserve the moral reputation of Jesus. One such critic, Moses Stuart, was an ardent advocate of the two-wine theory, for, as he wrote, it would be "impossible to suppose the wine fermented and yet leave the character of the holy Savior unscathed."

So convinced were the total abstainers of the superiority of their moral conviction that the most extreme of them argued that it didn't matter what Jesus did or what scripture said. If Jesus drank, then he would have to go. Said one of these radical reformers:

What?! Accept a brewer, distiller, or manufacturer of intoxicating wine as my Savior?

Convince me that Jesus of Nazareth was such, and I will relinquish on the instant a faith I have fostered for more than thirty years, and will unite in the cry, "Away with Him! Crucify Him! Crucify Him!"

What was becoming increasingly clear was the tension between the ambiguity of the Bible and the clarity of cultural convictions that desperately required its moral sanction. "If the duty of total abstinence from all intoxicating drinks cannot be fairly made out from the unforced testimony of the word of God, we should...be left without the greatest of all sanctions to one of the best of all causes." The Cold Water Army thought it was reading the signs of the times through the lenses of the Bible. In fact, it was attempting to read the Bible through the lenses of the signs of the times. The question of temperance raised the even greater moral question of how to interpret the Bible, whose cultural context was clearly at odds with the contemporary culture, without compromising the moral authority of the Bible or falling into a dangerous relativism or situationalism. Contrary to conventional wisdom, the nineteenth-century crisis of biblical authority had less to do with the higher criticism and the assaults on the Bible of Darwin and nineteenth-century science than with the increasingly frustrating task of translating biblical morality wholesale into the contemporary culture without doing violence to either.

By 1958, when Prohibition was but the fading memory of a failed social experiment, the great defeat for cultural Protestantism in America, a way out of the nineteenth-century debate between biblical practice and biblical principle was finally cleared in the matter of drink. In the conservative Protestant journal *Christianity Today*, Roland Bainton, professor of ecclesiastical history at Yale Divinity School, wrote an article titled "Total Abstinence and Biblical Principles." He began: "With regard to the use of alcoholic beverages, my practice and teaching are those of total abstinence. This stand is based on biblical principles, but I am free to confess that it is not based on biblical precepts or biblical practice."

What could he possibly mean? Bainton remained utterly unconvinced of the earlier arguments from the Bible for total abstinence. Any unforced reading of the word of God must conclude that at best the Bible is itself indifferent to the prohibitionist principles. The two-wine theory is utterly without merit, and to impugn the moral character of Jesus because without such a theory he is seen to have drunk wine is both ignorant and arrogant. For Bainton the issue was not biblical precedent but Christian principle. Such a view, he recognized, was contrary to much of Protestant America's bibliolatry, the worship of the text of scripture and its elevation as the sole norm of faith and practice. The Bible, for Bainton, was a book of principles, and not of precedents. The principles that governed his own behavior in the matter of drink clearly were contrary to much of biblical practice, but like the spirit which is superior to the letter, the principles rather than the precedents are meant to guide Christian living.

Bainton derived his principles from the New Testament. First, as Paul writes in I Corinthians, the body is the temple of the Holy Spirit, and therefore ought not to be abused. The second principle, also Pauline, is that the stronger should bear with the weaker, and thus set an example that the weak can follow. This is derived from Romans, where Paul says that while for some the eating of meat and the drinking of wine is no problem, they should abstain out of regard for those for whom it is a problem: "Do not, for the sake of food, destroy the work of God. Everything is indeed clean, but it is wrong for anyone to make others fall by what he eats; it is right not to eat meat or drink wine or do anything that makes your brother stumble." (Romans 14:20–21)

Making the biblical case for or against temperance is of course not really what Bainton's essay is about, and although he was concerned enough to make the best possible case for his position of total abstinence, the principle he introduced to do so is in many ways far more significant than the cause for which it was employed. In addressing a moral issue with both public and personal implications on the basis of Christian principles derived from a reading of the Bible, rather than simply on the basis of biblical practice and precedent, Bainton liberates us from a simpleminded bondage to texts whose context may be unrelated and unhelpful to our own. In other words, to be biblical may well mean to move beyond the Bible itself to the larger principles that can be derived from the Christian faith of which the Bible is a part, but for which the Bible cannot possibly be a substitute. To determine with what Christian principles one reads the Bible is to undertake an enterprise that requires more rather than less engagement with the Bible and with the cultures of its interpretation. It involves a rather daunting effort to see beyond the diversions of text and context, and of precedent and practice, and into the far more complex landscape of principle and teaching by which the whole is made considerably larger than the sum of its parts. Contrary to popular thinking, this invariably means giving more attention to the Bible, and more rather than less care to its study and interpretation.

The Bible must be understood not as a thing in and of itself but as a part of the whole teaching and practice of the Christian faith. The confrontation between our social and moral presuppositions is what we bring to the text, and what we find in the text and in its context is something we will have to face. That conflict, if it is to be resolved, must be done not on the basis of expedience but on the basis of the Christian principles with which we interpret biblical practice. To argue policy from biblical situations is to be limited to the textual imagination of the biblical context. Bainton requires a more demanding criterion: that we seek after the lively Christian principle that transcends the particularities of the Bible situation and with which we understand both those situations and our own. Not only is the Bible to be subject to this scrutiny, but so too are those who would take the Bible seriously, and this demand may well be the most dangerous and uncomfortable of all demands for those most accustomed to concealing their self-interested agendas behind the protective camouflage of the Bible. Difficult and demanding as such a principle of interpretation may be, it is, I suggest, the only viable way to negotiate, as biblically minded people, between hard texts and changing times, without doing damage to the text, the times, or to ourselves. How we have gone about this business in the context of some of the more demanding issues of our day is the subject of the next chapters.

CHAPTER 5

THE BIBLE AND RACE:
THE MORAL IMAGINATION

IN the summer of 1995, one hundred and thirty-two years after the Emancipation Proclamation, one hundred and thirty years after the end of the Civil War, and twenty-seven years after the death of Martin Luther King, Jr., at their annual meeting the Southern Baptist Convention, America's largest Protestant denomination, apologized for the role it had played in the justification of slavery and in the maintenance of a culture of racism in the United States. The Baptists did more than apologize. They took on the more morally rigorous and theologically appropriate term of "repentance" to describe their action in adopting a resolution on the floor of their convention. For many this was a radical step, for while no one was prepared to embrace the historic arguments either for slavery or for racial segregation, there was no general enthusiasm to appear to repudiate either the faith or the conduct of their cultural ancestors. For others this was hardly news at all. In their not altogether unsuccessful efforts to be a national rather than a regional church, the Southern Baptists have for a generation sought to distance themselves from the more vivid racism of their past, and have increasingly extended the right hand of fellowship to African Americans who earlier would have been excluded, or would have excluded themselves from such fellowship.

For still others, including some African Americans, the apology and the act of repentance was too little too late: "We knew you were wrong, the world knew you were wrong; why did it take *you* so long to learn that you were wrong?" This was the question, uncharitable but pointed, that many African Americans asked of their newly repenting brethren, and in the age of the ubiquitous nonapology apology—when people

116

routinely issue apologies not for what they did but for what you think they did, or for the consequences of what they did, or for the feelings that estrange you from them, but neither confess to what they did nor repudiate what they did— the apology can be seen to be a morally artful dodge that implies responsibility but avoids confession and confrontation with the sin or the crime. This is why, for example, morally ambiguous apologies such as those offered by Japan for its part in World War II prove unacceptable to those with a sense of grievance. When an Englishman treads on your foot in a crowded car on the London Underground, simultaneously with the offending deed he mutters "Sorry," which, as we all know, is not an expression of regret but a statement of intention. When politicians "apologize," they usually say something like this: "If I have given offense, I am sorry that you see it that way; and thus, for your error in perception of my actions or intentions, I apologize." We all recognize that artful dodge.

The Southern Baptists are more than Southern Baptists, however; they are Christians as well, and hence they are engaged in an act of repentance that in theological and biblical terms is a much more demanding exercise. It requires that one confront the sin, the sinner, and the sinned against. It demands confession, the asking of forgiveness, and the expression of an intention for what the Book of Common Prayer calls Amendment of Life. Only in that sequence of actions can pardon or forgiveness be granted;

otherwise it is merely an exercise in self-exorcism. Most Americans understood the moral implications of an incomplete process of repentance when Gerald Ford "pardoned" Richard Nixon for crimes and misdemeanors to which Richard Nixon had never confessed. The process was manifestly incomplete, and despite President Ford's genuinely noble efforts to put all that unpleasantness behind, it was never settled, nor did it ever disappear, for the essential ingredients of confession, contrition, and amendment of life were absent.

Cultural apologies in which one segment of society apologizes for its crimes against another are very rare indeed, and most entities follow the famous dictum of the Duke of Wellington, "Never apologize, never explain." Spain has never apologized to what is left of the indigenous peoples of South America for the destruction of the native culture in the name of Christian imperialism. The United States has yet to utter a word of contrition for its treatment of the Native Americans, or for chattel slavery. In modern times, only Germany has taken public responsibility for its atrocities in World War II and apologized both to the Jews and to Israel. The example of President Richard von Weiszäcker, in his speech of May 5, 1985, to the German Bundestag, stands nearly without parallel in the acceptance of moral responsibility. When Harvard's Henry Rosovsky read this speech, he said that he felt "as if a stone had been lifted from his heart." A decade later,

France's President Jacques Chirac, in a ceremony commemorating the end of World War II, issued a similar apology to the Jews of France for French complicity in acts against the Jewish people during the occupation. It is within this context that we take seriously the brave actions of the Southern Baptists in their resolution of repentance concerning American slavery.

While apologies and repentance in the matter of slavery are fascinating topics and worthy of more attention than can be paid them here, of even keener interest is the role that the Bible plays both in the debates on slavery and in the actions that have ensued in the repudiation of slavery and racism. If the ancestors of the Southern Baptists understood their system of slavery and racial apartheid to be based upon their reading of the Bible, what does this tell us about how people in general, and the Southern Baptists in particular, interpret scripture? What biblical or extra-biblical principles, explicit or implicit, are at work? What does this say to us about changed understandings of an unchanged text? It is abundantly clear that the Southern Baptists rejected neither the faith nor the Bible of their mothers and fathers, but they have certainly changed their minds as to what scripture says and to what scripture means, and that change has engendered enormous changes in the social consequences. How is the moral consensus changed without changing the contents of the Bible?

Slaves, be obedient to those who are your earthly masters, with fear and trembling, in singleness of heart, as to Christ.

(Ephesians 6:5)

God is no respecter of persons.

(Acts 10:34)

There is neither Jew nor Greek, there is neither slave nor free, there is neither male nor female; for you are all one in Christ Jesus.

(Galatians 3:28)

As previously noted, I grew up in the 1940s in the relatively benign climate of Plymouth, Massachusetts, where there had been since the Revolutionary War a small community of colored people, as we were then called. We were not the first persons of color in the land of the Pilgrims' pride, for we had all heard of Abraham Pierce, the "blackamoor" who had settled in Duxbury in the 1630s. We were by and large an insular and contented lot, long integrated into the Yankee culture and regarding much of it as our own. We were not, however, unaware of the legacy of slavery from which our ancestors had either escaped or been freed, and we were mindful through the Negro newspapers, to which some subscribed and which were circulated to all, of the larger issues of race in the country. Whenever we read of racial troubles in the north or of lynchings in the South, or of egregious instances of discrimination in the armed forces, or in the local police and fire departments, where some of our people served, the elders among us would murmur something about "poor Aunt Hagar's children." When my own parents remonstrated with me for not doing my homework, or for not doing it well enough, they would say, "You are meant to be more than a hewer of wood and a drawer of water."

These were biblical allusions, common parlance among black people for centuries, and they reflected the biblical literacy and Christian culture of black Americans descended from the slaves imported into America. Hagar was the slave girl who bore Abraham's first child, Ishmael, and when Sarah, Abraham's wife, bore him a legitimate heir some thirteen years later, both Hagar and Ishmael were banished from the household and sent into the desert on foot. The story is in Genesis 21. In Joshua 9 we read of a remnant of Canaanites who had not been slaughtered by Joshua but who were condemned to perpetual slavery in the land. To them Joshua says, "Now therefore you are cursed, and some of you shall always be slaves, hewers of wood and drawers of water for the house of my God."

As we have seen, the definitive Old Testament text for slavery and the subjugation of one race to another is found in the story of Noah. Thus, within the first third of the first book of Moses, almost as the first act of the second creation, the seeds of racism are sown and the foundations for slavery, segregation, and apartheid are laid. And slavery is no stranger among the patriarchs.

The greatest of them, Joseph, has listed among his successes as Pharaoh's minister for production the enslavement of the people whose forced labor was orchestrated in behalf of Pharaoh. "He made slaves of them from one end of Egypt to the other....Then Joseph said to the people, 'Behold, I have today bought you and your land for Pharaoh. Now...sow the land, and at the harvest you shall give a fifth to Pharaoh.'" (Genesis 47:21–24)

The culture of the New Testament was one in which slavery was quite common, and neither Jesus nor Paul condemn the practice; rather, they assume it to be one of the social givens of the day. Paul, with great eloquence, argues for the leveling of distinctions and the unity of spirit that is to be found in the fellowship of Christ, that is, among those who are called to be Christians; but he is equally clear that such spiritual freedom does not overcome the human circumstances in which one is found. In I Corinthians 7, he argues that everyone should lead the life that the Lord has assigned to him, and into which God has called him; everyone should remain in the state in which he was called. He says, "...this is my rule in all the churches....Were you a slave when called? Never mind. But if you gain your freedom, avail yourself of the opportunity. For he who was called in the Lord as a slave is a freedman of the Lord." Paul means that insofar as the Lord is concerned, the distinction between slave and free, as in Ephesians between male and female, is of no account. It is clear to Paul, and now made clear to the Corinthians, that in this life the distinctions *do* count. "So, brethren," he writes in I Corinthians 7:24, "in whatever state each was called, there let him remain with God."

The letter of Paul to Philemon would seem to amplify this position. Paul asks his fellow Christian, Philemon, to treat his slave, Onesimus, "no longer as a slave…but as a beloved brother." This does not mean that Onesimus is any less a slave than he was, and Philemon is not ordered to release him from slavery on the ground that chattel slavery is inconsistent with Christianity, or that one Christian cannot hold another Christian as a slave. None of that is said. What is asked of Philemon by Paul is that he treat his slave as a Christian brother, and what is implied is that in the Lord, Paul, Philemon, and Onesimus are moral equals. It is clear that the institution of slavery is not condemned. Onesimus is not set free, and Paul sees no apparent contradiction is asking a free Christian brother to treat his Christian slave as a brother in Christ. As one black commentator critical of Paul noted, "Paul never met a social status quo that he didn't like." Not only did New Testament morality fail to liberate the slaves or even to mitigate their lot in this life, but it required of the slaves obedience to their masters, even those masters who were not Christian, as a part of their duty to Christ. Slaves were free only to obey, and these arrangements were ordained of God, sanctioned by the patriarchs, tolerated by Jesus, approved of by Paul, and enshrined in the Bible.

With such an array of texts and precedents extending throughout all of scripture it would not be hard, even today, to make a biblical case for slavery. Nowhere does the Bible condemn it; everywhere in the Bible it is the practice. The curse of Ham provides the justification for the subjugation of one tribe or race to another, and the counsels of Paul forbid tampering with a lawfully established institution. That Paul sees slavery as annulled in the kingdom means only that until the kingdom finally does come, what is, prevails; and what is, is slavery.

In antebellum America all of these arguments were well known. Slavery might offend the conscience or the moral sensibilities, as it clearly did with George Washington, who freed his slaves upon his death, and with Thomas Jefferson, who imagined a world without slavery but could not quite see his way clear to making such a world, but to those who took both slavery and the Bible seriously, the one supported the other. As we have seen, what perhaps more than anything else offended the southern Christian slaveholder before the Civil War was the northern notion that he suffered a guilty conscience, was a hypocrite, and could not possibly be a good Christian, since he held slaves. Such southerners took comfort not only from their sense of a superior civilization, but from their Bibles as well. Their peculiar institution was built upon a firm biblical foundation.

When in 1856 the Reverend Thornton Stringfellow, a Virginia Baptist, published his sermon "A Scriptural View of Slavery," he argued that God himself had sanctioned slavery through Noah, Abraham, and Joseph, and that the biblical record was unambiguous. When a convention of Confederate ministers in Richmond, Virginia, in April 1863, published their "Address to Christians Throughout the World," making the case for the morality of the Confederate cause as Christians, they said of slavery that they knew it more intimately than their critics. "We are...alive to all their interests; and we testify in the sight of God that the relations of master and slave among us, however we may deplore abuses in this, as in other relations of mankind, is not incompatible with our holy Christianity, and that the presence of the Africans in our land is an occasion of gratitude on their behalf, before God." Arguing that the South had done more than any people on earth for the African race, the ministers further argued that "the practicable plan for benefitting the African race must be the Providential plan—the Scriptural plan." To make their biblical position clear, the ministers cite I Timothy 6:1–2, where the Apostle instructs the young minister of Jesus on the subject of slavery:

Let as many servants as are under the yoke count their own masters worthy of all honor that the name of God and his doctrine be not blasphemed. And they that have believing masters, let them not despise them because they are brethren; but rather do them service because they are faithful and beloved, partakers of the benefit. These things teach and exhort. If any man teach otherwise, and consent not to wholesome words, even the words of our Lord Jesus Christ, and to the doctrine which is according to godliness, he is proud, knowing nothing, but doting about questions and strifes of words, whereof cometh envy, strife, railings, evil surmisings, perverse disputings of men of corrupt minds, and destitute of the truth, supposing that gain is godliness: from such withdraw thyself.

They could have cited with equal approval Titus 2:9–10, "Bid slaves to be submissive to their masters and to give satisfaction in every respect; they are not to be refractory, nor to pilfer, but to show entire and true fidelity, so that in everything they may adorn the doctrine of God our Savior." And they could have added Paul's advice to the Ephesians, repeated also in Colossians, where he urges slaves to be obedient to their masters in the same way that they would obey Christ, "not in the way of eye service, as men-pleasers, but as servants of Christ, doing the will of God from the heart, rendering service with a good will as to the Lord and not men." Masters are required to treat their slaves in the same way, "...and forbear threatening, knowing that he who is both their Master and yours is in heaven, and that there is no partiality with him." (Ephesians 6:5–9)

Southern Christians were quick to point out

that slavery was not an accidental or an incidental matter in biblical times, and that the Apostle Paul took considerable pains in nearly all of his letters to regulate slavery, a social fact that he accepted, within the ethics of a Christian society. Acceptance of the reality of slavery was not necessarily approval or endorsement. In heaven, where there is neither marriage nor giving in marriage, as Jesus points out, there is presumably no slavery, no master and no free, for as Paul says, in Christ there is neither free nor slave. On earth and in this life, however, for as long as it lasts, marriage and slavery obtain. Paul endorses neither, and neither does he condemn either. He accepts both. For the southern apologist for the compatability of slavery and Christianity, the principle that what is not proscribed in scripture is permitted *is* the principle. Southern slave-holding Christians demanded that they be judged on the basis of their conformity to the body of ethical and moral precepts regulating the relationships between slaves and their masters as recorded beyond dispute in the New Testament.

The Challenge to Scripture

It may be argued that the issue of slavery in the New World stimulated one of the most controversial debates about the nature of scripture and its interpretation since the formation of the scriptural canon at the end of primitive Christianity, anticipating both in scope and in intensity the turmoils characteristic of the battle between scripture and science of the eighteenth and nineteenth centuries, and the debates about authority and interpretation that pitted modernists against fundamentalists in the twentieth century. In many ways this was the first battle for the Bible and the conflict between its letter and its spirit, exposing its interior contradictions and pitting biblical ideals and principles against biblical practice and example. This was not a debate about authorship or translation, or the finer points of exegesis. Nor was it a dispute about the proper role and use of scripture in relation to the teachings of the Christian faith, the sort of debate that provoked and enlivened the controversies of the Reformation and the Counter-Reformation period. This was a dispute about the authority and morality of the Bible itself, and about how it ought to be read, interpreted, and applied.

Those who wished to challenge the morality of slavery found that they had to challenge both the authority and the interpretation of scripture. They found also that it was not as easy as it might appear, for, as we have seen, the biblical case for slavery was both strong and consistent. There was, however, a moral case to be made, and the morality for that case was made from the Bible itself. Here, the Bible's moral principles argued against the social practices to be found within the Bible, and as we saw in the biblical debate on temperance, principle in the hands of the reformers took precedence over practice, and claimed for itself the sanction of the Bible.

The issue of slavery was first debated in the West in the context of the Spanish empire and its ruthless approach to the indigenous peoples of its New World possessions. The Most Catholic King of Spain and his Imperial Ministers regarded the native peoples of Latin America as so many biblical Canaanites to be exterminated or enslaved. The land was regarded as a gift from God to the Spaniards, just as the Old Testament lands were God's gift to the children of Israel. They found in their reading of the Old Testament, particularly in the first five books of Moses, ample precedent for their campaign of conquest and subjugation in the New World. This Iberian conquest of what we now call Latin America, fueled by the joint enterprise of Spain and Portugal, had as one of its stated goals a missionary dimension and a desire to claim these benighted lands for Christ and the Catholic Church. Bernal Díaz, one of the conquistadores who served with Cortés in the campaigns in Mexico, recorded in his memoirs: "After we had abolished idolatry and other abominations from among the Indians, the Almighty blessed our endeavors and we baptized the men, women, and all the children born after the conquest, whose souls would otherwise have gone to the infernal regions."

The conquest and plunder of the native cultures at the hands of Cortés and Pizarro, under both papal and governmental auspices, is well known, as is their introduction of Negro slavery. Pizarro's treachery is particularly infamous. It was he who murdered the emperor of the Incas, Atahualpa, by giving the hapless sovereign the choice of being burned at the stake as a heathen or of being baptized and strangled as a Christian. These excesses were applauded by Christians at home and justified on biblical grounds, but there were some Spanish Christians for whom these outrages, particularly slavery, were intolerable. Arguing against the notion that the Spanish conquest was a just war against infidels, supported by scripture, opponents criticized bitterly these actions, also on biblical grounds. Chief among these critics was a reform-minded missionary, Bartolemé de Las Casas, the bishop of Chiapas in Mexico, who in 1550 wrote *In Defense of the Indians,* in which he argued that the biblical texts used to justify the enslavement of the native populations were all historically conditioned and, in fact, overruled and superseded by the biblical principles of love and charity toward neighbors and enemies as exemplified in the teachings of Jesus. The Bible could not be used to justify actions contrary to the moral law of Christ. His arguments did not prevail, but they are important because they mark a significant instance of the use of scriptural principle against scriptural practice, and the establishment of a hierarchy of moral values within scripture based upon the teaching and practice of Jesus.

Two centuries later, English evangelists John Wesley and George Whitefield would make the same case against the slave trade in English North America. They argued that the holding of slaves, although permitted in scripture, was inconsistent with an understanding of the New Testament's paramount teachings on spiritual rebirth, sanctification, and evangelism. Slaveholders were guilty also, in this view, of gross materialism and greed, in that they regarded slaves as property for gain and profit. The New Testament teachings against materialism and obsession with worldly goods were principles to be invoked here, and slaveholders should release their slaves and make Christians of them as an exercise in evangelism.

These arguments from scripture, amplified by a zeal for social reform not found in scripture but inspired and sustained by scripture, became the basis for the antislavery crusades in England throughout the eighteenth and nineteenth centuries, which, under William Wilberforce, led to the abolition of the English slave trade in 1833, and the provision by Parliament in that year of twenty billion pounds in compensation for the slaveholders. This was not accomplished without objection and appeals to the Bible, and no less a figure than James Boswell, biographer of Samuel Johnson, wrote, "To abolish a status which in all ages God has sanctioned and many have continued, would not only be robbery to an innumerable class of our fellow subjects, but it would be an extreme cruelty to the African savages, a portion of whom it saved from massacre and introduced to a happier life."

In America, the antislavery cause accelerated in the aftermath of the Revolution, and the major evangelical Calvinist denominations criticized slavery as inconsistent with the biblical principles of justice and mercy as found in the prophets Isaiah, Jeremiah, Amos, and Ezekiel, and with the American ideal of an elect and chosen nation in covenant with God. Such arguments were the basis of Samuel Hopkins's 1776 sermon "Dialogue Concerning the Slavery of the Africans." The Quaker John Woolman, in his *Considerations on the Keeping of Negroes,* and his *Journal,* both published on the eve of the Revolution, argued that slavery was inconsistent with New Testament principles, and based his arguments on Matthew 6:19 and Matthew 25:44.

In the first third of the nineteenth century these arguments would be amplified and fortified by the spirit of social reform throughout the northeastern portion of the United States and by argument—reminiscent of the "two wine" theory in the crusade for temperance—that suggested that the kind of slavery in the Greco-Roman world with which Saint Paul was familiar, and in which he acquiesced, was notably different from the kind of chattel slavery that had been introduced into the West by the African slave trade. The American version of slavery was far more brutal and unacceptable than the biblical one, and hence the clear teachings of the New Testament did not apply. By this reading, slaves were not obliged, as a Christian duty, to obey their masters, and masters, as a Christian duty, were obliged to release their slaves. David Walker, an African American, wrote in 1829 his *Appeal to the Coloured Citizens of the World,* in which he condemned the slaveholders as acting contrary to the substance of Peter's famous sermon in Acts 10, where at verse 34–36 the Apostle says, "Truly I perceive that God shows no partiality, but in every nation anyone who fears him and does what is right is acceptable to him. You know the word which he sent to Israel, preaching the good news of peace by Jesus Christ." Against those Christians who did not repent of their slave-holding Walker invoked the punishment of the returning Christ, in Revelation 22:11–12: "Let the evildoer still do evil, and the filthy still be filthy, and the righteous still do right, and the holy still be holy. Behold, I am coming soon, bringing recompense, to repay every one for what he has done."

Abolitionism, essentially a radical and secular political reform movement, would take its moral mandate from this sense of injustice and judgment. Its agenda was not to reform the Bible, but to use, according to its members, the clear moral principles of the Bible and its social sanction to obliterate slavery from the nation. The abolitionists had no patience with the exegetical niceties of their Christian slaveholding opponents, and thought of them as Pharisees who, while straining a gnat from their soup, would willingly swallow a camel. They knew that the devil could quote scripture for his own purposes, and their purpose was to destroy the devil and all his works, and to redeem scripture itself.

One could argue that the chief victim of the Civil War was not the vanquished South, but the Bible. Its authority had been challenged. Those who had trusted in it to preserve the righteousness of the southern case for slavery were utterly defeated and disappointed. Those who had been used to a clear and consistent view of biblical morality and authority were saddened, and perhaps surprised, to see that the Bible could be read in so many different ways, and could be heard to speak in contradictory and divisive terms. We tend to think that the Bible suffered at the hands of the new and rampant science, and that Darwinism, with its challenge to the intellectual authority of the Bible, compromised its unity and credibility. It may well be argued, however, that the battle for the Bible that counted and contributed to a radically different way of interpreting its messages was substantially a moral one, and the issues were by no means settled by the military cessation of hostilities at Appomatox Court House. Brothers went to war and shed blood in the most divisive form of human conflict, a civil war, and did so in large measure on the authority of mutually exclusive readings of scripture. Those who "won" won the right to view themselves as on the right side of the battle for the Bible. Those who "lost," however, contrary to all logic, neither capitulated their reading of the Bible to their victors, nor abandoned the Bible for themselves.

A historian of the Southern Baptists, writing of the period 1865 to 1900, noted that in accepting the defeat of the South in the Civil War as "providential" and "the will of God," they absolved themselves of responsibility and never repudiated either secession or slavery, the ostensible cause of the conflict. In fact, to the notion that the war might have been God's means of abolishing slavery, one Southern Baptist correspondent of the period responded that the very idea was preposterous, as it was well and widely known that slavery was approved of in both the Old and the New Testaments. While for others God might have overruled their views on slavery through the means of the terrible war, they would accept God's will but they would not change their minds. In 1869, a writer to *The Christian Index*, a Southern Baptist journal of opinion, said, "Now I would certainly be opposed to the restoration of slavery in this country, but I have undergone no change on the righteousness of slavery, nor can I change until convinced that our Bible is not the book of God."

Racism is the mother of slavery, segregation is the child of slavery, and all were believed to be amply supported by the Bible. As the Southern Baptists were not willing to give up their Bibles, neither were they willing to change their reading of the divine arrangements for society as described in the Bible. Their accommodation to the new world order imposed by their loss of the Civil War was the system of racial segregation that emerged to preserve the southern way and, like slavery, was found to be sanctioned in the Bible. In the struggles against racial desegregation, which began in earnest in the South after World War II, and the desegregation of the armed forces at the executive order of President Truman, himself a Southern Baptist, the South, in the memorable phrase of Senator Harry Flood Byrd of Virginia, offered "massive resistance," arguing that "you can't legislate morality," and that "you can't go against the Bible." The incident that inspired Martin Luther King, Jr.'s famous "Letter from Birmingham Jail" was a letter addressed to him from largely Southern Baptist clergymen who, in the name of civil peace and scripture, urged him to end his crusade for civil rights. Part of their argument was that King's actions were unbiblical and uncharitable, and that no one in the name of religion should be coerced into changing his mind on deeply held, devoutly held, principle.

Minds and hearts are indeed very difficult to change, and especially so when the unchanged mind and heart are sustained in their convictions by the sanctions of the Bible, to which all authority is submitted, and when those convictions reinforce and are reinforced by the cultural consensus—those extra-biblical lenses through which scripture itself inevitably is read. Minds and hearts were already changing in the culture of the South, however, and the source of that change was not necessarily the culture imperialism of the alien North, but a changed reading and hearing of scripture. For example, in 1956 Floyd Bryant, a self-confessed "sixty-three year old white man, a Baptist, and a Southerner," wrote an article in *The Southern Baptist Review and Expositor* under the title, "On Integration in the Churches." This is what he wrote:

> Throughout the first sixty years of my life I never questioned but that Peter's confession that "God is no respecter of persons" (Acts 10:34) referred exclusively to the differences among white Christian persons. Neither did I question that segregation was Christian, and that it referred to the separation of white and Negro people. Three years ago (1953) these views were completely transformed. I became convinced that God makes no distinctions among people whatever their race and that segregation is exclusively by God in the final judgment. I exchanged the former views which I had absorbed from my environment, for the latter views which I learned from the New Testament. I came to understand the meaning of Paul's plea, "Be not conformed to this world: but be ye transformed by the renewing of your mind, that ye may prove what is that good, and acceptable, and perfect will of God." (Romans 12:2)

Fixed Text and Changed Minds

Here we have an instance, and a remarkably vivid one at that, in which the mind and the heart are changed because scripture requires that in Christ minds and hearts be changed—or transformed, in Paul's language. What is remarkable is that the text itself remains fixed and unchanged. No new translations have emerged to clarify textual issues. No hidden or lost manuscripts have been unearthed that would unfix long-settled opinion. No startling revelations external to the biblical text have been discovered with radical new information. What has changed, however, is the climate of interpretation, indeed, the lenses with which we read the texts and tell the tales. The texts have not changed but we have, and the world with us. Scripture, like Jesus Christ himself, may be the same yesterday, today, and forever, but our capacity to read scripture and to appropriate Jesus Christ and his teachings is not. No one in contemporary America, except perhaps the most hard-bitten white supremicist, would read scripture with regard to race in the same way as Southern Baptists read it a century ago, or even thirty years ago; and no one feels that some travesty of scriptural integrity has happened because of that fact. The racial theories based on the tortured inheritance of the sons of Noah, upon which racism in America and apartheid in South Africa were based, have yielded to Saint Paul's notion of the new creation in Christ and the transformed, renewed mind. The very same Paul who was seen as the apostle of the status quo is now also, and by the same people, seen as the apostle of liberation.

It is not scripture that has changed, but rather

the moral imagination by which we see ourselves, and see and read scripture. It is that moral imagination that tells us what we see and hear in scripture, and it is that same imagination that allows us to translate those transforming images into the world in which we find ourselves. The moral imagination, liberated from slavery to the literal text, also liberates from the cultural captivity of context both ancient and contemporary, and is informed by nothing less than what Christians call the Holy Spirit. That is why the Book of Hebrews describes scripture as "sharper than a two-edged sword." That is why scripture is referred to as "the lively oracles of God."

Anticipating the act of the Southern Baptists by two years, no less a Southern Baptist and American icon than Billy Graham defined racial and ethnic hatred as a sin. Writing in *Christianity Today* in October 1993, of the culture of which he has been so conspicuous a part, Graham said:

> Tragically, too often in the past evangelical Christians have turned a blind eye to racism or have been willing to stand aside while others take the lead in racial reconciliation, saying it was not our responsibility. (I admit I share in that blame.) As a result, many efforts toward reconciliation in America have lacked a Christian foundation and may not outlive the immediate circumstances that brought them into existence.

Then, with the authority of the preacher who has lived intimately and publicly in the culture to which he now speaks, Billy Graham concludes:

> Our consciences should be stirred to repentance by how far we have fallen short of what God asks us to be as agents of reconciliation....Of all people, Christians should be the most active in reaching out to those of other races, instead of accepting the status quo of division and animosity.

C. Eric Lincoln, the distinguished social historian of black America, when asked in the summer of 1995 to comment on the Southern Baptists' repentance, said, "Just think of all the violence and bitterness we might have been spared if the Southern Baptists had repudiated racism sooner." This doubtless is true, and the sentiment of some that this is too little, too late, while ungracious, is surely understandable. This, though, is not about timetables, nor is it really about correcting a historical grievance; it is about how we read the Bible, and about the creation of the moral imagination that allows us to do so. In that same moral imagination it is never too late to be right, or to be good.

CHAPTER 6

THE BIBLE AND ANTI-SEMITISM: CHRISTIANITY'S ORIGINAL SIN

THE Harvard University Choir, arguably one of the great choral groups in America, has enjoyed that reputation over a very long period of time and refreshes it regularly with an astonishing output of good singing. Under a succession of distinguished choirmasters it has embraced the world's greatest choral literature, and when it sings the incomparable repertoire of Palestrina, Schutz, Mozart, and Bach on a Sunday morning in The Memorial Church, it preaches as no mere prose preacher can. Where words fail, or at best divide, music succeeds at the most fundamental and ultimate level of communication, and many an undergraduate singer, indifferent to theology, unmoved by the Bible, and perhaps even hostile to religion, has been brought to the borders of heaven itself by the experience of singing this great choral literature of the Christian West.

It was a profound experience of a quite different sort with which I was confronted after a University Choir performance of Bach's *St. John Passion* on a Good Friday evening some years ago. The rehearsals had been long and intense, the performance, on the most solemn evening of the Christian year, was perfection itself, and on the next day, Holy Saturday, the day before Easter, one of the undergraduate singers came to see me. She was in tears, and they were not of joy. Her dilemma was that she loved the music of Bach to which her singing in our choir had introduced her, and the most demanding and satisfying aesthetic experience of her young life had been achieved in the performance of the evening before.

As her fellow singers had, she had steeped herself in the music and in the countless rehearsals that had made the performance itself almost something of an anticlimax. True singer that she was, she knew that the true experience was in the rehearsals. The actual performance, however, had unhinged her. She was Jewish, she knew German, and she was torn apart because the cultural experience that had given to her and to so many others such pleasure was also the very same cultural experience that had destroyed her people and that remained a constant threat to the integrity of her own cultural identity. While her aesthetic self said, "This music is beautiful, and Bach is a genius, and these are the most exquisite sounds known to the human ear," her existential self said, "This text is against me and my people, and combined they represent everything horrid and hateful that has ever happened to any Jew at the hands of any Christian. How can this be good music or God's music? How dare I participate in it, much less enjoy it?"

I could listen to her and try really to hear what she was saying. I could talk on and on about contextualization, and art transcending politics, and the ironic hope that beauty could cancel wickedness, but I knew in my heart that I had little of real substance to say to her because she was right. The beauty of Bach's passion was grounded in the horrid realities of Christianity's original sin of anti-Semitism, amplified, alas, by the Lutheran culture of post-Reformation Germany within which Bach had flourished and done his best work.

As a footnote to this, I asked my colleague, the university choirmaster, why the *Passion* was not sung in English, since an English translation of the text had been provided while the performance in the darkened church had been given in flawless German. I expected him to give me some artistically correct apology for authentic performance practice in an effort to reproduce the effect of the Lutheran services of the eighteenth century where these passions would be performed, but he did not. With a pastoral sympathy equal to his capacity for making great music, he said, "In German it is less harsh; we can have much of the beauty without most of the pain." That "pain" was not the suffering of Jesus. It was rather the pain that Christians, in the name of that suffering Jesus, have imposed upon the Jews.

Another instance of the painfulness of Christianity occurred early in my ministry in The Memorial Church. My predecessor had extended the hospitality of the university's church, a consecrated Christian space lean in the architectural vernacular of Harvard's New England Protestant heritage, for use of the Jewish community at the time of the autumn High Holy Days. Space for meetings was ever in short supply, and the addition of space in The Memorial Church was a welcome relief. I was delighted to continue the happy custom, finding it congenial that this house of prayer for all people was in fact being used hospitably for all people. A crisis, however, arose when for the first time in this relationship one of the functionaries making arrangements for the Jewish services asked that the one cross, carved into the woodwork of the rood screen that separates nave and chancel from choir, be covered up. This had never before been requested, and I confessed to a certain reluctance to agreeing to the request, arguing that it would not make the space any less Christian to the Jewish worshipers, and it would give considerable offense to those who would regard the covering of the cross as an act of gross insensitivity to the Christian faith.

It was explained to me then that at the High Holy Days, in addition to the young people of the university who would throng to the services, there would also be many older people and for some of these the sight of a Christian cross in the place of their most intimate and significant devotions would represent neither hospitality nor generosity of spirit. It would represent the horrors of two thousand years of Christian anti-Semitism and, for many, more immediate memories of the twisted cross of the Holocaust. No hospitality at all was better than a hospitality, however generous and sincere, that invoked such terrors upon one's guests. I had long known, in something of an abstract way, the painful fallout of Christian anti-Semitism, but never before had I been confronted with the unavoidable fact that what was dearest to me in all the world, the sign and symbol of all that was true and good and holy, was not merely a "stumbling block," to use Saint Paul's freighted phrase in his letter to the Corinthians, but a gallows—a sign of all the perversity of which this fallen world is capable.

We never resolved the matter, for life is too untidy for a solution that would put all of our anxieties to rest, but we did reach an accommodation with Solomonic implications. We decided that rather than exclude symbols, we would include them, and we commissioned the manufacture of a Torah screen with suitable inscriptions in Hebrew, from Hebrew scripture, which on the High Holy Days would enrich the worship of all God's people in this particular space. The very untidy nature of this episode forced me as a Christian minister to face the remorseless tensions between the exclusive and inclusive elements of my Christian faith.

Not all Christian ministers, however, are allowed the luxury of learning within a climate of thoughtful dialogue all that they need to know on these matters. The case of the Reverend Bailey Smith, formerly president of the Southern Baptist Convention, America's largest Protestant denomination, comes to mind. On August 22, 1980, Smith was quoted as saying,

"I'm telling you, all other gods besides Jehovah and his son Jesus Christ are strange gods. It's interesting to me...how you have a Protestant to pray, and a Catholic to pray, and then you have a Jew to pray. With all due respect to those dear people, my friends, God Almighty does not hear the prayer of a Jew. For how in the world can God hear the prayer of a man who says that Jesus Christ is not the true Messiah? It is blasphemous. It may be politically expedient...because no one can pray unless he prays through the name of Jesus Christ. It is not Jesus among many. It is Jesus, and Jesus only. It is Christ only. There is no competition for Jesus Christ."

Nearly every major paper in the country carried an account of Dr. Smith's remarks, usually under a headline such as GOD DOES NOT HEAR JEWISH PRAYERS. The reactions were swift and predictable. Marc Tenenbaum, national Interreligious Affairs director for the American Jewish Committee, called the remarks "morally offensive, really a defamation of four thousand years of loyalty," and accused Smith of "invincible ignorance." The director of the Interfaith Witness at the Southern Baptist Mission Board, said that Smith's remark, "instead of furthering understanding, actually impedes it." The editor of *The Bible Recorder*, the journal of the Baptist State Convention of

North Carolina, said that he felt sorry for Southern Baptist missionaries working in Israel. "These words," he said of Smith's remarks, "could easily negate all the fine spadework that former SBC president Jimmy Allen and others have done there." Smith's remarks were apparently broadcast all over Israel, in Hebrew and in English, on the eve of Yom Kippur. Even Ronald Reagan got into the debate during his campaign for the presidency. Distancing himself from Jerry Falwell and from Bailey Smith, Mr. Reagan said, "Since both the Christian and Judaic religions are based on the same God, the God of Moses, I'm quite sure those prayers are heard....But then, I guess everybody can make his own interpretation of the Bible, and many individuals have been making differing interpretations for a long time."

Smith himself said, "I was emphasizing the distinctive nature of Jesus Christ. I still believe it is blasphemous to say that Jesus Christ is not the Messiah or Savior." He went on to say, "As a Christian minister I must proclaim what the Bible says in I Timothy 2:5: 'For there is one God, and one mediator between God and men, the man Christ Jesus.'" Letters of support appeared in Southern Baptist denominational periodicals indicating that Smith's position was by no means out of the mainstream of Southern Baptist opinion. One, typical of these, concluded: "The very name of Jesus is an offense to the Jew. But the only way they can ever be saved, and we will never get them or anyone else saved by compromising the gospel of Jesus Christ in order to make it palatable to the natural mind."

The writer based her argument on Acts 4:12: "Neither is there salvation in any other: for there is none other name under heaven given among men, whereby we must be saved." To her, Smith had got it right, and the criticism he was seeing from around the world simply confirmed the truth of what he had to say. "There is no other God but by the way of the cross. And we should never compromise the word of God in order not to offend the world."

The controversy died down as the nation turned to the presidential elections of November 1980, and Bailey Smith and Rabbi Ronald B. Sobel, head of the National Program Committee of the Anti-Defamation League of B'nai B'rith, announced the establishment of a joint working group and a seven-point program which, they argued, "represents an important step forward for Baptists and Jews." The controversy seemed settled, but the relationship between the views of Dr. Smith, which proved so offensive to many, and the Christian scriptures upon which they appear to be based, is an issue that has been with us since the earliest days of the Christian community, and will not go away, and is not easily resolved. The critical question is whether it is possible to believe in Jesus Christ as Savior and Lord, and to believe the New Testament as the living and true word of God in which Jesus is revealed, and to *not* be anti-Semitic? Or, as a contemporary New Testament scholar has put it, "When reading the Bible, must the

Good News for Christians always be bad news for Jews?"

What Does the Bible Say About Jews?

And all the people answered, "His blood be on us and on our children." Then he [Pontius Pilate] released for them Barabbas, and having scourged Jesus, delivered him to be crucified.

(Matthew 27:25–26)

Then what advantage has the Jew?
(Romans 3:1)

And there is salvation in no one else, for there is no other name in heaven given among men by which we must be saved.

(Acts 4:12)

For you, brethren, became imitator of the churches of God in Christ Jesus which are in Judea; for you suffered the same things from your own countrymen as they did from the Jews, who killed both the Lord Jesus and the prophets, and drove us out, and displease God and oppose all men by hindering us from speaking to the Gentiles that they may be saved, so as always to fill up the measure of their sins. But God's wrath has come upon them at last!

(I Thessalonians 2:14–16)

Given what the Bible clearly says, and if one

takes what the Bible says seriously, how can anyone fault Bailey Smith for what he said? The conventional wisdom is that the Bible, and particularly the New Testament, defines how Christians are to see themselves and to see others in relation to themselves. Must the Christian identity be sacrificed, muted, or compromised in order to satisfy the sensibilities of others, particularly of Jews? One Christian point of view toward anti-Semitism, alas of long-standing, is that anti-Semitism would disappear if all Jews simply accepted Jesus as the Messiah and became Christians. "Completed Jews," as the Jews for Jesus describe Jews who affirm the messiahship of Jesus, would then accept the essential truths of the Christian scriptures as true not only for Christians, but true for themselves as well. The Christian ambition for the conversion of the Jews, a conversion regularly prayed for from the Middle Ages until fairly recent days, in the Christian liturgies for Good Friday, would then be accomplished, and the New Testament prayer attributed to Jesus, "that they all may be one," would be answered.

The Conventional Wisdom

The conventional wisdom for most modern Christians is that we differentiate ourselves from the harsh and cruel anti-Semitism of former times. We do not engage in persecution of the Jews in the brutal fashion of premodern Europe. We are not like the medieval Christians, who, on their way to the crusades to rescue the Holy Land from godless Islam, also boasted of slaying Jews as they traveled. We recoil at the cruel pogroms of Europe, the expulsion of the Jews from Christian countries, the creation of ghettos, the blatant discrimination, great and small, against the Jews in the most civilized countries of Europe. Some of us wince at Shylock in *The Merchant of Venice,* and at Fagin in *Oliver Twist,* and feel a guilty pleasure when we like the music of that colossal anti-Semite Richard Wagner. Culturally, we have, over a very long period of time, become sensitive to the overt social and political anti-Semitism that has stained all Western societies, and we recoil at any egregious manifestations of Jew-baiting and discrimination. Tolerance and the American sense of fair play keep us, as a rule, aware of the risks to ourselves and to our society of anti-Semitism, and we recognize in the Father Coughlins of an earlier generation, and in the David Dukes of our own, the blatant dangers to our cherished civic pluralism.

Yet, while recognizing the social and cultural dimensions of anti-Semitism, and while seeking to redress past grievances and to prevent new ones, we nevertheless should remember that anti-Semitism is at heart a religious phenomenon, and for Christians, at the heart of religious conviction and identity, sanctioned by the Bible and by the culture of interpretation that shapes how we read and hear the Bible. Temperance was an issue in which the Bible was used to support an extra-biblical concern; the Bible represented a divided mind on the issue of slavery; but, and alas for the case of anti-Semitism, the Bible seems to be hardly ambiguous at all. We could argue with Bailey Smith's politics, his good sense and judgment, his cultural sensitivity, his sense of propriety, and his responsibility as a public figure of significant influence; how, though, could we argue with his reading of the New Testament, which seems not only to justify his position toward the prayers of Jews, unpalatable as it may be, but represents as well the way in which his fellow Christians for nearly two thousand years have read the same texts and reached something of the same conclusions? This is not to say that all Christians and all readings of Christian scriptures are inherently anti-Semitic. It is to say that the virus of anti-Semitism is in the bloodstream of inherited Christianity, and that it takes enormous effort and will to address that painfully indisputable fact.

The "original sin" of Christianity is not so much the fall from grace in the Garden of Eden and the consequent loss of innocence; for Christians the original sin of anti-Semitism has to do with the fact that in the name of the risen Christ and the loving Jesus, and in pursuit of the righteousness and virtue of his service, we Christians, in the name of good and of God, are responsible for the systematic destruction of God's chosen and beloved people, the Jews. "As a Christian," wrote a 1937 prizewinning essayist in a little book, *How to Combat Anti-Semitism in America*, published by *Opinion*, a journal of Jewish life and letters, "I find it difficult to look a Jew in the eyes without a sense of shame. As a member of one of the great majority groups that outnumber the Jews of the world by more than a hundred to one, I feel like a cad and a coward because of anti-Semitism." The essay was titled "A Job for Christians." And so it is.

It is not an easy job, however, for how can the average reader of scripture be expected to read the account of the crucifixion in Matthew 27, and not see in Holy Writ that "the people" in verses 25 and 26, the Jews, accept responsibility for the death of Jesus when they demand that Pilate, the governor, crucify him? Not only do they accept responsibility for themselves, relieving the Roman civil authorities of it, but they accept responsibility for their children as well. "His blood be on us and our children," invites both the epithet of "Christ killers," and a blood curse upon all Jews down through the centuries. Repeated in Latin homilies, and enshrined in the great passion music of Christian composers, this attribution of Jewish acceptance of guilt for the death of Jesus reminded Jewish Christians and Christian biblical scholars that in the Hebrew Bible bloodguilt or illicit bloodshed pollutes the earth. Such contamination, according to Numbers 35:33–34, can be expunged only by shedding the blood of the killer or killers. "You shall not thus pollute the land in which you live," says Numbers, "and no expiation can be made for the land, for the blood that is shed in it, except by the blood of him who shed it." This is nothing

153

less than a license to kill in the name of avenging the blood of Jesus. It is not the heirs of Pontius Pilate and of Roman civil authority who are to make expiation; it is the Jews. This was not some abstract point of theology or some obscure matter of biblical exegesis. This was clear to anyone, anywhere, who ever bore a grudge against a Jew. Is it any wonder, then, that when Jews see a cross they both fear and expect a knock on the door in the middle of the night?

Responsibility for the death of Jesus—indeed, in orthodox Christian doctrine, the death of God—is grave enough. Continuing obduracy in the face of the claims of Christianity compounds the original grievance against the Jews. Refusing to recognize Jesus—whose name is above every name—as Lord, and hindering those who do, is the sin of the Jew who is called variously in the epistles "stiff-necked," "hard of heart," and even, by the early Christians, "enemies of God." In the English prayerbooks descended from the Latin rites of the Roman Catholic Church of ancient times, among the so-called solemn collects on Good Friday until very recent days would be found one that numbers the Jews among Turks, infidels, and heretics and, after asking God's mercy on them, prays:

> ...and take away from them all ignorance, hardness of heart, and contempt of thy word; and so fetch them home, blessed Lord, to thy flock, that they may be saved among the remnant of the true Israelites, and be made

one fold, under one shepherd Jesus Christ our Lord.

Recent revisions of the Book of Common Prayer have softened this collect considerably, and the English version is itself a toned-down version of the old Roman collect, which referred to the "perfidious Jews."

With the destruction of the Jewish Temple in c.e. 70, Gentiles saw themselves proven right and the Jews wrong. The Jews' punishment had now begun, and all that had been theirs, the covenant and promises of the Hebrew Bible, even the very name Israel, now passed into the possession of the Christians. Augustine, one of Christianity's most significant thinker since biblical times, would write in the fourth century that "all that was concealed in the Old [Testament] was revealed in the New [Testament]," meaning that the very Hebrew scriptures themselves were now in full possession of the Christians.

All of this is deeply rooted in the subconscious identity of the Christian inheritance, where, on the basis of reading and hearing the Bible, and of being faithful to the Church whose book it is, to be a Christian would appear to require that one be anti-Jewish, and it confirms at the heart of the Christian faith what Krister Stendahl, sometime bishop of the Church of Sweden, calls "the most persistent heresy of Christian theology and practice." What will it take to unmask this demon and set us all free?

"Unless the church is reconciled with the Israel of God," writes Clark M. Williamson in a *Christian Century* piece of October 13, 1993, "The Church's Mission and the People of Israel," "it is hard to see how it can claim to be reconciled with the God of Israel." Fifty years after the Holocaust and the nearly successful attempt to rid the world of the Jews, and nearly as many years after the founding of the State of Israel, what can be news about the relationship between Christians and Jews? Despite the memorials to the Jewish dead of the German campaign against the Jews, and the sustained visibility of the new Jewish state rising out of those ashes; despite the vigilance of the Anti-Defamation League and the best of intentions, anti-Semitism remains an ugly fact of life for both Jews and Christians. The most fundamental place to address its root causes is in the Bible, and it is in the aftermath of Auschwitz that this process has at long last begun. We have needed new lenses through which to read old texts, new experiences through which to filter old truths and preconceptions. If any good can come out of the world's descent into the abyss that was Auschwitz, a thoroughgoing reassessment of the biblical basis for Christian anti-Semitism is one such good. Some of the best and the brightest of the new generation of biblical scholars have been addressing themselves to this matter for some time. The harvest of their scholarship is both considerable and radical, radical in the correct sense of that much-maligned word, which means getting back to the root.

No one argues that Adolf Hitler functioned as a Christian in the promulgation of his racist theories, but it can hardly be doubted that centuries of anti-Semitic readings of Christian scripture gave him cultural permission, indeed encouragement, to do as he did. If the connection for the Christian is difficult to sustain, it is not for the Jew, who, through the voice of Elie Wiesel, recalls that the German officers and staff who conducted the daily work of the prison camp at Auschwitz received communion weekly in the Catholic parish church. The work of Satan and the work of God in this horrible proximity seemed to go hand in hand. If for the Jew the question after Auschwitz, as Richard Rubenstine once put it, is "Where is God?," then for the thoughtful Christian the question is exactly the same. For a generation, biblical scholarship has sought to find and disseminate an honest answer.

Could We Have Got It Wrong?

Perhaps the most visible public theologian practicing today is Professor Hans Küng, director of the Institute for Ecumenical Research at the University of Tübingen. He has been described as the Pavarotti of theology, not so much because he shares the enormous popularity of the Italian tenor who brings to ordinary people in the Hollywood Bowl the high culture of opera but because he takes theology out of the seminary, and even outside the church, and into the popular discourse of our age. Now nearly twenty years ago, as custodian of a set of endowed lectures at Harvard, I invited Professor Küng to address the university on the subject of his then new and very popular book, *On Being a Christian*. For three nights he held forth in the university church, filled to capacity with the great, the good, and the generally curious and eager. Priests and nuns from all over New England mingled with street people and with the university crowd. Each evening, in an almost parody of the German professor, Küng delivered himself of a set of theses that he proposed to answer, an intellectual's catechism of the Christian faith. He took no prisoners, condescended to no one, and put in a bravura performance. The format was as old as a medieval disputation; the content was refreshingly, even stunningly, radical. He caught and kept the rapt attention of one of the most secular audiences on earth, and he did so by making them think, perhaps many of them for the first time, about the consequences of thinking about holy things.

In the years since, Hans Küng has neither been silent, to the dismay of his ecclesiastical Fathers in God in Rome, nor has he been unproductive. In 1992 he published *Judaism: Between Yesterday and Tomorrow*, in which he addresses head-on the vexed topic of anti-Judaism in the New Testament. Asked if he would conclude that the New Testament is simply an anti-Jewish collection of documents, Küng said, "The apologetic positions of Christians in former times should not be replaced with any polemical position associated with our times." Conceding that there are elements of anti-Judaism in the New Testament, he said that "we have to understand them in their historical context. We also have to strive at all costs to avoid interpreting them in the light of the anti-Judaism which lies within ourselves and within the Christian community." In an interview on his book with James H. Charlesworth of *Explorations*, Küng was asked how we translate the Greek New Testament so that it reflects its social and narrative context but cannot be used to inflame hatred for the Jews in our communities. To this he replied that "translations implying that Jesus was a non-Jew and that the Jews were against him are inappropriate and misrepresentative." For Küng, as for so many scholars of the New Testament and its relationship to anti-Jewish sentiment, the question of translation and the circumstances of the writing itself—text, context, and subtext, indeed, even pre-text, as we might say in the literary trade—is critical, and a matter too important to be left to the experts.

An example of the importance of understanding context is the gospel of John, widely regarded as the most anti-Jewish of the four gospels. There are constant confrontations between Jesus and "the Jews," and the Jews are made to represent an ossified orthodoxy critical of Jesus and eager to do him harm and to prevent his teaching from being heard. The Jews claim to speak for Abraham, but Jesus tells them that they do not understand Abraham, nor do they act as Abraham did. Even the seemingly innocent miracle at Cana is interpreted in the form of anti-Jewish polemic, a fact that could easily be missed in our earlier fascination with the matter of wine and water. At the hands of a good exegete, the wine that had been exhausted quickly became the old covenant, the law, or the Jews; and the new wine, the best, which was served last and caused the comment of praise and surprise, this was the gospel now preached by Jesus. Within the very first miracle in this gospel the distinction is made between those who followed the old way, the Jews, and those who were now the beneficiaries of the new, the followers of Jesus, who became Christians. The climate of comparison and opposition is established at the very start of the gospel.

Biblical scholars are quick to point out that the gospel itself is not anti-Semitic, but that "the text nurtures anti-Semitism in the church today." Robert Kyser, in "The Gospel of John and Anti-Jewish Polemic," tells us that it is important for the reader of John to remember that everybody in the discourse of John is Jewish. There are no "Christians" there; they are all Jews. Second, we are to remember that "the gospel [of John] was written in response to the exclusion of the Johannine church from the synagogue, and the subsequent dialogue between these two religious parties." In other words, the gospel is one side of a bitter family quarrel. Third, we are to remember that, as in the case with most quarrels, and particularly with those of family, the arguments are heated, even exaggerated, and the literary form for a heated and exaggerated form is a polemic. Invective, exaggeration, hyperbole, sharply cast distinctions—this is all the stuff of polemic; and in the gospel of John the polemic is addressed to one group of Jews by another group of Jews.

However, those leaders of the synagogue responsible for the expulsion of the Christian Jews, so the theory goes, can also be seen to be responsible for the death of the Lord. Historical circumstance has now been introduced to support the polemic, and "herein lies a dreadful danger. It [the Gospel] is now read and interpreted outside of its original situation and beyond its original purpose. With the passing of centuries the historical organ becomes more and more remote, less and less known or knowable." What was situational has become normative, and the tragic consequences are only too well known to us.

Another example of a critical misreading is to be found in the letter of Paul to the Romans. The history of interpretation is the history of the presuppositions that interpreters bring to their work. Biblical interpretation is a cumulative affair and, like a giant snowball, it gathers momentum on the basis of its previous movement and picks up much in its path which becomes incorporated into the mass. The three great commentaries on Romans are those of Augustine, Luther, and Karl Barth, and none of these was written after Auschwitz. This means that the presence of anti-Semitism in the text of a major Christian writing, and the moral and

161

social implications of such a reading for both Jews and Christians, were not yet the problems they would prove to be when after Auschwitz one was compelled to face the issue. Perhaps it is a perverse violation of the Clinton administration's policy of "Don't ask, don't tell." Do we really want to know if there is anti-Semitic content in our most sacred book? If there is, and if we know that there is, then whatever are we to do with that information?

The conventional wisdom about Paul is that he is a super-Jew who, after his conversion on the road to Damascus, becomes a super-Christian. He repudiates his Jewish past and wants his fellow Jews to join him now in his Christian faith, and when they decline the opportunity he turns the full force of his polemic against them. It is possible that this is too bald a cartoon of the knowledge of Paul on the part of the average Christian, but, in paraphrase of H.L. Mencken, one would not lose too much money in underestimating the theological knowledge of the average Christian in the late twentieth century.

What we learn from contemporary scholarship on Romans reminds us once again of the context in which Paul writes. He repudiates neither Judaism nor God's special relationship with the Jews. Indeed, the Torah of the Jews was, and remains, the way of salvation for them. Paul's argument is that the cross of Jesus is to Gentiles what the Torah is to Jews, and that both are means of salvation and righteousness. In other words, Jews need not become Christians to obtain the promises—in the Torah they already have the promises as Jews. By the same token, Gentiles need not become Jews and subscribe to the law, for Gentiles cannot do so and because of the cross of Jesus do not need to do so. Paul's argument is for an inclusive God who has provided for both Jews and Gentiles through the cross. God's promises, the radical nature of those promises, is that they are for both Jew and Gentile. What the Jew now has and has never lost is, according to Paul, now also available to the Gentiles, to whom he is an apostle. Contrary to popular perception, Paul never argues in Romans that the Gentile church has displaced Israel, nor does he argue that the Jews must embrace Christ. He does argue that as God spoke to the Jews through the law, he now speaks to those outside the law, the Gentiles, through Christ. Jews are meant to embrace the good news of Christ, which is that he is the means for non-Jews to know God. The gospel for Paul is not simply "Christ crucified"; it is rather that through Christ crucified the Gospel has been extended to the Gentiles.

These insights are the result of the fruitful work of Sidney G. Hill in his 1993 book *Christian Anti-Semitism and Paul's Theology*, in which he reminds us, "The church has missed Paul's assumption that the good news belongs to the Jewish people. The good news is discovered by Gentiles apart from the law through Christ. Paul's good news was never intended to be bad news for Jewish people, but because the church failed to see Paul's basic assumption, the good news for the Gentiles has become bad news for Jews." Paul never doubts the inclusion of the Jews in the providence of God, and he is inclusive of Jews without requiring them to become Christians, that is, to put their faith in Christ. "For Paul," says Sidney Hill, "Jews experience the righteousness of God through faith grounded in the living Torah, which includes the Abrahamic promise. Gentiles experience the righteousness of God through the faithfulness of Christ."

The notion of Israel's co-status before God, a Pauline concept so radical in the historic context of the Christian denigration of Judaism as inferior or superseded, is rooted in the irrevocable promises of God. Just as God did not abandon the children of Israel in the time of the wilderness, but led them through to the promises, neither, according to Paul, has he abandoned them now. The promises of God are sure, and so too ought to be the status of those to whom the promises are made. In the matter of election the mind of God does not change; if it did, Christians would have much to fear. "For Paul, the Jewish people are beloved for the sake of their ancestors. Their acceptance as God's elect is a present reality for Paul, whether or not they themselves are inclusive of Paul's gospel. For the gifts and call of God are irrevocable."

If So, So What?

If all of this is true, or even plausible, how is it that we have not heard this before, and what are the methods by which we hear it now? Fair question and fair comment. We did not see or hear this before because we had very little problem with what we did see and hear. Paul, the Jew-*cum*-Gentile, made sense in a biblical worldview where Jews were of little if any account at all. Jews were bit players upon the New Testament stage, present to drive the major argument that demonstrated that Christianity had succeeded where Judaism had failed, that God had chosen a new people, and that as a result of our win/lose mentality, present if not articulated in the history of Christian interpretation, we, that is, the Christians, won, and they, that is, the Jews, lost. History, we are told, even biblical history, is written by the winners. We do not ask questions about what isn't there.

But what isn't there is the fact that Paul was a Jew who embraced Jews as Jews and not as potential Christians, and that Paul embraced a God who also embraced both Jews and Gentiles, providing Torah for the one and Christ for the other. In ridding the New Testament of its Jewishness, that is, of the tensions of change and continuity within the Jewish religious community and its consequences for the Gentiles, it soon became permissible to rid the world of the Jews. If they had a place in the Christian cosmology, it was, as Augustine and many others would point out, to be reminded of how far they had fallen from God, and that the only way back was to cease to be Jews and to become Christians.

By this reading of Romans, and of much of

the rest of the Pauline writings, Paul would be appalled at Bailey Smith or with anyone else who said that the prayers of a Jew did not reach the ears of God. What utterly silly and profoundly unbiblical nonsense, and what terrible consequences have come from such unsound and dangerous readings of the New Testament. It does matter what the New Testament writers meant and wrote, and it matters even more that we understand, as clearly as our God-given minds permit, what they said, what they meant, to whom they said it, the context in which they said it, and the degree to which what they said and what they meant is now normative or situational. It simply will not do, it is a cultural luxury that we can no longer afford, if ever we could, for any Christian on the whims of an uninformed and culturally driven piety to read the Bible and to pronounce upon its meaning with any less effort than these questions require. The Bible is too important to be left solely in the hands of the ignorant and the powerful, and after Auschwitz we should know better than to do so.

CHAPTER 7

THE BIBLE AND WOMEN: THE CONFLICTS OF INCLUSION

IN 1971, in my second year as assistant minister in The Memorial Church, I drew duty on the October Sunday when the first woman invited to preach in the church's pulpit was due to appear. That woman was Professor Mary Daly, a Roman Catholic theologian from neighboring Boston College. In my ignorance I was unaware that she was a rising power in the rising tide of feminist theology, and that to many she was a symbol of all that needed to be said about women, the Bible, and the church, that hadn't yet been heard. My ignorance was nearly complete in that I had had no idea that I was to be witness to one of the defining moments in women's religious history in the United States.

Her sermon was titled "Beyond God the Father," which would also become the title of one of her most influential books; the essence of her message on that autumn morning was that women had outlived patriarchy and the need of a patriarchal church. She had come to tell us that. Much more of the sermon I cannot recall, but I do recall that she led a walkout, and from the pulpit invited women and sympathetic men to join her. Many had come to The Memorial Church that morning in order to do just that and at her invitation did so. The rest of us remained, sang the final hymn, "Love divine, all loves excelling," and wondered what had happened.

In the era of sit-ins, teach-ins, be-ins, and act-ins of all sorts, we should not have been surprised at a walkout. A few years before, James Forman, on behalf of a coalition of radical black activists, had walked in upon a service in New York's

Riverside Church and demanded the payment of "reparations." Church services then were literally sitting targets for various forms of social protest aimed at the Christian conscience. The greater the sense of grievance, the more provocative the level of confrontation. This, however, had not seemed like a confrontation, it had seemed more like a recessional; and what did it mean? Were these women walking out of the Christian church for good? Were they just walking out of this service? Would they leave in order to return? Under what circumstances would they return? How widespread was the intensity of these feelings as articulated by Mary Daly?

The aftermath varied. Some people were annoyed that the stately liturgy of The Memorial Church had been interrupted. A Roman Catholic woman of middle age, interested in the historical aspects of the first woman preaching at Harvard, and a Roman Catholic woman from Boston College at that, was angry, saying, "She was so rude she gave us all a bad name, a terrible abuse of hospitality." Certain undergraduates thought it had all been orchestrated as a rather theatrical ploy to get their attention and prove that the church was "with it." Some applauded the action as a much needed and long-delayed shot across the bow of the institutional church. Some, recognizing the truly revolutionary nature of her presence, were glad that she left and hoped devoutly that she and her ideas would never be heard again. Most were quietly confused, mildly interested, and basically eager to get on with whatever thoughts Mary Daly's exodus had interrupted. I felt that we had had a narrow escape, but that we had not heard the last of these matters, or from Mary Daly, and I was right.

In the quarter of a century since 1971, the liturgical, theological, and biblical agenda of the Christian church has been set by the concerns and issues of women who are determined that their experiences, hitherto repressed or marginalized, be taken into account and given priority within the church. No denomination has been spared wide-ranging and often deeply divisive debates about the appropriate place of women. An entirely new field of scholarship has emerged in which women have taken the critical tools once used to interpret them out of the picture and inserted themselves back in, creating academic programs and institutes where there were none, and bringing a fully matured generation of new feminist scholars into the academy. The largest section in any divinity school bookstore these days is the section on women. They have claimed the attention of every field and discipline, and they have stimulated creative work, and not all of it reactive, in all of these fields on the part of men as well.

The effect of this stupendous achievement can be witnessed on every hand. "Gender issues," once the private frustration and preserve of an inner circle of feminist scholarship, is now a generic concern. "Inclusive language," a concept once exclusive to this same circle, now generates the language of liturgy, scholarship, hymnody, and even the language of Holy Scripture itself. It is not simply language that is to be inclusive, however, it is to be concepts as well. Few and far between are the places today where one can speak of Christian brotherhood, the Fatherhood of God, or mankind, without a wince, an apology, a hiss, and usually all three. The very geography of our discourse has been changed without a single shot being fired or a single piece of national legislation being filed and passed. Add to these fundamental conceptual changes the increased presence and influence of women among the ordained clergy in many denominations, including most recently the Church of England and the Episcopal Church in Scotland, and the fact that even the pope, mightily opposed to women's ordination in the Roman Catholic Church, has given attention to the status of women within that communion, and we realize that we have been witness to one of the great revolutions—paradigm shifts, as the chattering classes would say—in the Western world. We have perhaps seen nothing like it since the Reformation.

What's All the Fuss About?

The issue of women in the churches would seem to have been settled long ago. Anyone who has spent any time in any of the churches would recognize that in most of them the dominant force is one of women. The congregations have women in the majority, the program for most churches is managed and supplied by women, initiatives in religious education and works of charity have long been the special province of women, and the moral and religious influences of home life have historically been shaped by women. In the African-American Protestant church tradition, women held places of great public honor and private influence, and were particularly influential in missionary movements both at home and abroad. Mothers of the Church, a derivative of the ancient title of Mothers in Israel, was a title of great esteem accorded to venerable women in certain traditions of the African-American church. The title implied both spiritual dignity and temporal influence, and pastors ignored that dignity and influence often at their peril. There were sample role models from the Bible as well, to affirm the presence and influence of women in the religious life of the churches. In the precedent and practice of the New Testament, the images are clear and the examples plentiful. We know that women took large and active parts in the work and worship of the Pauline church. Saint Paul's first convert in Europe, we discover in Acts 16, is a woman, and a professional businesswoman at that, Lydia.

One who heard us was a woman named Lydia, from the city of Thyatira, seller of purple goods, who was a worshipper of God. The Lord opened her heart to give heed to what was said by Paul. And when she was baptized, with her household, she besought us, saying, "If you have judged me to be faith-

ful to the Lord, come to my house and stay."
And she prevailed upon us.

(Acts 16:14–15)

We know her to be a devout Jew, as she is described as a "worshipper of God," and as she is worshiping on the Sabbath with other women outside the gate of the city and at the riverside, we can suppose that there were not enough men within the city to form a proper synagogue. As women could not be the founders of synagogues, what is impossible for Lydia as a devout Jewish woman becomes possible for her upon her conversion to the religion of Paul, and she is described as the founding member of the Christian community, which begins to meet in her house. Lydia behaves contrary to the social customs of the day. A Jewish woman, even as substantial a woman as was Lydia, ordinarily did not engage in theological discourse with men, and certainly not with strange men. Lydia has a conversation with Paul, and responds to that encounter by receiving baptism; and then she opens her household to Paul and his colleagues, a rather gutsy enterprise. As the first European convert of Paul and the founder of her own house/church, Lydia is taken seriously by the author of Acts, and is meant to be taken seriously by all who read about her; and in her house/church we can assume that she did more than merely provide refreshments and sit at the apostles' feet.

There are other women given prominence in Acts, which leads various commentators to suppose a special interest in women and the Christian church on the part of Luke-Acts. Sapphira, the wife of Ananias, is a woman of property and financial acumen, qualities that are not used to her spiritual advantage when with her husband she conspires to hold back some of their wealth from the common property of the church. The judgment upon her and her husband is swift and fatal, as we read in one of the more chilling passages in Acts 5:1–11. Ananias and Sapphira are often used to illustrate less than complete integrity in the apostolic church, but the point often missed is that as a woman she is given equal billing with her husband and shares equally in his dismal fate. Then there is Tabitha, described in Acts 9:36–41 as a woman "full of good works and charity," who is raised from the dead by Peter.

In Acts we are reminded that Paul was determined, in his preconversion zeal, to imprison both "men and women" who were members of the Christian communities subject to his persecution, and both men and women are baptized in response to the preaching of Philip in Samaria. We read of this in Acts 8. Women are frequently mentioned as responding to the effects of Paul's preaching, and three instances alone in Acts 17 attest to this:

> Some were persuaded, and joined Paul and Silas, as did a great many of the devout Greeks and not a few of the leading women.
> (Acts 17:4)

Many therefore believed, and not a few Greek women of high standing as well as men.
(Acts 17:12)

But some men joined him and believed... and a woman named Damaris and others with them.
(Acts 17:34)

In his account of his own ministry, Paul indicates that women were not only among his converts but were his colleagues in the work of the gospel. In Romans 16:1–2, he cites Phoebe: "I commend to you our sister Phoebe, a deacon of the Church at Cenchreae, that you may receive her in the Lord as befits the saints, and help her in whatever she may require from you, for she has been a helper of many, and of myself as well."

We must linger here a bit with Phoebe. In the Greek text, Paul uses three titles to describe Phoebe: *adelphe,* "sister," *diakonos,* "deacon," and *prostatis,* "patroness." These are not terms of endearment or descriptions of qualities or attributes, but rather titles of functions and roles that are ascribed to Phoebe by Paul. These titles have caused much discussion, and the second one, "deacon," the most controversy. The Revised Standard Version of the Bible translated *diakonos* as "deaconess," but most contemporary commentaries regard that as an incorrect translation. The term "deaconess" implies a Greek word not known to have been used in first century Greece, and it further implies a later usage in which a deaconess ministered almost exclusively to women and was in a subordinate role to men, who were deacons. Paul's clear use of the term "deacon" in reference to Phoebe implies no such restrictions. He applies the term to her in the same way he applies it to himself and to other colleagues in his ministry who preached and taught. Her activity may have been located in the church at Cenchrae, for she is described as a "deacon of the Church at Cenchreae," but her function, and the title she bears that reflects it, are equivalent to those of Paul and his male colleagues.

Her additional title of patron, helper, or protector—all translations of *prostatis*—implies that she was a woman of substance capable of providing necessary assistance to Paul and to many others. Like Lydia, she probably had a house large enough to accommodate a house/church, and a social position superior to that of Paul and most of his colleagues. One commentator goes so far as to suggest that Paul's relationship to her was one of client to sponsor.

Phoebe was thus no minor figure, and she clearly had a responsible position, which Paul himself took seriously. All of this comes to mind when I remember the debates of my youth in my local Baptist church, when the question of women was first raised. Deacons were by definition in our polity and tradition men of spiritual substance and authority who ruled with the pastor in all spiritual matters of the church and had explicit responsibility for sound doctrine and the relief of the poor. On Communion Sundays they sat in great state with the pastor at the Lord's Table, and they had charge of the sacraments, the admission of members, and their discipline. Deacons often were elected for life, and their office was the highest the church could offer a person not ordained. In some instances, deacons were even ordained to their office.

Deaconesses, however, were of another order, and first were merely the wives of deacons. Their job was to provide for the care of the Lord's Table, and to be devoted to acts of charity and kindness, but unlike their husbands, they were not to "bear rule" in the church. To make a woman a deacon was to go against both nature and the New Testament, but more important, it was also to go against the customs of the church and the culture of interpretation. My own mother, a Baptist preacher's daughter and a woman of strong convictions, not easily intimidated by men and not overly fond of the clergy, had no use for the idea of women deacons. She found the idea unscriptural, and while not lacking in self-confidence, she was not necessarily prepared to submit to the spiritual jurisdiction of women, especially those whom she know so well in her own church. She knew her Bible, but clearly she didn't know all that she needed to know about her sister Phoebe. In this uninformed prejudice she was not, and even today is not, alone.

There are other women whom Paul takes seriously in his correspondence. After speaking of Phoebe, in the same chapter of Romans he writes, "Greet Prisca and Aquila, my fellow workers in Christ Jesus, who risked their necks for my life, to whom not only I but also all the churches of the Gentiles give thanks; greet also the church in their house." (Romans 16:3–5)

Prisca, also known as Priscilla, is accounted "the most prominent woman of the New Testament," who, with her husband, Aquila. preached Christianity in at least one of the Roman synagogues and caused such a tumult among the Roman Jews that the Roman civil authorities expelled them, among others, from the city. They moved on to Corinth, where Paul first encountered them. (I Corinthians 16:19) They then moved on to Ephesus, where they formed a house/church and were active with Paul as fellow missionaries among the Ephesians, and it was probably here that they "risked their necks" for Paul, earning his commendation and the undying gratitude of which we read in Romans.

Some have argued that because Prisca's name precedes that of her artisan husband, she was of superior social rank to him, and it would not be unusual, as we have noted in our discussion of Lydia, that women of high rank were attracted to the Christian gospel and served with Paul. Others argue that her name precedes that of her husband not out of social distinction but because she was the more renowned Christian leader of the two. Such an honorific to distinguish spiritual precedence would be typical of Paul. We know that they returned to Rome after the death of the Emperor Claudius, and between Paul's writing of I Corinthians and Romans, perhaps as a vanguard of Paul's own visit to Rome, and they may in fact have delivered the letter to the Romans. This may well be why he commends them to his correspondents; we know that they established a house/church in Rome, and that their prominence as Christian leaders and colleagues of Paul was well known and well established.

Lydia, Phoebe, Priscilla: These were names to reckon with in the formative days of early Christianity, and well attested to in the Acts of the Apostles and in the Epistles of Paul. The presence of women in the circle of Jesus, as recorded in the gospels, is of equal significance. In the rush to tell the story of the birth of Jesus, the significance of Mary, especially for Protestants, is often lost, but in the Greek Church she has always borne the most exalted of all titles: *Theotokos,* "Bearer of God." The role of the holy women—Anna, the prophetess who, along with the aged Simeon, longed for the coming of the Lord, and Elizabeth, cousin of Mary and mother of John the Baptist—is well recorded. And in the genealogy of Jesus as recorded in Matthew, a list to which too little attention is paid in providing a context for Jesus, we find among his female ancestors three women of ambiguous sexual morality: *Rahab* the Harlot; *Bathsheba* the Adulteress; and *Ruth,* who slept with Boaz without benefit of marriage.

Although we know that Jesus did not have women among his twelve disciples, we know of his encounters with women throughout his ministry. Women were among the marginal peoples he healed: lepers, the blind, demoniacs, the afflicted and possessed. His long discourse with the Samaritan woman at the well, in John's gospel, makes of her something of an evangelist, and she has the same function as witness and disciple as John the Baptist, Andrew, and Philip. John 4:42 tells it all. We know as well of Mary Magdalene, who in the same gospel has the unnerving privilege of being the first to see the risen Lord, and thus is the first apostle of the resurrection; indeed she *is* the first apostle. We know as well of the social and spiritual intercourse that Jesus shared with Mary and Martha, both of whom can be described as strong women.

Given what we know of both the secular and the religious culture of the period of Jesus and the earliest generations of the forming Christian community, we also know that the attention paid to women, their proximity to Jesus, and their precedence and participation in the earliest Christian communities is nothing less than revolutionary in its time, and still astonishing to us in ours. Yet we know as well that the debate attending the appropriate role of women in the Christian church continues to be a vexed and divisive one, equal perhaps in moral and political ferocity only to that of slavery. If the New Testament had possessed even a small percentage of the positive testimonial to the role of slaves in the Christian community that it bears toward women, the biblical case against slavery, while it would still have to contend with enormous cultural prejudice, probably could have been made with the immense authority of its own transforming examples to carry the day. Such, however, as we know, was not the case. Ironically, the case against women's authoritative participation in the church is made on the basis of biblical principles clearly subordinated to much of biblical practice. The examples of Lydia, Phoebe, and Priscilla, to name only a few of the New Testament women, are subordinated to later biblical and cultural practices that repudiate the transformative character of the gospel and reinforce the prevailing habits and customs of a culture fearful of too much change. These liberating examples are silenced by a culture of male interpretation, and that silence has been maintained until very recently. The greatest irony is that the case against the role of women in the churches is made on appeal to the New Testament, as if Lydia, Phoebe, and Priscilla were not in it. Hence, the Bible is called to testify against the Bible, in the matter of women.

What Does the Bible Say About Women?

The Bible has a great deal to say about women, and the Old Testament is filled with a wide variety of female personalities and voices. There is Eve, the mother of all living. There are Sarah, Abraham's conniving wife; Hannah, the mother of Samuel; Jezebel, the foreign-born wife of Ahab; Delilah, who wormed Samson's secret from him; Ruth and Rahab, ancestresses of Jesus, and many more. In the wisdom literature, wisdom is herself feminine, and in certain of the prophetic books, Israel is feminine, and the land is fecund and maternal. The images in Hebrew scripture are many and varied, and the presence of women in these holy books has never been an issue. When Christians speak about "what the Bible says" with regard to women, however, invariably they mean the New Testament, and so is it here that we will look.

As in all the church of the saints, the women should keep silence in the churches. For they are not permitted to speak, but should be subordinate, as even the law says. If there is anything they desire to know, let them ask their husbands at home. For it is shameful for a woman to speak in church.
(I Corinthians 14:34–35)

Let a woman learn in silence with all submissiveness. I permit no woman to teach or to have authority over men; she is to keep silent. (I Timothy 2:11–12)

Mary Magdalene went and said to the disciples, "I have seen the Lord," and she told them that he had said these things to her.
(John 20:18)

For as many of you as were baptized into Christ have put on Christ. There is neither Jew nor Greek, there is neither slave nor free, there is neither male nor female; for you are all one in Christ Jesus. And if you are Christ's, then you are Abraham's offspring, heirs according to promise.   (Galatians 3:27–29)

Those four passages from the New Testament represent the tension between the New Testament's principle of transformation and renewal in Christ, by which the old and established order is overturned and transcended, and the apostolic government of the early church, where explicit rules of conduct and patterns of relationship for specific situation are seen to be normative and definitive for Christian conduct and order in the church. For many the problem of the New Testament and women is the reconciliation of the so-called "hard passages," with the gospel principle of participation and equality. The problem is compounded by the fact that both principles are expressed in practice, and both thereby share in the authority and primacy accorded scripture. The secular cynics may dismiss the whole dilemma with the often quoted notion that you can find any verse in the Bible to support any view you wish. The fact that this is more true than untrue does not dismiss the problem, but only compounds it for persons of goodwill who genuinely seek "the mind of scripture" in the ordering of their affairs. As we discovered in the discussion of slavery, the more seriously one takes scripture, the more difficult becomes the problem of its several, often contradictory, voices, and therefore the more urgent becomes the development of a persuasive principle of interpretation by which the differences are reconciled, the authority of scripture maintained, and the moral and theological life developed from its teachings affirmed. As the Protestant Reformation introduced as normative the principle of *sola scriptura,* fidelity to scripture has become the normative principle for the faith and practice of most Protestant churches. For many churches of this inheritance, a case is made or lost on how one "reads" scripture.

"Reading scripture," however, is not as simple as most Protestants would like to believe. Reading is a transaction, and by no means a neutral transaction. A text does not simply "say what it says," despite the rational good intentions of a sensible reader like Alice in Wonderland. We read more like Humpty-Dumpty than we would care to admit, for in reading it is a matter not only of what is written there but what we expect to find there, what we bring to the text, and what we take away from it. Reading, then, is hardly a clinical or neutral affair. There is that bewildering battery of text, context, subtext, and pre-text with which we must contend, which we in fact do automatically and subconsciously. The scanning of these interests is so automatic and instantaneous that we are as unaware of it as we are unaware of the infinite number of physical motions and electrical impulses that it takes for us to turn the handle of a doorknob. When that simple action is reduced to slow motion and recorded, or when we find that some injury or ailment makes it difficult or impossible to do, then, and perhaps only then, do we realize the complexity that is camouflaged by the apparent natural ease with which we have performed the function before we were required to take notice of it.

Reading is such a function, and particularly the reading of scripture. The reading of contentious or difficult passages involves both an encounter with the text and an extra-textual consciousness by which we are enabled to make sense and reconcile the foreign and contrary with the familiar and accepted. This context, as opposed to the historical and literary context of the text itself, I call the culture or climate of interpretation. For most readers of scripture, or of anything else, this is the only context that counts. The very notion, for example, of "hard passages" in a discussion of women and the Bible does not necessarily presuppose that there is a "problem" with the biblical context, although there may be. The problem that makes these passages hard is that what they appear to say is at odds with what we now think. In other words, the text is out of sync with our climate or culture of interpretation. Thus, in order to make sense of what the text says, it must in some sense be made to conform to our climate of interpretation. With all due respect to the pieties addressed to the mind of scripture and to its context, as in most things our context is the only one that really counts.

Remember how our temperance friends "read" those accounts of the scriptural use of wine, which clearly did not coincide with the moral content of their contemporary climate of interpretation? It was scripture that was made to conform. In the matter of slavery each side adapted the context and content of the biblical writings on slavery to suit the moral purposes of their own contemporary climate of interpretation, and that battle was settled not by an exegetical consensus but by might of arms.

The readings of scripture in the debates about the role of women in the church today tell us as much, if not more, about the climate of interpretation within which we are willing to undertake the reading in the first place as it tells us about the content, context, and "clear meaning of scripture."

For those for whom the writings in Corinthians and in Timothy are not hard, and who take them as normative practice for the church in all places and at all times, the problem is no problem. Why? Because the texts as they read them, and the climate of interpretation within which they read them, are not in conflict—at least, they do not believe them to be. The pope is not anxious to know if scripture and his reading of scripture are at odds on the matter of women priests. He has said over and over again that the question of the ordination of women to the priesthood is settled by the fact that Jesus did not call women to serve as his disciples. The practice and principle of scripture in the mind of the pope are consistent with his reading and interpretation of it. In this view he is joined by many conservative Protestants, with what is called a high view of scripture.

There is a substantial and growing body of Christians in all communions, however, for whom the biblical texts in question and the climate of interpretation are in fact out of sync. Many of these would argue that the texts themselves are out of sync within their own context, both of the gospel and of the particular message and example of Paul himself. It is this range of interests and views, stimulated by the larger cultural revolution by which women have determined to overcome their marginalization and cultural disenfranchisement, that has generated the theological revolution in interpretation of which we have spoken earlier with profound and massive implications for the ways in which we read and understand scripture. The most interesting, creative, and demanding scholarship in the field of biblical interpretation since the translations of the Bible into English has been generated in the last twenty-five years by what may be called the feminist initiative.

This frightens people—the very notion of a feminist initiative in the interpretation of scripture—in much the same way that good Christians of varied opinions were frightened by the abolitionists of the nineteenth century. Many have been and will be put off by the sense of an aggressive set of special interests that are brought to the interpretation of scripture with destabilizing consequences to the authority of the scripture, the order of the church, and the structure of society and of civilization itself. As we have pointed out before, however, it is not just feminists who have an interest in the way in which the Bible is read these days. In their fight for the Bible and the right both to take it and themselves seriously, feminist interpreters of scripture have much to teach us, and we ignore these lessons to the peril of scripture and of the church.

It has become a habit on the part of some evangelicals and religious conservatives to dismiss the mountain of female scholarship on the Bible with the taint of the most extreme and deconstructive dimensions of that scholarship, suggesting pagans and goddesses under every hermeneutical bed. Any challenge to the language of patriarchy or the thousand years of male interpretation is understood to be a challenge to the full wealth of conviction and part of a "liberal," "feminist," or "radical" conspiracy to subvert the faith once delivered to the saints. As in politics, there is clearly a paranoid style in much of the response to the new scholarship of women on the Bible. Of course, as in physics, every action generates a reaction. When feminist scholarship concludes that it is no longer appropriate to pray to "Our Father," and such masculine titles as "Lord" and "King" are excluded both from the text and from worship, the instinctual reaction of those who feel thus deprived of the familiar and useful language of piety is to reject the possibility that any helpful insights can be provided from such scholarship.

Language has become the battlefield for the conflict between old and new ideas, and the inclusive language debates with which Christian churches have contended in the last twenty years demonstrate just how hard and bitterly people will fight for the right to their language of choice. Perhaps even more than the ordination of women, the language issue has been the place where the conflicts of inclusion have been most painfully addressed. More perhaps than through the Bible itself, the popular piety of most Christians, particularly Protestants, has been expressed in the hymns people sing in church. The late New Testament scholar and poet, Amos Niven Wilder, once said that what incense is to the Catholic, hymns are to the Protestant: an indescribable, primal association of the personal and the holy. One learns the hymns of the faith in childhood. They provide a theological vocabulary that may be supplemented and improved upon by age and experience, but is never supplanted. It has been my experience time after time that what remains with the dying Christian is the hymns of childhood. And it is my experience as well as that of practically every other preacher that worship depends upon the hymns. The sermon may be good or bad, the liturgy indifferent, but the effect of the service depends upon whether or not the people know and like the hymns. And most people like the hymns they know and on that basis know what they like. Thus to tamper with the hymns is to get perilously close to the emotional center of the worshiper.

Women recognized this early on, knowing that the hymnic images are for most people the determining images and language of piety. Thus, to be excluded from the language was in their minds to be excluded from the fundamental experience of worship, or to be included under terms that did not affirm their particular identity as women. Women would ask, "Where am I?" when at funerals we sang Isaac Watt's great paraphrase, "Time, like an ever-rolling stream bears all its *sons* away." Even in so basic an act of Christian praise as the Doxology, which affirms, "Praise Him all creatures here below" and closes with the Trinitarian formula of "Father, Son, and Holy Ghost," women increasingly asked where they were in these classical formulations. When the congregation is asked to sing "Rise Up, O Men of God," are the women to remain seated, or are they to think of themselves as Elizabeth I did, as a man trapped in the puny body of a woman?

Challenges in scholarship are one thing. But challenges to popular piety, which strike at the heart of the believer and the language of devotion, with all of the fond and intimate associations that language evokes, are another thing. Congregations were set at each other over the battle for the hymns. Radical inclusivists were accused of Freudian-like "pronoun envy," and the hymns, once the point of commonality, became symbols of the great divisions among people. It is difficult to say if the scholarship of women generated the dis-ease with the language of hymnody, or if the distress at the exclusive language of hymnody generated the case for a new and compelling scholarship. Whatever the answer to this particular chicken-and-egg dilemma, hymns will never be quite the same again. For my part, I have been no more willing to edit out offending passages in hymns than I have been to edit out offending passages in scripture. But while it is not possible to write new Bibles that reflect the spirit of the age, it is not only possible, but essential, that we write new hymns to add to the storehouse of piety, hymns that include more people.

It seems to me that where the old hymns are concerned, we do not have to be like Oliver Cromwell's Puritan New Model Army, which took great delight in smashing the medieval iconography of the English cathedrals, justifying such vandalism in the name of God and of their revolution. Had they been more successful in their efforts than they were, we would be the poorer today. It was an English cleric friend of mine who, at the height of the revision of liturgical language in the English prayer book two decades ago, observed that the glories of English worship had survived Henry VIII, Oliver Cromwell, and Adolf Hitler, only to be done in by the heavy hand of the liturgical reformers of the 1970s.

Somewhere between a thoughtless veneration of the past and the total destruction of all that is out of step with the latest conclusions of the moment is where most of us within the church would like to stand, and it is possible that women may show us, at least in part, how to do this.

Dianne Bergant in her article "Women in the Bible: Friends or Foes?" divides the biblical scholarship of women into revisionists and reformists. The revisionists, or revolutionaries, as some of the feminist theologians prefer to be called, "contend that the Bible has not only outgrown its usefulness, but is, in fact, detrimental to the development of women— and men for that matter. They often seek to reconstruct history as it *should have been* remembered, not as it *has been* remembered." The tradition for this point of view is not simply exclusive, it is destructive, and therefore irrelevant. The reformers, on the other hand, while equally opposed to patriarchy, "maintain that the message of the Bible is itself intrinsically liberating." To get at that biblical message and its liberating truth depends, of course, on how the Bible is to be read.

Bergant defines herself as a reformist, which means to her that the biblical tradition is a source of revelation for her, and remains so in its contemporary reinterpretation. She makes the telling but not so radical point that every generation, "successive communities of faith," as she calls them, has struggled with the relationship between the received tradition and the demands of its own unique experiences. Technically, this process in the field of biblical interpretation is called canonical criticism, but so technical a term should not disguise the fundamental fact that each age can read what it has received only through the lenses of its own experience.

Anyone who considers the matter will realize that eighteenth-century Christians do not necessarily interpret the texts of scripture in the same way as twelfth-century Christians. Augustine did not read scripture in the same way as Paul, and Luther repudiated centuries of Roman Catholic interpretation. American fundamentalists read scripture very differently from nonfundamentalist communions—and in fact, very differently from the primitive church, although they would dispute that as a slander upon themselves and scripture. This is not simply a matter of relativity, as many with a high view of scripture would contend, but an unavoidable and perfectly understandable phenomenon of relevance. That women should do this is no more destructive of scripture than it was when Augustine, Luther, or Calvin did it. Scripture will survive such an inquiry, although there may be some reasonable doubt about the survivability of the exclusively male view of scripture.

Bergant's method is disarmingly simple, and I will describe it only briefly and without doing full justice to her discussion, simply to demonstrate that the best of this feminist scholarship is both accessible and constructive, taking both scripture and its interpretation as seriously today as ever it was taken in the great historical days of biblical interpretation. She calls her method "recontextualizing," and it involves (1) Looking carefully at the received tradition; how has this text come down to us in the history of interpretation? (2) Operating out of a feminist sensitivity to the contemporary context; how is the text received now? (3) Finally, pointing out how "the dynamics within the text" can achieve a significance within the community that now reads and hears it. This is really no more than the Saturday-night method of any responsible preacher who has to stand up in the pulpit on Sunday morning, text in hand: (1) What did it mean then? (2) How do we understand it now? (3) So what do we do with it, or what does it do with us?

Rather than terrorizing scripture or subverting the faithful, this particular example of a feminist hermenutic, one among many, I might add, actually works toward liberating both text and reader and is hardly a radical methodology—except, perhaps, in the including of perspectives hitherto excluded. Bergant concludes: "The result of such an approach is a reading that is both faithful and challenging. It is faithful because as 'word of God,' it is challenging; and it is challenging precisely because as open to God, it is faithful."

Options for the Hard Passages

A story of W.C. Fields has the old reprobate on what he thinks may well be his deathbed. When his doctor comes in to see him, he finds Fields leafing furiously through a huge Bible. Surprised at such a sign of piety in so notori-

193

ously profane a fellow as Fields, the physician asks, "What are you looking for?" Replies Fields, "Loopholes."

That may appear to be the only paradigm available to those who would look at the hard passages here and hope to find something other than a confirmation of the status quo, but there is more to it than that, and a survey of critical literature presents us with a range of opinion on how to "read" what we find here. These are not loopholes, but they are options, and we look at them now. The options, adapted from a technical but useful study by Arthur Rowe, are these:

1. Paul, a man of his time
2. Permanent principles
3. Particular problems
4. Not from Paul
5. Hermeneutical problem

The first option may well be called the principle of context. Paul writes as a man in a man's world. The roles of men and women in agrarian first-century society were prescribed by the circumstances of that society, where, with very rare exceptions, women were subordinate to men. In the three worlds of which Paul was a citizen, the Jewish, the Greek, and the Roman, women's societal roles were dictated by the subordination principle. His teachings on women, therefore, while reflecting the mores of his time, are no more relevant to an age where those mores no longer apply then, say, first-century standards of dress, of social etiquette, or of dietary rules. Paul is a social and political conservative. He does not, for example, advocate revolution against the state, and as we know, he requires that Christians obey lawful authority. Only in his theology, and in anticipation of the world to come, is he radical. So we should understand him, his social teachings, and those who imitate his teachings such as the writer of Timothy, as writing from within the social assumptions of the age of which they are a part.

The second option sees Paul enunciating in these hard passages permanent principles of behavior, normative rules for the organization of the church and the relations between men and women within those churches. Here we should not necessarily infer that one role is better and superior to, or less good and inferior to, the other; they are simply different and distinct. The model and order of creation to which Paul himself appeals is an example: The man is made first, and the woman second. This does not mean that the man is better than the woman, or the woman inferior to the man. It does mean that they are different, by order of precedence, and by function. Harmony is assured when that order is understood and the different functions in the relationship are appreciated and affirmed.

The third option looks at the hard passages in Corinthians and Timothy as addressed to particular and particularly troublesome situations in the places to which the letters are addressed. As we do not have all of the correspondence and do not necessarily know what it is that provokes Paul's response, we may well infer that women were party to some contentiousness in these churches. These then are Paul's instructions to put these troubles in those places, and at that time, to rest. These instructions are situation-oriented, and are not meant to be normative, and they certainly are not meant to inhibit the work of the Lydias, the Phoebes, and the Priscillas, and they do not negate the "equality principle" enunciated in Galatians 3:28, where all distinctions are leveled in Christ on the basis of baptism.

The fourth option is perhaps the most attractive for those who want to liberate themselves and Paul from Paul: These texts are not from Paul but from a "proto-Paul." One tempting theory, supported apparently by the earliest manuscripts, is that the instructions about women are to be found in the margin of the manuscript and not in the text, and they appear in their present places in the manuscripts by virtue of a later editorial decision on the part of a copyist. The problem remains, but at least it is not a problem of Paul's, and lacking that ultimate authority, can be "situationalized."

The fifth option is perhaps the most demanding, and that is that we must seek principles of interpretation that allow for the cultural presuppositions both of Paul and of the reader in making sense of these texts. In other words, if we expect to find women in a subordinate cultural position in Pauline times, we read that condition as normative in reading the text; and if in our own climate of interpretation we understand that subordination to be biblical, we are not surprised to find it there and affirm its presence and its application to our own time as well.

If one has no interest concerning the role of women in New Testament times, or now, for that matter, and if one does not see these hard passages as essentially inconsistent with the larger picture of the gospel as found in the New Testament, then, as we have said before, the problem is no problem. However, the last twenty-five years of New Testament studies with respect to the role of women both in the Bible and now in the churches makes this of interest, indeed, of concern, to everyone who takes the Bible and the churches seriously, even those who are opposed to any construction of these hard passages other than what they believe to be their clear, if painful, meaning. No less a resource than *The Women's Bible Commentary*, published in 1992, with the ambition, as stated in the introduction, "to gather some of the fruits of feminist biblical scholarship on each book of the Bible in order to share it with the larger community of women who read the Bible," says of I Corinthians 14:34–35: "The inclusion of these verses in the text of Paul's letter is particularly unfortunate, for their strong wording affects the way the rest of Paul's comments on women are read. They reinforce, for example, the conservative tendencies of Chapter 11, and obscure the more liberating aspects of Paul's statements about women."

From a brief review of these options we might

well conclude that rather than loopholes or ways out of a sticky situation, they are in fact variously related efforts to get into, and behind, and admittedly beyond, the texts. Women who might be expected willingly to toss out the offending passages, in much the same way as Thomas Jefferson edited out of "his" Bible all those Pauline passages not consistent with his view of the ethical and moral teachings of Jesus, have by and large done no such thing and have fought for the Bible, hard passages and all, and for the right to interpret them within and against the context of the larger principles for which Paul writes and which his own experience with women co-workers amplifies.

Although Christian traditions as diverse as the Roman Catholic Church and the Mennonite Brethren Church continue to affirm that such passages as I Corinthians 14 and I Timothy 2 are normative texts whose prohibition against the teaching of women "concerns the official function of teaching in the Christian assembly"—a phrase from the "Declaration on the Question on Admission to the Ministerial Priesthood," of the Sacred Congregation for the Doctrine of the Faith of the Roman Catholic Church—the overwhelming consensus of the vast literature on these texts since 1970 suggests that they are meant to be understood situationally, contextually, and not normatively. Despite the firmly stated desire of Pope John Paul II and his allies within significant portions of the evangelical Protestant communions to put the divisive nature of this debate to rest in favor of the Pauline status quo, the issue will not go away for women, nor for those who demand for them a role at the very least as central as the roles played by Lydia, Phoebe, and Priscilla.

With women bishops in the Anglican Church, women clergy throughout the ranks of the Protestant churches, an unremitting campaign for women within the Roman Catholic Church, and the prodigious scholarship of women and men on the frontiers of biblical study, this particular fight for the Bible is by no means over, but it certainly looks nearer to 1945 for the Allies than it does to 1940 for the Germans. Let no one mistake that this is a battle still in progress, however. As one critic has pointed out, the issue for the conservative position is not women. That tradition honors and cherishes women and their unique and biblically approved gifts, for without women the churches would not function, let alone flourish. The pope's most recent pastoral letter on women makes this point. The concern is not women, but rather the authority of scripture, the teaching tradition of the church, and the social, theological, and moral upheaval that is sure to come from selective principles of interpretation that relegate the teachings of scripture to the realm of first-century sociology and the control of a cadre of experts. If we are wrong, say the more perceptive and worried among these conservatives, on so clear a matter as the biblical warrant for the subordination of women, on what else could we be wrong, and what other changes, even less agreeable than these, are in store for those who worry that a

Bible diminished by interpretation is no Bible at all?

These are not new concerns or issues. They are as old as scripture itself, and they have arisen in every age when the prevailing climate of interpretation has been challenged. The conservative rabbis of biblical times raised the same issues about Jesus and Paul, and we heard the same anxious concerns expressed about the authority of scripture and the order of society in the debates about temperance, to a lesser degree, and far more urgently, about race within our own lifetimes. When Roland Bainton declared in the matter of total abstinence that he was giving precedence to biblical principle over biblical practice, and regarded doing so as biblical, he did not provide us with a way out but a way in to the fight for the Bible which is as old as the Bible itself, and as painful and new as each age's attempt to understand and appropriate that book for itself. Making that point upon a review of the New Testament discussions of women, Malcolm O. Tolbert concludes that one of our most fundamental mistakes in the reading of scripture, particularly of the New Testament, is to assume that the structures and the systems it describes are as sacred and authoritative as the principles it affirms. Not only is this wrong, it is idolatrous, even blasphemous, to use the word of God to affirm and maintain human privilege. It was wrong in the interpretation that God approved and encouraged chattel slavery, it was wrong in the maintenance of a climate in which the persecution of the Jews could be regarded as biblical, and it is wrong, unequivocally wrong, in imposing first-century social standards on the participation of women in the life of the church simply to preserve the abstraction of the authority of scripture and the preservation of a status quo favorable to those already in power.

Tolbert writes, "I do not understand the pattern of male dominance reflected in the Bible as an expression of the will of God. It is rather the reflection of the culture in which Jews and Christians as well as pagans lived. I am governed rather by the insights found in various key texts which make it possible for the Christian to criticize the structures of society and the Church. These passages, Mark 10:43 and Galatians 3:28, emphasize the ideals of servanthood and mutuality in relationships rather than the ascendancy of any one person or group of persons over others." He is of a large and growing company.

As long as there are people willing to read the Bible in this way over and against the powers and principalities that would have them read it otherwise, such people will fight for the Bible and for the right to read themselves into it rather than to be read out of it. In the vanguard of this battle, perhaps the most significant battle for the Bible since the debates over slavery, at least in the United States, the women have led the way, and one would like to think that Lydia, Phoebe, and Priscilla would be pleased.

CHAPTER 8

THE BIBLE AND HOMOSEXUALITY:
THE LAST PREJUDICE

AMONG religious people who wish to take the Bible seriously there is no more vexed topic today than that of homosexuality. The current debates recall the passion with which the topic of slavery was once debated within the context of American Christianity, but since the debate about homosexuality is very much alive and well with no immediate prospect of a moral or social consensus in sight, we have more than a historical or even anecdotal exhibition of the conflicts of values and interpretations, the hard texts and changing times we have been discussing in this section of the book. We have a contemporary, existential, deeply felt struggle that shows no sign of going away, that grows increasingly less civil, and upon which everyone has an opinion and a text upon which to base it.

The Hottest of the Issues

Theologians and biblical scholars have generated an enormous literature on the subject of the Bible and homosexuality, but the topic is so electric, and so much seems to be at stake, that few are willing to concede to the experts their personal conviction on this topic. Thus, perhaps more than any other social or theological issue of our day, this one engages us at our most fundamental level of existence and raises disturbing questions about our own sense of identity, of morality, and of the nature of settled truth. Now that the Cold War and the struggles against "godless communism" have receded into the background—and for the time being we have become convinced that we are likely neither to blow up our world in a nuclear holocaust, nor to destroy the environment by our immoderate use of aerosol deodorant—we can no longer be diverted from these issues of sexuality and religion, the very discussion of which violates all our conventional taboos.

Homosexuality is one of the issues in the current culture wars. One's position on homosexuality determines where one stands in the politically charged debates about virtue and values, and what was once called the "love that dare not speak its name" is now the topic that simply won't be quiet. Unlike the topics of other moral debates, homosexuality is seen not only as a social practice or condition upon which good hearts and minds may differ but as an issue so central to right conduct and belief that compromise or sweet reasonableness is thought to be capitulation to error, and therefore unacceptable. Thus, the debate is almost undebatable.

Our subject, however, is not homosexuality in general, but homosexuality and the Bible and the religious basis for the prejudice against homosexuality so often expressed by people of religious conviction. Nearly every such person who acknowledges an aversion to homosexuality does so on the basis of what he or she believes the Bible to say, and in their minds there is no doubt whatsoever about what the Bible says, and what the Bible means. The argument goes something like this: Homosexuality is an abomination, and the homosexual is a sinner. At Sodom and Gomorrah God punished the cities for the sin of homosexuality. Saint Paul and the early Christians were equally opposed to homosexuality, and homosexual practices are condemned in the New Testament church. Therefore, if we are to be faithful to the "clear teachings of scripture," we too must condemn homosexuality; it is the last moral absolute, and we compromise it at our own peril. The sufferings and persecutions homosexuals have endured over the centuries are signs of God's extreme displeasure with who they are and with what they do, and their behavior, as Saint Paul points out, is contrary to nature; and this then invites a terrible retribution. The AIDS epidemic is a terrible visitation, but it is the consequence, and only the latest one, of the sexual perversion of homosexuality. All of this can be summarized in the hate slogan of the notoriously homophobic Baptist preacher Fred Phelps, who pickets the funerals of gay men dead of AIDS with the sign god hates fags. The source of that conviction and of its more subtle variations, we are told, is the Bible.

In preparing for her novel *The Drowning of Stephen Jones,* based upon the true story of a young gay man tossed from a bridge to his death by a group of young gay-bashers, author Bette Greene interviewed more than four hundred young men in jail for various forms of gay-bashing. Few of the men, she noted, showed any remorse for their crimes. Few saw anything morally wrong with their crimes, and more than a few of them told her that they were justified in their opinions and in their actions by the religious traditions from which they came. Homosexuality was wrong, and against the Bible. One of those interviewed told her that the pastor of his church had said that homosexuals represented Satan and the Devil. The implication of his logic was clear: Who could possibly do wrong in destroying Satan and all of his works? The legitimization of violence against homosexuals and Jews and women and blacks, as we have seen, comes from the view that the Bible stigmatizes these people, thereby making them fair game. If the Bible expresses such a prejudice, then it certainly cannot be wrong to act on that prejudice. This, of course, is the argument every anti-Semite and racist has used with demonstrably devastating consequences, as our social history all too vividly shows.

Although most contemporary Christians who have moral reservations about homosexuality, and who find affirmation for those reservations in the Bible, do not resort to physical violence and intimidation, they nevertheless contribute to the maintenance of a cultural environment in which less scrupulous opponents of homosexuality are given the sanction of the Bible to feed their prejudice and, in certain cases, cultural "permission" to act with violence upon those prejudices. This is the devastating theme of Daniel Jonah Goldhagen's 1996 book, *Hitler's Willing Executioners: Ordinary Germans and the Holocaust,* published to much dismay in Germany. Goldhagen argues that it was the cultural permission of Germany's Christian anti-Semitism, based of course upon a reading of the Bible, that allowed the nasty work of the Holocaust to be done not only by military specialists but by people whose attitudes were based upon centuries of Christian teaching. The unforgiving indictment of Goldhagen's thesis is not reserved solely for those who were "simply following orders," but extends now to all branches of a society whose moral obtuseness made it impossible for most of them to see anything wrong with those orders, or with their terrible consequences.

In the case of the Bible and homosexuality in contemporary American culture, the tragic dimensions of this biblically sanctioned prejudice among the most devout and sincere people of religious conviction are all the greater because no credible case against homosexuality or homosexuals can be made from the Bible unless one chooses to read scripture in a way that simply sustains the existing prejudice against homosexuality and homosexuals. The combination of ignorance and prejudice under the guise of morality makes the religious community, and its abuse of scripture in this regard, itself morally culpable.

A good deal of significant scholarship in recent years has been devoted to those verses in the Bible that are adduced as definitive in determining the Bible's view of homosexuals and homosexuality. We will look at these verses in light of some of this scholarship and with one continuing question in mind: When the Bible speaks of homosexuality, does it mean what we mean when we speak of homosexuality?

Given the appeal to the Bible in the case against homosexuality, one would assume that the Bible has much to say on the subject. It has not. The subject of homosexuality is not mentioned in the Ten Commandments, nor in the Summary of the Law. No prophet discourses on the subject. Jesus himself makes no mention of it, and homosexuality does not appear to be of much concern to those early churches with which Saint Paul and his successors were involved. One has to look rather hard, and with a user-friendly concordance, to find any mention of homosexuality at all. This should come as no surprise, because the word *homosexuality* itself is an invention of the late nineteenth century and does not occur in any of the original manuscripts from which the English Bible is descended. As historian John Boswell has pointed out in his magisterial 1980 study, *Christianity, Social Tolerance, and Homosexuality:*

In spite of misleading English translations which may imply the contrary, the word "homosexual" does not occur in the Bible; no extant text or manuscript, Hebrew, Greek, Syrian or Aramaic, contains such a word. In fact none of these languages ever contained a word corresponding to the English "homosexual," nor did any language have such a term before the late nineteenth century.

Victor Paul Furnish, in his 1985 book *The Moral Teaching of Paul,* informs us that the term *homosexuality* was not coined until the latter half of the nineteenth century when it was used by a Hungarian writer commenting on the Prussian legal code. Furnish goes on to remind us that the King James Version of 1611 makes no mention of *homosexuality* or of any of its cognates, and that the first use of the term in an English Bible is to be found in the Revised Standard Version of 1946. More recent translations apply the word *homosexuality* to biblical situations that the translators assume correspond to the meaning of the word, and thus today, depending upon your translation of choice, you may or may not see *homosexuality* in the Bible. There is no doubt, however, that you would not have found the word in any Bible in any language before 1946. The significance of this process whereby contemporary meanings associated with the term *homosexuality* and its cognates are applied to biblical situations from which the contemporary understanding may well be absent is one we will discuss in reviewing the texts in question.

What Does the Bible Say About Homosexuality?

The traditional sets of texts from the Old and New Testaments to which people appeal in seeking the Bible's teaching on homosexuality are these:

1. Genesis 1–2 The Creation Story
2. Genesis 19:1–9 Sodom and Gomorrah, with the parallel passages of Judges 19 and Ezekiel 16:46–56
3. Leviticus 18:22 and 20:13 The Holiness Code
4. Romans 1:26–27 Regarded as the most significant of Saint Paul's views
5. I Corinthians 6:9 and I Timothy 1–10 Pauline lists of vices

As Jeffrey S. Siker has pointed out in the July 1994 issue of *Theology Today,* to argue that the creation story privileges a heterosexual view of the relations between humankind is to make one of the weakest arguments possible, the argument from silence. The Genesis story is indeed about Adam and Eve, not Adam and Steve, as the critics of homosexuality delight in admonishing. "Heterosexuality may be the dominant form of sexuality, but it does not follow that it is the only form of appropriate sexuality." What the story does do is reflect the world experience of those human beings who wrote it. Of course they would privilege the only way available to perpetuate the race, and they would do so with the aid of their own cultural lenses.

Despite the efforts of modern "creationists" to cast Genesis in the mold of nineteenth-century science, the authors of Genesis were intent upon answering the question "Where do we come from?" Then, as now, the only plausible answer is from the union of a man and a woman. That biological fact is attended by the cultural assumptions of the world in which the writers lived. Woman, for example, was subordinate to man. The creation story in Genesis does not pretend to be a history of anthropology or of every social relationship. It does not mention friendship, for example, and yet we do not assume that friendship is condemned or abnormal. It does not mention the single state, and yet we know that singleness is not condemned, and that in certain religious circumstances it is held in very high esteem. The creation story is not, after all, a paradigm about marriage, but rather about the establishment of human society. John Boswell describes early Christian attitudes toward marriage as a "compromise with the material world," and for at least one half of its first thousand years, the church valued lifestyles other than family units, preferring priestly celibacy, voluntary virginity even in marriage, and monastic community life. The creation story is the basis and not the end of human diversity, and thus to regard it as excluding everything it does not mention is to place too great a burden on the text and its writers, and too little responsibility upon the intelligence of the readers, and on the varieties of human experience.

Sodom and Gomorrah

The story of Sodom and Gomorrah in Genesis 19:1–9 is perhaps the most famous instance in scripture where homosexuality is seen to be condemned, and from the name of the destroyed city of Sodom came the term *sodomy*. According to Boswell, "Throughout the Middle Ages the closest word to 'homosexual' in Latin or in any vernacular, was '*sodomita*.'" In an extensive etymological note, he points out that the term *sodomy* "has connoted in various times and places everything from ordinary heterosexual intercourse in an atypical position to oral sexual contact with animals. At some points in history it has referred almost exclusively to male homosexuality and at other times almost exclusively to heterosexual excess." On the term *sodomite,* Victor Paul Furnish in *The Moral Teaching of Paul* notes, "In every instance in the King James Version where the term 'sodomite' is used, the reference is to male prostitutes associated with places of worship." The sodomites in this context, he points out, are condemned not because they have sexual relations with other men, but because they serve the alien gods of the Canaanite and Babylonian fertility cults.

We do not know what the grave wickedness

of the city of Sodom was, but it was grave enough for God to send two angels to warn Abraham's nephew Lot of impending doom. It was God's intention to destroy the city before the arrival of the angels, and so the punishment that befell the city had to do with its previous and notorious state of wickedness and not with the menacing treatment accorded the angels while they were partaking of Lot's hospitality. It may well be that the men of Sodom knew that their fate was sealed when they saw the arrival of Lot's guests, and perhaps it was for that reason that they wished to "know" them, either carnally, as a further expression of their wickedness, or perhaps, if merely socially, to reassure themselves that these were not the angels of doom. The temptation here is to assume the use of "know" in this instance to be carnal knowledge, and that the wicked men of Sodom further justified their reputation for wickedness by attempting to violate the laws of hospitality with the rape of these strangers. Lot, of course, refused their demands, and in a perverse gesture of hospitality of his own, offered his daughters to the lusting mob. They wanted the strangers, not the daughters. The angels gave their protection to Lot's household, and struck blind the Sodomites at the door. The next day Lot and his family, with the exception of his wife, who disobeyed and looked back at the city, were spared the destruction of fire and brimstone.

The conventional wisdom is that the city of Sodom was destroyed because its inhabitants practiced homosexuality. That was its great wickedness. Even if we credit the Hebrew word "know" in the demands of the Sodomites, however—"that we might know" the strangers—in a carnal sense, we should not neglect the fact that the fate of the city was determined well before the ugly incident at Lot's door. It was in behalf of that errand of doom, in fact, that the angels came at all. Boswell informs us that this particular form of the Hebrew verb "to know" is rarely used in a sexual sense. It occurs nine hundred and forty-three times in the Old Testament, and in only ten of these does it have the sense of carnal knowledge. More to the point, the passage in Genesis 19 is the only place in the Old Testament where it is generally believed to refer to homosexual relations. Sodom is referred to throughout the Old Testament as a place of wickedness and is synonymous with it, but nowhere does it state that homosexuality was the wickedness in question. Among the sins attributed to Sodom in other books of the Old Testament are pride—in the books of Ecclesiasticus and Wisdom in the Apocrypha—and in Ezekiel, in addition to pride, "Fulness of bread, and abundance of idleness was in her and her daughters, neither did she strengthen the hands of the poor and the needy." (Ezekiel 16:48–49) In the New Testament, Jesus himself is under the impression that Sodom was destroyed because it was a place lacking hospitality; we find him saying as much in Matthew 10:14–15, and in Luke 10:10–12.

What is revealing about all this is that nowhere

in the Old or New Testaments is the sin of Sodom, the cause of its sudden and terrible destruction, equated with homosexuals or with homosexuality. The attempted homosexual rape of the angels at Lot's door, while vivid and distasteful, is hardly the subject of the story or the cause of the punishment, and no one in scripture suggests that it was. Homosexual rape is never to be condoned; it is indeed, like heterosexual rape, an abomination before God. This instance of attempted homosexual rape, however, does not invalidate all homosexuals or all homosexual activity. Jeffrey S. Siker makes an excellent point when he says in his article in *Theology Today* that "David's sin of adultery with Bathsheba does not make all heterosexual expressions sinful!" In the matter of Genesis 19 and the "obvious" conclusion that God here enunciates in fire and brimstone his condemnation of homosexuals and homosexuality, there is less than meets the eye.

The Law of Leviticus

Leviticus 18:22 reads, "You shall not lie with a male as with a woman; it is an abomination," and Leviticus 20:13 reads, "If a man lies with a male as with a woman, both of them have committed an abomination; they shall be put to death, their blood is upon them." The statements are clear, but the context and application are not. It is clear that this so-called Holiness Code is designed to provide a standard of moral behavior that will distinguish the Jews from the Canaanites, whose land they have been given by God. The price of the land, as it were, is a new standard of behavior. The Jews are not to worship the Canaanite god Molech, nor to adopt any of the practices of the people who do. The sentence to be carried out when this Holiness Code is violated is death. Children who curse their parents are to be put to death. The sentence for adultery for both parties is death. The punishment for incest is death. The punishment for bestiality is death. "You shall therefore keep all my statutes and all my ordinances, and do them; that the land where I am bringing you to dwell may not vomit you out. And you shall not walk in the customs of the nation which I am casting out before you, for they did all these things, and therefore I abhorred them. But I have said to you, 'You shall inherit their land, and I will give it to you to possess, a land flowing with milk and honey.'" (Leviticus 20:22–24)

These rules are designed for a very particular purpose and in a very particular setting. Their purpose is nation building; their setting is the entry into a promised but very foreign land. These are fundamental laws for the formation of a frontier community. In addition to honoring one's parents and keeping the Sabbath, showing appropriate hospitality and abstaining from idol worship, the people are forbidden to permit cattle inbreeding, or to sow fields with two kinds of seed, or to wear garments made of two different kinds of materials. Fruit trees may not be harvested until the fifth year, and the kosher laws must be kept. Round haircuts are forbidden, as are tattoos, and consultations with mediums and wizards. A man may not have sexual relations with his wife while she menstruates. These and many other actions are condemned because they defy purity and weaken the cultural identification of the children of Israel; and so great is the principle of ritual and ethnic purity that to violate it is in most cases to warrant the sentence of death.

We can understand the context: cultural identity, protection, and procreation. In this context homosexual conduct is a risk to all three of these necessary frontier ambitions. We have, however, long since ceased to live as God's frontier folk in the promised land. Not only is the cultural context markedly different, but so for Christians is the theological context. Indeed, to what extent can Christians be said to be bound by these rules of the Holiness Code when even Saint Paul, himself a Jew and an heir of this very code, says that the Gentiles, that is, the non-Jewish Christians, have the gift of the Holy Spirit without the necessity of the Law of Israel? In Acts 10:47, of these non-Jewish Christians, the Apostle Peter asks, "Can anyone withhold the water for baptizing these people who have received the Holy Spirit just as we have?"

For Jesus and Saint Paul, the ritual purity of which Leviticus speaks with such passionate detail is plainly irrelevant; they are both concerned with purity of heart. Boswell argues that a distinction is made between what is ritually impure and what is intrinsically wrong. Homosexuality in Leviticus is condemned as ritually impure, the key to this conclusion being the fact that the word *abomination* does not usually describe something intrinsically evil, such as rape or theft, but something that is ritually impure, like eating pork or engaging in intercourse during menstruation. An abomination is by definition what the Gentiles do, but that in and of itself is not necessarily evil or a violation of the Commandments. Thus homosexuality is an abomination in Leviticus not because it is inherently evil but because the Gentiles do it, and it is therefore ritually impure.

When Christians ignore most of the Holiness Code and regard its precepts as irrelevant to a New Testament understanding of purity of heart, and yet cite the Levitical prohibitions against homosexuality as the basis of their own moral position on that subject, one is led to wonder what is behind the adoption of this prohibition and the casting away of the others. Once again the "clear meaning" of scripture in the matter of homosexuality seems more expedient than compelling.

What Saint Paul Says and Means

We turn now to the New Testament and the writings by and attributed to Paul, in Romans, I Corinthians, and I Timothy.

Paul's most significant comments on what we call homosexuality occur in Romans 1:26–

27. "For this reason God gave them up to dishonorable passions. Their women exchanged natural relations for unnatural, and the men likewise gave up natural relations with women and were consumed with passion for one another, men committing shameless acts with men and receiving in their own persons the due penalty for their error." The first thing to be remembered here is that Paul is not writing about homosexuality in Romans—neither about homosexuality as he would have understood it nor about homosexuality as we now understand it. He is writing about the fallen nature of humankind. It is this fallen nature, this "corrupted will" to use a favorite phrase of Saint Augustine, that has caused both Gentile and Jew to suppress the truth by their wickedness. They are able to know what is knowable about God: his invisible nature, his eternal power and deity. The creation itself bears witness to this. The nature, power, and goodness of God are not hidden. There is therefore no excuse for this ignorance of God. The people knew God but did not honor God. They were not grateful to God. They substituted their own minds and their own thinking in place of God. As Paul says in Romans 1:21, "They became futile in their thinking and their senseless minds were clouded." In other words, the creatures ignored the Creator, and they themselves became the objects of their own worship and veneration. They became worshipers of self, caught up in their own egos, and they gave to created things the glory and dignity that belong

to the Creator. This is what he means when he says that in the fallen state of total self-absorption and self-deception, human beings, "claiming to be wise...became fools, and exchanged the glory of the immortal God for images resembling mortal man or birds or animals or reptiles." This is the golden calf of the Old Testament all over again, the worship of the Canaanite and Babylonian fertility gods, and, in Greco-Roman civilization, the worship of worldly wisdom and philosophy.

We become what we worship. It is this sophisticated psychological insight that Paul applies to those who worship a lie rather than the truth, who submit themselves to images rather than to the divine reality. Such people are disordered, that is, they have their priorities wrong; they have lost their perspective. God's judgment is that they will reap the consequences of these lesser, inferior gods. This is what is meant at verses 24–25: "Therefore, God gave them up in the lusts of their hearts to impurity, to the dishonoring of their bodies among themselves, because they exchanged the truth about God for a lie and worshipped and served the creature rather than the Creator, who is blessed for ever!" As a consequence of this, in the jargon of contemporary psychology, God let them "bottom out." As H. Darrell Lance points out in his 1989 article entitled "The Bible and Homosexuality," in *The American Baptist Quarterly,* "As a result, God let his creatures follow their own corrupt ways."

These corrupt ways include intellectual self-deception and the sexual practices of the pagan world. These fallen ones are described as "filled with all manner of wickedness, evil, covetousness, malice. Full of envy, murder, strife, deceit, malignity, they are gossips, slanderers, haters of God, insolent, haughty, boastful, inventors of evil, disobedient to parents, foolish, faithless, heartless, ruthless." (Romans 1:29–31) This is the context in which Paul, at verses 26 and 27, discusses what we call homosexuality, and he never takes up that subject in Romans again, for it was merely one of the many consequences of the fallen state.

When modern readers scrutinize Romans 1:26, with its discussion of "dishonorable passions," "unnatural relations," and "shameless acts," conditioned as we are by the characterization of homosexual behavior prevalent among us since the late nineteenth century, which in the current cultural debate is described both loosely and pejoratively as the "gay lifestyle" and the "homosexual agenda," we are tempted to give a content to those words and a profile, largely negative, to those behaviors, and are persuaded by our own infallible opinions that Saint Paul is "obviously" talking about the same thing as we are. The hard question we must persuade ourselves to ask is, is this so?

In their discussions in a statement on "Issues in Human Sexuality," members of the House of Bishops of the General Synod of the Church of England write: "Passions are more than emotions; they are emotions out of control. Dishonorable passions are a disordering of God's purpose." They go on to say, "Paul takes for granted an ordering of things in which the body and its sexual desires have their place and their proper honor; but the sexual acts of which he is now speaking dishonor the body." Paul is speaking here of passions out of control, that become an end in and of themselves, that are in fact idolatrous. Dishonorable passions refer to the worship of sexual pleasure, an excess to be condemned with all other excesses.

The "natural relations exchanged for unnatural" among women, at verse 26, and among men, at verse 27, who "likewise gave up natural relations with women and were consumed with passion for one another," does not describe the conduct of homosexuals, but rather of heterosexual people who performed homosexual acts. As Boswell reminds us, the whole point of Romans 1 is a discussion of people who know what is right but who, because of their arrogant willfulness in their fallen state, choose to act contrary to that knowledge. In other words, "Paul did not discuss gay persons but only homosexual acts committed by heterosexual persons." It is not clear that Saint Paul distinguished, as we must, between homosexual persons and heterosexual persons who behave like homosexuals, but what is clear is that what is "unnatural" is the one behaving after the manner of the other.

We must further point out, as has nearly all contemporary scholarship on this point, that "nature," as Paul here utilizes the concept, has nothing to do with a theory of Natural Law, which comes into the picture some centuries later, nor is he referring to the "order created in Genesis by God," as H. Darrell Lance reminds us, "but to a common idea taken from pagan culture." "Nature," for Paul, is something more akin to "customary" or "characteristic"; it is not to be confused with that which is innate, inherent, or immutable. Among the Jews, homosexual behavior was not customary. It was in fact uncommon, "unnatural," compared with the customs of the Greco-Roman world. As Boswell puts it, "For Paul, 'nature' was not a question of universal law or truth, but rather a matter of the character of some person or group of persons, a character which was largely ethnic and entirely human." Nature is not, in the thinking of Paul, a moral force.

The "shameless acts" of which Paul speaks may well refer to the assumption that homosexual acts, whether experienced by heterosexuals or homosexuals, always involved lust and avarice, an act of will, and an unavoidable degree of exploitation where the stronger took advantage of the weaker. In these same-sex relationships the passive partner, the female role, was taken advantage of by the active partner, the male role; and in the most disagreeable form of homosexual activity known to Paul and his contemporaries, pederasty, the adult male exploited for sexual purposes the younger male.

The homosexuality Paul would have known and to which he makes reference in his letters, particularly to the Romans, has to do with pederasty and male prostitution, and he particularly condemns those heterosexual men and women who assume homosexual practices. What is patently unknown to Paul is the concept of a homosexual nature, that is, using Paul's sense of the word "nature," something that is beyond choice, that is not necessarily characterized by lust, avarice, idolatry, or exploitation, and that aspires to a life under the jurisdiction of the Holy Spirit. All Paul knew of homosexuality was the debauched pagan expression of it. He cannot be condemned for that ignorance, but neither should his ignorance be an excuse for our own. To base the church's principled objections to homosexuality and homosexuals on the basis of Paul's imperfect knowledge is itself unprincipled, and indeed quite beside all of the heroic points that Paul intends to make in Romans 1.

In I Corinthians 6:9, the reference to homosexuals among the list of those who will not inherit the kingdom of God actually has as its context in Chapter 5 a startling case of heterosexual immorality, and of a kind not even found among the pagans: "For a man is living with his father's wife." (I Corinthians 5:1) Paul is so horrified by this that he demands that the man be expelled from the community, and it is this violation of the accepted standard of Christian behavior that leads Paul into another discussion about how Christians ought to live, and how they ought to put their old lives behind them. This passage is not about homosexuality; there is no reason to believe that the Corinthian church was troubled on that topic. We must remind ourselves that when Paul speaks of what we call homosexuality, he is speaking again of what can be called the "Gentile sin," whose characteristics are those of which we have already spoken: willful, lustful, exploitive, avaricious, self-deceiving, self-absorbed, and thus idolatrous. Of course someone who fits this profile is unfit for the kingdom of heaven. Victor Paul Furnish reminds us that in these examples of wickedness, such as I Corinthians 6:9–10, the vices listed are "understood by Paul to be symptomatic of sin, not as its roots and essence." In other words, because one is sinful one behaves in these ways. In I Timothy 1:10, "sodomites" are to be found on the list of the lawless and the disobedient for whom the law is laid down. "Sodomite," as we now know, refers almost exclusively to a male prostitute, and is not a Pauline synonym for "homosexual," as we understand that term.

The Silent Text and Doctrinaire Prejudice

In his study *Christianity, Social Tolerance, and Homosexuality*, John Boswell concluded his chapter on the New Testament texts having to do with homosexuality with these words:

> The New Testament takes no demonstrable position on homosexuality. To suggest that Paul's references to excesses of sexual indulgence involving homosexual behavior are indicative of a general position in opposition to same-sex eroticism is as unfounded as arguing that his condemnation of drunkenness

224

implies opposition to the drinking of wine.

Jeffrey S. Siker, in the July 1994 issue of *Theology Today,* concludes his study of the biblical texts with these words:

Thus the Bible has relatively little to say that directly informs us about how to address the issue of homosexual Christians today. The Bible certainly does not positively condone homosexuality as a legitimate expression of human sexuality, but neither does it expressly exclude loving monogamous homosexual adult Christian relationships from being within the realm of God's intentions for humanity.

Victor Paul Furnish, in the conclusion of his chapter on homosexuality in his 1979 book, *The Moral Teaching of Paul,* writes:

Since Paul offered no direct teaching to his own churches on the subject of homosexual conduct, his letters certainly cannot yield any specific answers to the questions being faced in the modern church....It is a mistake to invoke Paul's name in support of any specific position in these matters.

As early as in 1964, German theologian Helmut Thielicke, in the volume of his *Theological Ethics* dealing with sex and homosexuality, after a thoroughgoing discussion of all of the relevant biblical passages, wrote, "There is not the slightest excuse for maligning the constitutional homosexual morally or theologically." He went on to observe, however, that the continuing willingness to do so on the part of the Christian churches has nothing to do with the biblical texts, and very much to do with what he calls "doctrinaire prejudices."

Doctrinaire prejudices, which at the same time distort the theological problem presented by homosexuality, manifest themselves also in the fact that the value-judgment, "homosexuality is sinful," is not isolated from an objective assessment of the phenomenon but is rather projected into it, and the result is that one arrives at an *a priori* defamation of those who are afflicted with this anomaly.

Yet the matter remains unsettled. In an article in *Christianity Today*, "Why Is This Important?" Stanton L. Jones gives three reasons. "First, the church's historically high view of the authority of scripture is threatened by efforts at revising the church's position on homosexuality." His second reason is that if homosexuals are defined primarily by their sexual inclinations, this definition is contrary to the fundamental definition of Christian identity. The third and most critical reason, however, is this: "We can only change our position on homosexuality by changing our fundamental stance on biblical authority, by changing our core view of sexuality, and by changing the meaning and character of Christ's call on our lives."

The first of Jones's objections, that the authority of scripture is challenged by a revision of the church's position on homosexuality, does not take account of the fact that the authority of scripture seems not to have been challenged by the revision of the church's position on women, Jews, and slavery. Nor does he appear to take into account the fact that, high view or not, the scripture has so little to say about homosexuality that it cannot be called upon to resolve the contemporary church's debates about homosexuality or address itself to the modern complexity of human sexuality. It should also be noted that it is not homosexuals who define themselves by their sexual desires, but it is invariably the case that persons opposed to homosexuality define it and homosexuals exclusively in sexual terms. Finally, of course, what Jones sees as a "problem" is in fact the only intellectually and spiritually responsible way forward. We must change our position on homosexuality if that position is based upon a prejudicial and uninformed reading of scripture. Our fundamental stance on biblical authority ought by no means to be an absolute; that is a form of Protestant idolatry. Indeed, our core view of sexuality ought to change, and must, and the "meaning and character of Christ's call on our lives" thus is not merely changed but enlarged to reflect a dynamic and inclusive gospel.

What is at stake is not simply the authority of scripture, as conservative opponents to homosexual legitimization like to say, but the authority of the culture of interpretation by which these people read scripture in such a way as to lend legitimacy to their doctrinaire prejudices. Thus the battle for the Bible, of which homosexuality is the last front, is really the battle for the prevailing culture, of which the Bible itself is a mere trophy and icon. Such a cadre of cultural conservatives would rather defend their ideology in the name of the authority of scripture than concede that their self-serving reading of that scripture might just be wrong, and that both the Bible and the God who inspires it may be more gracious, just, and inclusive than they can presently afford to be.

The biblical writers never contemplated a form of homosexuality in which loving, monogamous, and faithful persons sought to live out the implications of the gospel with as much fidelity to it as any heterosexual believer. All they knew of homosexuality was prostitution, pederasty, lasciviousness, and exploitation. These vices, as we know, are not unknown among heterosexuals, and to define contemporary homosexuals only in these terms is a cultural slander of the highest order, reflecting not so much prejudice, which it surely does, but what the Roman Catholic Church calls "invincible ignorance," which all of the Christian piety and charity in the world can do little to conceal. The "problem," of course, is not the Bible, it is the Christians who read it.

This is where I come in.

A few years ago I found myself speaking at a rally in Harvard Yard, at the request of an organization of gay and lesbian undergraduates who had found themselves the objects of an attack against them on religious grounds by a conservative undergraduate periodical. The articles in the periodical, all written by undergraduates, most of whom were conservative Roman Catholics, argued that homosexuality was bad for the individual, bad for society, and should be condemned on religious and biblical grounds as well as on the empirical evidence of the unhappy lives of homosexuals. The purported purpose of this periodical was pastoral, no malice was intended, and while it was meant to be provocative and to attract attention, it was also meant to persuade, by the power of its arguments from Christian tradition and contemporary social analysis, that homosexuality was an unsound position and an unsafe and destructive lifestyle.

In its efforts to attract attention and to provoke, the periodical was a roaring success, and the response was outrage on the part of the Harvard homosexual community. It should be pointed out that this community was a diverse and secular one, and that while many of its members were doubtless devout practitioners of a number of religious faiths, it would be less than accurate to call the community as a whole particularly visibly religious, and the rally itself was hardly a churchy affair. It was arranged to be located in the traditional gathering place for protest and demonstration in Harvard Yard, on the large platform that forms the south porch of The Memorial Church, the scene not only of hundreds of rallies over the years but of the annual Commencement exercises. When the Harvard community has something on its mind, it gathers on these steps to express it.

In the days after publication of these articles and before the rally itself, the college community was ablaze with debate and controversy, and many felt that a line in college civility had been crossed. Rarely in the memory of many had one group of students taken to print to castigate its fellow students, and quickly the issue of homosexuality and religion fell second to questions of fairness, fair play, and civil discourse. At Harvard, where tolerance and diversity had long assumed the status of sacred cow and secular icon, the challenge to these virtues assumed in the minds of many a form of blasphemy. Some homosexual students said that they no longer felt safe from physical attack if they could be subjected in print to such an aggressive assault. What may have been genuine desire on the part of the young authors to present their strongly argued positions as a way of opening a vigorous debate on an issue of enormous moral significance had the effect of most polemics. Fears and anxieties were raised where few had been before, discourse was inhibited rather than stimulated, and the moral climate of the community was poisoned. What was meant to be robust debate was perceived to be theological thuggery, and the situation could not continue unaddressed.

It was to this situation that I, and a number of other members of the faculty and administration, were invited to speak. I accepted the invitation both because I recognized the precariousness of the situation and because I believed I had something to say that would not necessarily be said by my secular colleagues on the platform. I fully appreciated the fact that I was not asked to speak because of any radical credentials that I may have had: I had none and was not thought to have any. After all, I was the man who had prayed for Ronald Reagan at his second inaugual and preached for George Bush at his first. Some knew I was a Republican, and others knew I had been consistently on the "wrong" side of the divestment issue in the debates on South Africa. I was opposed to divestment. I knew that I was invited to speak as a representative of the establishment and, together with certain of my colleagues, was expected to lend a patina of respectability to an occasion that otherwise might be easily written off as homosexual hysteria. I also knew that no one wanted me to be "religious." Religion, in fact, was part of the problem here and not part of the solution, or so it was thought by my secular friends.

I knew all that, and yet I also knew that the only ground on which I could stand in this particular instance was religious ground, and so rather than a pious elegiac on civility, or an exercise in political outrage, I determined that I would make my best effort to represent my understanding of the Bible and the Christian faith as it applied to the heart of the present discontents. As the university's pastor and preacher, as a Christian, and as a homosexual, I decided to reclaim by proclaiming a vision of the gospel that was inclusive rather than exclusive, and to do so as a Christian who was more than the sum of the parts of which I was made. I did so. I did so because I wanted all and sundry, but particularly these young homosexuals and their polemic antagonists, to see that there was more than one way to read the Bible and to understand the imperatives of the Christian faith. Certainly I wanted to contribute to the cooling down of local passions, but admittedly I also wanted to win minds and hearts, or at least to awaken them, to a view of the Christian faith which in dispute valued charity and humility over mean-spiritedness and arrogance. I thought of Edwin Markham's poem about the circle:

> *But Love and I had the wit to win:*
> *He drew a circle that shut me out—*
> *Heretic, rebel, a thing to flout.*
> *But Love and I had the wit to win:*
> *We drew a circle that took him in.*

I warned of the dangers of Christian absolutism, with the appropriate references to the Spanish Inquisition and the Salem witch trials, and I dismissed the easy references to scripture and the rather glib social analysis as unworthy of thinking or charitable Christian debate. I gave my speech, and naively thought that my disclosure of my own homosexuality would serve to substantiate the Christian message of reconciliation in diversity and equality in Christ. I, however, rather than my message, became the subject of attention.

The ensuing tempest drove me to an ever more intense study of both the relevant passages of scripture and the theories of interpretation, hermeneutics, as we call it in the trade, by which they are to be explained and understood. Despite some student calls for my resignation or dismissal, and threatening noises from clergy in my increasingly edgy denomination of American Baptist, I nevertheless found this experience to be one of the most formative and rewarding of my ministry. I prayed a lot, and was prayed for, and the support of friends who were secular and could not understand the problem, and of religious friends who did, and did not, and of strangers who heard not me but what I had said, served to sustain me in the difficult times. I got much mail, most of it a pleasure to receive. All that was not a delight to read, however, had to do with the Bible. Many of my critics, chiefly from within the religious community, asked if I read the same Bible they did, and if I did, how then could I possibly reconcile my position with that of scripture? When arguments failed, anathemas were hurled and damnations promised. The whole incident confirmed what had long been my suspicion.

Fear was at the heart of homophobia, as it was at the heart of racism, and as with racism, religion—particularly the Protestant evangelical kind that had nourished me—was the moral fig leaf that covered naked prejudice. I further concluded that more rather than less attention must be given to how we read the scriptures, what we bring to the text, what we find in the text, and what we take from the text. This transaction has brought me to the present moment, and I am grateful for that.

It Seems to Be All About Sex

It is all well and good to discuss what the Bible says or doesn't say about homosexuality, and it has been the purpose of this chapter to do just that. But when it comes down to cases, homosexuality is not about the Bible or texts. It is all about sex, and that is what tends to make it rather difficult to talk about in polite society, particularly in the religiously saturated culture of the United States that is still squeamish about the subject of sex. This squeamishness doesn't deny the hedonistic basis of much of our popular culture; entertainment and advertising, perhaps our two chief "art forms," are suffused with sex. Calvin Klein makes a sexual statement with every promotion of his underwear. The soap operas glide on a film of sexual frisson, and the substance, if we can call it that, of television situation comedies and nightclub stand-up comics is laced with sexual innuendo, and often with considerably more than innuendo.

The paradox of our culture is that while we are hardly averse to sex and its all too prominent place in our public consciousness, we are still awkward in talking about it. Perhaps this is not surprising in a sophisticated civilization that persists in all sorts of childish euphemisms for body parts and functions and refers to what other cultures call simply the toilet as the "rest room." This reticence in speech is explained by many as a result of modesty. In honest discussions about homosexuality, however, this reticence gets in the way. When we ask just what is wrong with homosexuality, we are forced to ask what for many is the far more difficult question, what is the purpose or function of sex?

Taking its cues from much of its inherited Jewish morality of sex, the early Christian church had little doubt that the chief function of sex was to procreate. When the Hebrew Bible commanded that humankind be fruitful and multiply, as is recorded in Genesis 1:28, the Hebrew writer meant that from the posterity of Adam would come the Messiah. Fecundity was not simply to replicate the race, but to provide the means for the Messiah to enter into the world. Every male child was in fact a potential Messiah, as King Herod, in Matthew's gospel, knew only too well. Thus, for the Jews, any sexual activity that interfered with the possible birth of the Messiah was forbidden. The wasting of seed through nonprocreative sex was destructive not only to the survival of the race but to the redemption of the race through the Messiah. Masturbation, coitus interruptus, and, understandably, sex without the possibility of issue, that is, homosexual activity, was proscribed.

Not only did the early Christians have this moral inheritance as a part of their identity, they also had the negative examples of pagan sexual practices, which to them upheld private pleasure and satisfaction, together with aspects of exploitation and degradation, at the expense of the best interests of society. For Paul and his contemporaries, the end of the world would soon be at hand, and for them the Messiah had come in the form of Jesus Christ. Paul, interestingly enough, does not endorse the procreative aspects of sex, and in fact seems to prefer celibacy as the higher vocation. For those for whom the call of celibacy was too high, he issued his famous edict that it was "better to marry than to burn"— not in hell but with desire for the satisfactions of sex. In I Corinthians 7 he discusses the conjugal relations that ought to obtain between Christian husbands and wives. Nowhere does he mention that the sole purpose of such conjugality is the procreation of children. That emphasis would come later with the Church Fathers, who, seeing that the end of the world was not yet at hand and that the church needed to be replenished, grudgingly gave the mandate of sex for procreation. They were grudging in that they, like Paul, held celibacy to be a higher vocation than marriage. And as such Church

Fathers as Jerome, Augustine, Origen, and Tertullian all knew either by experience, as was certainly the case with Augustine, or by keen observation, the pagan pleasures of sex, which they themselves had renounced upon their conversion to Christianity, they wished to separate "Christian sex" from "pagan sex" by imposing a strictly moral purpose on it.

Augustine and the Invention of Shame

To minimize carnal pleasure, Augustine and his colleagues endowed the act of intercourse with the burden of shame. Lust was the sinful desire that could only be mitigated by purposeful, procreative, and unpleasurable sex. The very organs of sex, the genitals, were called by Augustine pudena, from the Latin *pudere*, "to be ashamed." Thus the genitals were instruments of shame because what they facilitated was itself a shameful, disgusting, but necessary act. Augustine reconstructs, "resitualizes," as modern biblical critics would call it, the Eden story and transforms it from a story of creation and disobedience to a tale of the discovery of sexual shame, making sex, and not disobedience, the original sin by which all of the subsequent race was tainted at birth. It is in this way that he reads Psalm 51:5, "Behold, I was brought forth in iniquity, and in sin did my mother conceive me." As Reay Tannahill points out in her eminently readable *Sex in History,* for Augustine and the moral theology he was developing, "The body was no more than a flawed vessel for the mind and spirit, and it was now up to the Church to propagate Christian morality in these terms."

He succeeded beyond his wildest dreams, if the austere Augustine may be credited with wild dreams. Celibacy became the badge of moral authority. Marriage was a concession to human weakness and the need for companionship, children, and sex. And sex within marriage was tolerated not for pleasure but for the morally worthy purpose of producing more Christians— but even children were described as a "bitter pleasure," of which the pangs of childbirth were both sign and punishment. Somewhere in the twelfth or thirteenth century, marriage was made a sacrament, which meant that like all sacraments it could not be dissolved. Jesus' judgment on divorce, "Whoever divorces his wife and marries another commits adultery against her; and if she divorces her husband and marries another, she commits adultery" (Mark 10:11–12), confirms Paul's textually older prohibition on divorce in I Corinthians 7:10–15. According to Tannahill, "One marriage...should supply enough companionship for any man; second marriages were adultery, third fornication, and fourth nothing short of 'swinish.'"

Given these strictures and the intrinsic sense of sin attached to sex, it is no wonder that sexual activity outside of marriage that gave only pleasure or sensation because it was incapable of performing its moral duty of producing issue was held in deep revulsion. The Bible, we may say, was utilized to reinforce this position, but

238

as we have seen, the Bible was evidence for the prohibitions rather than the basis for them. Homosexuality was thus by definition, together with masturbation and other forms of nonprocreative sexual activity, deviant, and the degree to which these deviations gave pleasure only compounded the sin of lust.

What the homosexual did was different, and hence the homosexual was different, and in a religious world that increasingly prized conformity in all things, but particularly in sexual matters, the difference branded the homosexual a threat to the moral order, the equivalent of a heretic in the church or a traitor to the state. This is the position when Saint Thomas Aquinas arrives, whose teaching formed a basis of moral philosophy for the treatment of homosexuality up to the present. Until fairly recent times, homosexuality was regarded first as sin, then as crime, and then as illness. These cultural identities all stem from what homosexuals do or cannot do sexually, and the source again is not the Bible but the moral assumptions of the Church Fathers with which they then read the Bible and interpreted it as part of the teaching tradition of the church.

What the Homosexual "Does"

Andrew Sullivan, the Roman Catholic and openly gay former editor of *The New Republic*, tells of an encounter with Patrick J. Buchanan on *Crossfire*, Buchanan's television talk show. The subject was same-sex marriage, with

Sullivan in favor of it and Buchanan opposed. Thundered Buchanan, "Andrew, it's not what you are. It is what you do!" A good Roman Catholic knows that what homosexuals "do" is to have sex in which the possibility of procreation is excluded. Since the only purpose of sex is to procreate, when that is by definition not possible, the sexual activity is also by definition "unnatural" and proscribed by church teaching. Sullivan points out in his *New Republic* essay, however, that the Roman Catholic Church permits the marriage of infertile couples in church and allows them sex. Couples in which the wife is past childbearing are also allowed to marry in church and to have sex although the procreation options are closed. By a miracle a childless couple could have a child, but as Sullivan points out, if we appeal to the miraculous, why are God's miracles necessarily limited to heterosexual couples? If homosexuality is an objective disorder, then what is infertility? Sullivan's argument is that the church has accommodated itself to nonprocreative sex in marriage. By what logic other than circular does it oppose homosexual nonprocreative sex in a marriage that also in every other way conforms to the church's definition of the marriage state?

In his recently published essay "By Their Fruits" in *Our Selves, Our Souls and Bodies*, Boston College Professor of Theology Charles C. Hefling, Jr., raises this timely discussion to a new level of clarity. Writing firmly within the tradition of Anglican moral theology, Hefling argues that to say that homosexual conduct is wrong because the Bible says it is "is not to answer but to dismiss the question."

He puts the question in the way he thinks it should be asked: "Are there sound reasons for revising the traditional account of what the wrongness of homosexuality consists in? Is the idea that physical intimacy between men or between women can only be unnatural an idea that the best available understanding of the relevant facts will no longer support?" In other words, are we able to advance beyond the moral hypothesis of Saint Augustine and Saint Thomas Aquinas that the sole natural function of sex is procreation?

Beyond Procreation

The answer is yes. There is a widely shared consensus developed over time that "sex is good in more ways than one." He cites the 1958 resolution of the Ninth Lambeth Conference, the decennial meeting of the bishops of the worldwide Anglican Communion, which on the subject of intercourse said, "Sexual intercourse is not by any means the only language of earthly love, but it is, in its full and right use, the most revealing....It is a giving and receiving in the unity of two free spirits which is in itself good....Therefore it is utterly wrong to say that...such intercourse ought not to be engaged in except with the willing intention of children." The Roman Church teaches that the sexual act must have two core elements: the procreative, which means an openness to the possibility of new life, and the unitive, which means a commitment to faithfulness. The Lambeth ruling makes it clear that the procreative does not take precedence over the unitive, and in fact the unitive is an equally valid context in which the sexual act may take place. Fruitfulness in marriage, as Hefling argues, can be real without being visibly obvious. Or, as he neatly summarizes it, "Sex can be productive without being reproductive." On this basis Hefling argues that "homosexual intercourse is not, in and of itself, the unnatural vice that tradition condemns."

Sex Redeemed

Hefling has not devoted this careful and constructive analysis merely to the advocacy of what is called "gay marriage," which is of course a civil affair and very much before the public in the congressional debates on the so-called Defense of Marriage Act. Hefling is suggesting that the church, his own Anglican Communion and by implication all other churches, advance the conversation to the point where the relevant question is what are the appropriate Christian expectations placed upon those permanent, monogamous, faithful, intimate relationships within which the sexual act takes place, whether the relationship be heterosexual or homosexual. "Have same-sex relationships the same potential for sacramental meaning and power" as heterosexual relationships? He believes they have because "they can, and do signify a natural good." Sex thus understood is not only redeemed, it is also redemptive.

PART THREE

THE TRUE AND LIVELY WORD

"Give grace, O heavenly Father, to all
Bishops, Pastors, and Curates, that they
may both by their life and doctrine set
forth Thy true and lively word."
—Thomas Cranmer,
The Book of Common Prayer, 1662

CHAPTER 9

THE BIBLE AND THE GOOD LIFE

OVER the years of my ministry I have come to two conclusions about people and the Bible. The first is that people really do desire to be and to do good. They want to know what makes a good life, and they want such a good life for themselves and for those they love. The second is that people have an instinctive belief that the Bible is an important book and that it is significant in helping them learn about the good life, but that most of them do not know how to read the Bible, finding it a confusing mystery and not understanding what is in it or how to make sense and meaning of what is in it. Thus the good life remains an elusive goal and the Bible an unknown, even unknowable book. Is it wrong to expect the Bible to provide a key to the good life? Is that not using the Bible in a self-serving way? Am I stupid for not being able to figure out on my own what the Bible says and means? Do I have to be a fundamentalist or a biblical scholar to answer these questions? These two questions and their attendant anxieties consume the interests of many modern men and women, who are, in the words of Carl Jung, "in search of a soul."

In the autumn of 1995 I went to preach in one of New York City's oldest and most historic churches, the First Presbyterian Church on lower Fifth Avenue in Greenwich Village. This was the church in which Harry Emerson Fosdick preached his famous 1923 sermon, "Shall the Fundamentalists Win?" The liberal Fosdick, a Baptist by ordination, created such a fuss among the more conservative Presbyterians that he was forced out of the friendly and relatively liberal pulpit of the First Church by a less than friendly denomination. As a consequence, the Riverside Church was founded to provide an unfettered pulpit for his preaching. There are some who would suggest that the transformation of America's traditional churches, from the main line to the sidelines, began with this confrontation. The First Church has a proud history, but until recently most churches with a proud history faced an uncertain future. The movement was away from these old establishments, the balance of power was shifting to the more conservative, evangelical, and nondenominational religious powerhouses in the suburbs of the South, the Heartland, and the Far West. For twenty-five years we have heard of the slow death of the once-thriving inner-city churches. They have been killed off by dead preaching, aging congregations, costly physical plants, the changing demographics of America, and unfavorable statistics.

By all measures then, the First Presbyterian

Church should have been dead on its feet years ago. Surrounded as it is by a half-dozen institutions of higher learning in one of New York's trendiest and most secular neighborhoods, one might have expected to find a small and faithful congregation of the elderly, holdouts against an inevitable decline, huddled within these nineteenth-century Gothic walls much like the old praying women muttering their beads in the neglected darkness of Orthodox churches in the secular Soviet Russia of two generations ago. Yet the place was filled to the doors with a vibrant, varied, and energetic congregation. Many came from the suburbs into the city for services, and as many, if not more, were New Yorkers from nearby; even more were new Presbyterians and new Christians. I was delighted and surprised. On the Sunday in question nearly forty new members were received into the church, and this, I was told, happened three times a year. Most of these were young adults, and many were young parents. From the little biographical summaries the pastor made as each person came forward I learned something of who they were and why they were joining this church. Many had been brought up in church but had fallen away; others had never known a church, had discovered this one, and had decided to sign on. None, it seemed, was merely going through the motions; all were intentional and articulate about why they were there and what they wanted. What they wanted could be summed up in three words: The Good Life.

The Good Life to many now has a decidedly

comfortable, consumerist, and secular ring to it. Following the gospel of *Wall Street*'s Gordon Gekko, that "greed is good," the good life means as much of this world's goods as can be carried away and charged. He who dies with the most toys wins. We all know about the Greedy Eighties, that decade of rampant materialism in which our cultural values were defined by television's *Dynasty* and Alexis Carrington, and *Dallas* and J.R. Ewing. Junk bonding was the national sport, and self-indulgence was a constitutional right. Excess was in, moderation was only for those who could not accelerate or excel. Luxury was both a goal and a reward, and Godiva chocolates turned one of the world's most ordinary of confections into a pricey status symbol. Cityscapes exploded with steel and glass temples to the gods of commerce; banks, insurance companies, and brokerage houses sprang up everywhere. Malls, the horizontal version of these monuments to the credit economy of things, killed off the pokey downtowns of Middle America, and became self-sustained suburban pleasure domes. The word was "development," and the developers became the apostles of the new age of instant and trouble-free prosperity. This was as close to heaven as the Brie-and-bottled-water set wanted to get, and a *New Yorker* Thanksgiving cartoon of that era captured the mood: It showed one Pilgrim saying to another as the *Mayflower* was putting in to Plymouth Harbor, "Religious freedom is my immediate goal, but my long-range plan is to go into real estate."

The Harvard undergraduates I knew in those days, when asked what they wanted out of life, would say that they wanted "the good life," or "a good life," and by that most of them meant, like their college generation across the country, and perhaps the world, economic security, marital happiness, and a license to pursue the pleasures of this world. "I'm not greedy," one once said to me. "I just want all I can get, legally, of course." Many of these have now learned the truth of the sad aphorism "Be careful what you pray for, for you just might get it." Since no one aspires to be lower class, and our democratic and anti-elitist principles deny the existence of an upper class, everybody in America of whom account is taken is middle class. Political parties and their partisans are devoted to the interests of this middle class, and the values and virtues of this class are taken to be normative, worthy of emulation and preservation. Affirmative action and high taxes "hurt the middle class"; high interest rates and government regulations "hurt the middle class"; and in fact, if Newt Gingrich and most of the Republican candidates for high office are to be believed, government itself is lethal to the health of the middle class.

It does not take a degree in sociology to know that this vast entity known as the middle class is unhappy, and woefully so. Elsewhere we have discussed some of the reasons for this discontent, and they are familiar to us all, but one of these discontents, not often discussed, is a discontent not with the failures of our system but

251

with the unsatisfying nature of our system's success. In the Needy Nineties, over and over again I have heard from people who by the standards of the day have made it, or are making it, the plaintive and at times resentful question, "Is this all there is? Isn't there more to life than this?" This is not a question of greed but of need, an acknowledgment that what has been sold as the good life is not all it was cracked up to be.

Some years ago I gave the commencement address at a very posh girls' day school in Manhattan. Many of the brightest and the best of the girls went on to Radcliffe and to other elite colleges, and soon thereafter would make their way into the expanding stratosphere of the establishment once reserved for their brothers. They were able, aggressive, and entitled young women on the threshold of conquering the world, and I rejoiced in their achievement, was happy to celebrate with them, and wished them well. I took as my text on that bright sunny morning in midtown that wonderful passage from Jesus' Sermon on the Mount in Matthew 6, where he asks, "Is not life more than food, and the body more than clothing?" Neither for Jesus nor for me was this a hostile question, and he goes on to invite his listeners, as I did, to "consider the lilies of the field, how they grow; they toil not, neither do they spin, yet their heavenly father provides for them. Are you not of more worth than these?" It is one of the most lyrical passages in all of literature, one well suited to the overachieving anxieties of prep school. It concludes with the sound advice, "Therefore do not be anxious about tomorrow, for tomorrow will be anxious for itself." Jesus knew his audience, and I thought that I knew mine, and I think the girls liked it, or at least they told me so.

All were not pleased, however, and at the reception the father of one of the girls came up to me with fire in his eyes and ice in his voice, and told me that what I had said was a lot of nonsense. I replied that I hadn't said it, but that Jesus had. "It's still nonsense," he said, not easily dissuaded by an appeal to scripture. "It was anxiety that got my daughter into this school, it was anxiety that kept her here, it was anxiety that got her into Yale, it will be anxiety that will keep her there, and it will be anxiety that will get her a good job. You are selling nonsense."

He was one unsatisfied customer, and I recognized the type, for I have watched Harvard parents drive their children not only to college but to distraction with their anxiety that they get the credentials for the good life. If the parents are wealthy they want their kids to learn practical skills to manage and to keep the wealth intact; if the parents are poor they want their kids to get the practical skills to move up the economic and social escalator, both for the kids and, vicariously, for themselves; and if the parents are from the middle class, they want their kids to be responsible and to get the practical skills, and so forth. Few parents tell their children to smell the roses or consider the lilies or become a poet or a potter or a painter, and when the child, wonder of wonders, discovers his or her muse and wants to take Music or Fine Arts or a seminar on Hindu religion instead of "something useful, like economics," they are anxious because of their parents' anxieties. College, to some students, and, alas, to most parents, is the very expensive ticket to the good life.

It is a pity, but it is also a truth that for many it is only when the good life turns sour or proves inadequate that it is seen to be not good enough. If Wordsworth were still taught and known as our grandparents knew him, we could say,

> *The world is too much with us:*
> > *late and soon,*
> *Getting and spending, we lay waste*
> > *our powers:*
> *Little we see in nature that is ours.*
> *We have given our hearts away,*
> > *a sordid boon!*

The poem may be less known than of old, but the truth is even less so, and I think we have reached that point where so many thousands of able, disappointed, and questing people are prepared to exchange the good life for the life that is good. That is what brought so many of those people to the First Presbyterian Church in New York City. That search is what is beginning to fill up the waste places of America's churches across the continent.

Some sociologists of this phenomenon

describe the yuppie return to religion as the result of parenting, that these young people are seeking spiritual security for their children in the same way that they want them to have straight teeth, the best day care, and early violin lessons. This spirituality is just one more consumer objective to be satisfied. The consumer mentality is hard to break, and there is the very real ecclesiastical version of comparison shopping: looking for the church with the best parking, the most congenial day-care programs, the best choir, and the most user-friendly preaching. What is wrong with this? Why shouldn't we rejoice that people take the same care in seeking out spiritual guidance as they do in looking for a dentist or a podiatrist for the family dog? Who are we to dismiss disillusion with what this world offers as the good life as an inadequate reason for seeking out the life that is good, and for those things that make for life rather than just for a living?

We should congratulate those who see that what they have is less than meets the eye, we should encourage them in their search for meaning and transformation, and those of us in the religion business should pray to God that we are able to help them in their search for the living waters. Perhaps one of the most remarkable phenomena of our age, at the end of what we like to call "modernity," is this palpable search for the good, for goodness, and for God. Some will call it a revival. I do not, for it suggests that people are looking for that which they once had and lost. I prefer to call it a pilgrimage, whose characteristic is the search for that which has not yet been achieved. This is not a backward, nostalgic, sentimental retreat into the religious certainties of an earlier age. This is not your father's Chevrolet, as a very effective advertisement for the newest model once put it. Because this movement arises out of the despair and disappointments of our experience of a true secularity, this is truly countercultural, new, and full of adventure; and that others in other times have discovered what these now seek is a sign of encouragement in the pilgrimage.

An Elusive Book

The people of whom I have been speaking have a sense that the Bible has something to do with the true good life that they have been searching for. They know it is a holy book, but they don't quite know why, or how it is so, and that is in part because they have no real sense of what the holy is. That is not because they are an ignorant or insensitive lot, but rather because they have been the products of a spiritless, godless, and remorselessly mundane world in which the notion of a transcendent and ultimate other has been erased from our collective memory. The culture that has shaped and formed the culture in which they live and against which they must now contend has been so arrogantly and aggressively hostile to what cannot be quantified, measured, bought, or sold that it is no wonder that wonder itself has been held hostage to sensation and feeling, but not to meaning or to awe. The reigning ideology of our age, the notion that we are the solitary centers of the universe and that in our splendor we are quite alone, means that we are left with just the consoling conceit that we are the only ones who have ever asked the great questions of life, that we alone have suffered, feared, loved, lost, and sought for something beyond our grasp and control. Ralph Waldo Emerson's dreadful hymn to "Self-Reliance" has persuaded us not only that we are on our own but that we ought to be, and that we are failures if we cannot make it as solitary, self-sufficient voyagers.

Somehow, despite all this, people sense that there may be something in the Bible for them although they are not certain what it is and how to find it, and are fearful of confessing their ignorance in the matter. The answer is not to give these seekers the full benefit of a thousand, or even of the last twenty-five years, of biblical scholarship. That would be like a thirsty person trying to get a drink of water from an open fire hydrant. Biblical scholarship is important. I have made its importance central both to my preaching and to my teaching, and to this book as well. People do need to know, and deserve to know, what the Bible is and is not, and how it came to be, and what can and cannot be expected of it. No one should be in the position of a devout Catholic layman of whom I recently heard, who, now in late life, said that he was brought up in the pre–Vatican II church which told the laity not to read the Bible, and that all they would need to know about it the priest would tell them. "Now," he said, "in my old age I would like to read it for myself, but I don't know how."

The Bible has a talismanic quality, with magical, even oracular powers attributed to it. This is why brides are given a Bible bound in white to take down the aisle on their wedding day; this is why oaths in court are sworn on it, and why presidents take their oaths on it as well. Many are the stories of soldiers in war whose lives were saved when a bullet meant for them was stopped by the leather-bound Bible in the breast pocket of their battle dress. "Swear on a stack of Bibles" is the ultimate request for truthfulness, and "It's in the Bible" is the ultimate clincher to a religious argument among Christians. In our churches the place of honor given to the physical artifact of the Bible would confirm that impression. In Catholic churches one knows that the place of highest honor is the Tabernacle, in which the consecrated elements of the Eucharist are to be found, the very body and blood of Christ. It is to this that the priest and all others make their acts of veneration. In Episcopal churches the faithful make an act of reverence before the cross, both on the altar and when it passes them in procession, but in most Protestant churches it is the Bible that is the object of the devotions of the faithful. In certain churches the open Bible is to be found propped up between two candles on the Communion Table or altar. On Protestant pulpits the Bible is displayed, and in biblically minded churches the preacher makes much of the well-leafed floppy Bible in his left hand, to which he points with his right. Bibles are placed in cornerstones of buildings. The Gideons place them in bedside-table drawers in hotels and motels across the world, and the queen of England is presented with a Bible at her coronation.

We are supposed to be a people beyond symbols, living in an age when symbols have lost their potency, but as a symbol of what we aspire to and do not know, the Bible remains. The question also remains: What do we do with it? How do we get at it? Surely it is not to be read as we would read a catalog, a textbook, or a novel, is it?

One of the reasons that fundamentalist and evangelical churches have experienced such profound growth in recent years has to do with the emphasis they place upon the Bible. It is not necessarily the theology of fundamentalism that draws people in, and within the broader evangelical tradition there is a wide diversity of opinion on many matters of faith and practice. What these traditions have in common, and what fundamentalism offers in particular, is the assurance that they know what the Bible says, and are capable of telling the inquirer in such a way as to satisfy every need. For many this is an answer to prayer; they want to know what the Bible is about, and here is a place that will tell you all that you need to know, and then some.

There are many who have a desire to make use of the Bible, to come to know it, and to discover within it the things that make for the good life they now seek. They do not wish to become either biblical scholars or Christian fundamentalists. They feel awkward with the concept of "using the Bible," wondering, perhaps, if profane hands can "use" holy things. Yet they worry as well that if they don't make some effort to explore the deep things of God, which they believe the Bible speaks to, they will be hostage to anybody and everybody who knows more about it than they do. One very intelligent young woman told me that she was driven to consider a more intentional study of the Bible because when she was visited by the Jehovah's Witnesses, she, a lifelong churchgoer, knew that what her visitors were saying about the Bible was nonsense, but she had no basis on which to argue with them. "They knew more than I did," she said, "and that made me mad and embarrassed." I have heard variations of this concern when young Christians try to argue with fundamentalist lay evangelists or street preachers.

Arguments about scripture generally are unprofitable, and no one has ever been persuaded from his or her position in a biblical argument by the weight of superior scholarship; and so it is not my purpose here to provide tips on how to read the Bible, or strategies on how to best your antagonist in an argument about the Documentary Hypothesis or the Mosaic Authorship of the Pentateuch. The scholarship is available to be consulted, and it ought to be. Bible "study" should be that, and not just the steadfastly uninformed piety of the reader reflecting on "what this verse means to me." God has given us a mind, the church has given us the benefit of its teachings, and the best of biblical scholarship has given us unparalleled resources with which to assist our understanding. It is not piety but arrogance that refuses to take advantage of these opportunities for edification.

Five Questions in Search of an Answer

My concern now, however, has to do with the relationship between the search for the good life and the Bible's ability to help in that search. The needs of the age can be summarized in five question which those in search of the good life are likely to ask, and to which I believe the Bible provides an answer. The questions are these:

1. Am I the only one who is confused?
2. What can I trust?
3. Am I on my own?
4. Can I feel good about myself?
5. How can I face the future?

Am I the Only One Who Is Confused?

Critics of the Bible have often said that its moral authority is compromised by the fact that it is filled with so many less than exemplary characters. No less an exemplary character than Helen Keller said of the Bible, in her autobiography, "There is much to the Bible against

261

which every instinct of my being rebels, so much that I regret the necessity which has compelled me to read it through from beginning to end." Thomas Paine, writing in his anti-religious tract *The Age of Reason*, complained of the "obscene stories, the voluptuous debaucheries, the cruel and torturous executions, and unrelenting vindictiveness with which more than half the Bible is filled." What engages the reader of the Bible is the fact that it is filled with people very much like the reader, people who are confused and confusing, who are less than exemplary but who nevertheless participate in a developing encounter with God. If the Bible were just about the successful and the pious it would be little more than a collection of Horatio Alger tales or Barbara Cartland romances. It could aspire at best to the status of *Aesop's Fables* or a Norse epic. What makes the Bible interesting and compelling is the company of human beings who through its pages play their parts in the drama of the human and the divine. In the sense that Bible stories tell our story, the human story in relationship to the divine, they are true. They are not true because they are in the Bible; they are in the Bible because they are true to the experience of men and of women.

Take, for example, the common theme of reluctance to accept responsibility that God wants to confer. None of the prophets took on their assignments willingly or gladly. Moses complained that he was not eloquent enough and that people wouldn't believe him. Isaiah claimed himself unworthy, "a man of unclean lips." Samuel was just a little boy. Ezekiel was sent out to preach to dead bones. Jonah refused to go to Nineveh, and yet God took these people and turned them into something for his purpose.

Esther we know of because hers is the only book in the Bible in which the name of God does not appear, and yet we know she was used of God, and had been "called to the kingdom for such a time as this." Rahab the Harlot, who saved Joshua's spies, and Ruth, who gleaned in Boaz's field and became an ancestress in the genealogy of Jesus, and Sarah, who laughed when she learned that in old age she was to bear a son to Abraham—none of these were heroic in the Greek sense of heroic. They were not even celebrities in the American sense of people being famous for being famous. They were ordinary people for whom God had a use, and the adventure of their stories is their discovery of their use of God's use of them.

No one who has ever suffered and wondered about the goodness of God can read the book of Job without a sense of profound recognition. No one can read the Psalms without a sense of the Psalmist's psychological insight into the depth and breadth of human experience. I once advised a woman about to undergo surgery for cancer to read the Psalms straight through, preferably in the King James Version. I wanted her to read the whole thing in one or two sittings in order to have an immersion experience in the soul of the writer, and I wanted her to read it in an unfamiliar yet evocative translation where there would be rhythmic power and imagery just slightly anachronistic so that she would have to enter into it and not simply be carried along by the familiarity of it all. She did as I suggested, and when I asked her how it went, she replied that she had had no idea that the Psalmist knew who she was, her precise condition, and what she needed and when. "When he rejoiced, so did I," she said, "and when he howled and cried out, I did too." She was not alone.

I hated Lent as a child because the Passion story that gained in momentum as we got nearer and nearer to Easter was all about my impetuous namesake, Peter. Poor Peter, he never got it right. He was always promising more that he could deliver. He walked on water, and then fell in. He promised never to deny Jesus, and then he did, not once but three times. His flaws were mine, his anxieties mine, and then, when I thought about it, his redemption and rehabilitation were also mine, and that was not so bad.

The apostles of Jesus never seem to understand what is going on, and yet he loves them. They forsake him but he does not forsake them, and each one of their ordinary, shabby lives is transformed after an encounter with the living Jesus. They finally do "get it," and we rejoice that they do.

The Bible is filled with the companionship of the confused and seeking, men and women made of the most ordinary stuff who often fail to understand, who make mistakes, whose humanity is transparent, but who encounter the living God and whose lives thereby are changed. When Paul says that he regards no one any longer from a merely human point of view, he means that in Christ the limitations of the human perspective are overcome. People are not taken out of this life, but are given strength and power and purpose to live in it. In Romans 12, Paul invites the members of the Roman church to present their bodies as a living sacrifice to God, and in so doing they are not to be conformed to this world, but transformed by the renewing of their minds. In other words, they are to grow and change and become something and somebody other than what they now are.

Think of Nicodemus, that wise doctor of Israel, in John's gospel, who comes to Jesus by night to learn of life. He is very much confused and uncertain, this Nicodemus, when he hears Jesus say, "You must be born again." So, too, are so many modern-day people confused when they hear that phrase, "born again." To so many it sounds like a statement of spiritual achievement, a destination at which one has already arrived, and when it is uttered with the spiritual pride with which so many American Christians utter it, as a badge of spiritual and moral superiority, we can understand why people are confused and mightily put off. What "born again" in the gospel means, however, is literally to begin all over again, to be given a second birth, a second chance. The one who is born again doesn't all of a sudden get turned into a super-Christian. To be born again is to enter afresh into the process of spiritual growth. It is to wipe the slate clean. It is to cancel your old mortgage and start again. In other words, you don't have to be always what you have now become. Such an offer is too good to be true for many, confusing for most, but for those who seek to be other than what they are now, who want to be more than the mere accumulation and sum total of their experiences, the invitation, "You must be born again," is an offer you cannot afford to refuse. The Bible is an account of that great company of people who have both sought and found a way. We should take them seriously, for they have much to tell us.

What Can I Trust?

The world is longing for something worthy of its trust. So too are most men and women— longing for something to trust in, longing for someone and something worthwhile to give one's heart and life and love to. We are not too stingy, as the conventional wisdom goes; we are too generous, too trusting, and thus over and over again we give away our hearts and our trust to that which is not worthy of them. This is called idolatry, and because we must worship something we are tempted to worship anything, giving completely to that which can respond only partially, if at all. The sin of idolatry which is denounced in the Ten Commandments is denounced not so much for what the worshiper does not give God, but for what the false gods cannot give the true worshiper: "I am the God who brought you out of Egypt." The emphasis is where it should be, on the one who performs the action. Because of the action performed, liberation from slavery, the God who accomplishes this deserves and demands priority. A false god, or an idol, is by definition one who neither has nor can deliver the goods.

Political dictators do not gain the loyalty of their adherents, at least at first, by coercion. Those of us opposed to them like to think that that is the case, but I suggest that it is not necessarily so. Dictators win the loyalty of their people because people are anxious to have someone and something in which to believe and to whom they can give that loyalty. Dictators rely upon trust first, then upon gratitude, and only after these two, on fear and on terror and the repression that goes with them. Anyone who has watched any of those old newsreels and documentaries on the rise of the Third Reich notices with some chagrin that the German people listened to Hitler and heard him gladly, not because they were coerced into doing so but because they wanted to trust him and they were grateful for what he was able to do first for their spirits and their imagination, and then, by implication, for the state.

Paul Tillich wrote famously of "ultimate concern," and attracted the attention of a generation deeply eager to find something worthy of its ultimate loyalty and trust. Writing in America's most popular magazine, *The Saturday Evening Post*, in the middle of a postwar revival of religious interest that saw so great a boom in the building of new churches that the phenomenon was called "the edifice complex," Tillich titled his article "The Lost Dimension in Religion," and argued that despite the apparent institutional success of Christianity, the real dimension had been lost: "If we define religion as the state of being grasped by an infinite concern we must say: Man in our time has lost such an infinite concern. And the resurgence of religion is nothing but a desperate and mostly futile attempt to regain what has been lost."

I think he was right. The religious boom of the 1950s was a blip and not a movement, and those main-line Protestant churches that largely profited from it were set up for a terrible fall from which many have yet to recover. In less than a decade the revival of religion in the America of the 1950s, expressed largely through statistics and buildings, was over, and the resurgence was indeed a "mostly futile attempt to regain what has been lost." For Tillich what was lost was that "state of being grasped by an infinite concern," and it was replaced by the sense of human achievement, power, and progress, of which the conquest of outer space was the most significant sign. "The loss of the dimension of depth is caused by the relation of man to his world and to himself in our period, the period in which nature is being subjected scientifically and technically to the control of man. In this period, life in the dimension of depth is replaced by life in the horizontal dimension."

We did put our trust in technology, economic

success, and gave our utter institutional loyalties to the government, to the universities and colleges, and to the church. Technology failed us; we were not warmed but chilled by the terrors of our technology, epitomized by nuclear energy. Our economy turned sour and continues to bedevil us. The government lied to us in Vietnam and in Watergate, and continues to stumble in disrepute. Our colleges and universities turned first into laboratories of discontent, out of which came the angry violence of the late 1960s and early 1970s, and since then have been unable to give a lead to the nation, or even to stem the dumbing-down of the culture. The churches, particularly those in whom such confidence was placed in the resurgence of the 1950s, have been reduced to mere observer status as men and women in search of a soul look elsewhere for meaning.

These objects of trust all failed, and unambiguously so, proving themselves unworthy of one's ultimate loyalty; and yet, because of these manifest failures, the issue of a loyalty worthy of our trust is even greater now than it was then. Hence the search for the good life is purer, more acute, and much less distracted by these idols and false gods than it was in the good old days, which is why this present search is not a revival or a resurgence, but rather a pilgrimage. It is also why for so many people it begins within, in the interior reaches of the soul.

The Bible knows all about false gods and idols, things unworthy of our loyalty. Its first moral tale, that of Adam and Eve, is not about sex or even about disobedience. We might say that it is about a false trust in the benevolence of knowledge, for it was the fruit of that tree that got the first society into trouble. "O put not your trust in princes, nor in any child of man; for there is no help in them," we read in Psalm 146. "Some put their trust in chariots, and some in horses," says Psalm 20:7–8, "but we will remember the name of the Lord our God. They are brought down and fallen; but we are risen and stand upright." The Bible, if nothing else, is a book about the dangers of false trust:

Put no trust in a neighbor,
  have no confidence in a friend,
  guard the doors of your mouth
  from her who lies in your bosom,
For the son treats the father with contempt,
  the daughter rises up against her mother,
  the daughter-in-law against her mother-in-law;
  a man's enemies are the men of his own
  house.
But as for me, I will look to the Lord, I will wait
for the God of my salvation; my God will hear me.
                              (Micah 7:5–7)

A book that knows this about the human condition must also know a lot about God. We can trust what that book has to say about the source of trust. It is not the Bible but the God of the Bible in whom we find someone, something, worthy of our loyalty, our ultimate concern, our trust: "In returning and rest you shall

270

be saved: in quietness and trust shall be your strength." (Isaiah 30:15)

For tired people weary of noise and striving after that which gives no reward, a book that promises this is worth taking seriously; and now, perhaps, having exhausted ourselves and all of the alternatives, we may just begin to do so.

Am I on My Own?

Despite the crowded conditions of this planet, most of us think ourselves alone and on our own in the matters that count. The two groups that I know best speak of loneliness as if it were patented for them alone. Students in their private confessions of soul, while they are anxious and fearful and full of the insecurities of youth, speak more often of loneliness than of anything else, and in those fears, anxieties, and insecurities they think of themselves as utterly alone and the first to feel this way. "It's not that I'm homesick," said one young undergraduate in a moment of unguarded candor, "but I do feel as if everything I do now depends entirely upon me and on me alone. I looked forward to being on my own, but now I'm not so sure."

The other group I know well, the clergy, have as their besetting anxiety the fearful fact of loneliness. "In the end," said one of my colleagues, "we are all Lone Rangers. Lawyers, doctors, even computer programmers stick together; we are all soloists." We might like to think of ourselves as Henry David Thoreau with his three chairs, "one for solitude, two for company, and three for society," but the demands and disciplines of solitude are too much for most of us who have no woods into which we can retreat.

We celebrate individualism and autonomy in America, and we like to think of ourselves as beyond merely following the crowd. Yet we abhor silence, and we mass together whenever we can, in sports stadia, rock concerts, and in that crowd that is defined not by physical proximity but by the deadening uniformity of the shared experience of television. Like those crowds that flock to Times Square to see in the New Year, we flock together and dare not be alone lest we discover that we are not only alone but on our own. No one knows, no one cares. This is not the fear of mere physical isolation; rather, this is what Joseph Conrad once called "moral solitude." This is what he says:

Who knows what true loneliness is—not the conventional word, but the naked terror? To the lonely themselves it wears a mask. The most miserable outcast hugs some memory or some illusion. Now and then a fatal conjunction of events may lift the veil for an instant. For an instant only. No human being could bear a steady view of moral solitude without going mad.

Moral solitude is more than the lack of companionship and fellowship; it is that, but it is more than that. It is the loss of the sense of accountability and responsibility that at first appears to be the benefit of autonomy, but turns out to be, together with autonomy, itself a liability.

We all know the cliché that in Africa, the archtypical "primitive" society, it "takes a whole village to raise a child." We utter that cliché with a sense of longing and of loss, for most of us remember those villages from which we sought an early escape. When I was growing up, a small-town boy in the town of Plymouth, Massachusetts, now fifty years ago, I remember that the whole town was part of a conspiracy to deprive me of my liberty. "They" were all in it together, my school teachers, my pastor and Sunday school teachers, the cop on the beat, the butcher, the baker, the candlestick maker, they were all in league with my parents, and there were no hiding places. I remember once when I was fifteen years old and able to go to the "adult" movies when "adult" was not a euphemism for "pornographic," I decided that I wanted to see what was then the controversial film *The Sandpiper*, with Elizabeth Taylor and Richard Burton, who were at the height of their notoriety. I knew that it was about a scandalous clergyman, and the presence of Elizabeth Taylor promised a little sizzle. So after school I put up my money to catch the matinee. I knew the ticket taker, and worse, she knew me. She left my money underneath the opening of her booth, and said, "Does your mother know you're here?" I took back the money and fled. Mother probably would not have minded for she was a very sensible woman, but I minded that she would know what I had done, innocent as it seemed to me, even before I got home from the Old Colony Theatre. She would have cared, as did the ticket taker, and I would be accountable. The village, inhibiting and stifling as it was, worked.

My college generation is the one that overthrew the old village concept of college life. We so harassed the college administrations of our day, heady as we were with the new wine of autonomy and revolution, that they caved in to our "nonnegotiable demands." We killed requirements and regulations against our freedom, and with these we slew the biggest dragon on the campus, the doctrine of *in loco parentis*. No longer did the college stand in place of our parents. We were now customers and consumers, and the college was our shopping mall.

We are now running these colleges and more often than not are bemused and confused when our students demand that the college take a moral stand, say on divestment in corporate malefactors of great wealth, or that it give institutional support to the values and needs, say, of minority communities. When a controversial speaker comes to town and is likely to give offense to somebody, colleges are criticized for not taking "community values" and "community sensibilities" into account. To many, institutional refuge in the principle of absolute "free speech" seems an abdication of moral responsibility and institutional accountability. Parents, and the general body politic, insist that colleges interfere more than they have done in the private lives of their students as far as drinking and drugs are concerned, and wholesale development of quasi-legal codes of conduct under the rubric of sexual harassment have made deans and college administrations far more intrusive than they ever were in the bad old days of parietal rules and the old-fashioned disciplinary rules that defined and punished "conduct unbecoming the college." The difference between "now" and "then," of course, is that "then" there was a reasonably broad consensus on what "conduct unbecoming" was.

At Harvard Commencement, from ancient times the president confers degrees upon the various candidates with a little formula suited to the special qualities of the profession for which the candidates have been presented. The candidates in law, usually rowdy and surly as they rise to be admitted, are granted their degrees with the president's ironic certification that they are fit "to assist in shaping those wise restraints that make us free." Although the repute in which lawyers are held has perhaps never been lower, I think that all of us have an increasing appreciation of "those wise restraints," if we could only figure out what they are; and that such "wise restraints" are necessary is not merely a concession to Thomas Hobbes's mordant view of human nature, but an affirmation of an ancient view that we are not and cannot be "on our own." Neither our souls nor our society can afford the luxury of such a liberty.

Most of us do not need a seventeenth-century political philosopher to tell us this. We know and fear the moral solitude that deprives us of the fellowship of our fellow pilgrims, and it is this desire for fellowship, not just company but fellowship, that is the ambition of the men and women of our day in search of Paul Tillich's "lost dimension." It is a commonplace that conservative churches are growing at such a fast rate because people want quick and easy certitude, and in an age of anxiety and uncertainty they want absolutes and infallibilities. So-called liberal churches in their statistical decline denigrate the success of their evangelical competition, and argue that it is bought with the price of cheap grace and an inability to handle the ambiguities of modernity, but I suggest that while fundamentalism does offer a whole host of absolutes on to which people can cling, the reasons for spectacular growth cannot be attributed alone to the search for certitude. I would argue that people are seeking companionship, fellowship, in their pilgrimage, and that the sense of community, of being in a place that cares, where people are accountable to and responsible for one another, is an even greater and more desirable quality than theological certitude. On matters of doctrine, despite all claims to the contrary, we know now only in part and will know fully only when we are with the Lord, but we do not have to wait for the day of the Lord to know and to experience the benefits of a beloved community of memory and hope. The secret of such a community is that it stands apart from the secular culture and is not its mere reflection. It has something to offer the lonely soul who seeks soul-mates in the soul-denying culture of purely rational, secular, and utilitarian mainstream culture.

Robert Wuthnow's helpful book, *Christianity in the 21st Century: Reflections on the Challenges Ahead*, suggests that our model for religious community in the new millennium will not come from a reconstruction of the "primitive" church of biblical times or from a re-creation of the "prosperous" church of the 1950s American ideal. Rather, Wuthnow suggests that a lesson can be learned from the cults and the Twelve-Step groups that proliferated as church substitutes in the 1970s. What did they have to offer? These groups first "drew on and created a distinct past of their own," and that past did not simply mirror "a vague vision of secular progress." Second, they drew people apart from the larger social environment into smaller, self-contained, self-defined, and disciplined communities within which new identities could be formed and affirmed. Third, they focused on the nonrational and invented rituals and forms of meaning that got people "out of their heads."

Many of us know the dangers and excesses of many of these New Age movements; we have smiled wryly at the image of overweight white men beating drums in the suburban woods, and at rational women's rediscovery of the appeals of witchcraft and the goddess community. The reappropriation of the ancient symbols of fire, blood, and water in group-invented liturgies make many of us wonder and some of us worry about the reaccreditation of what some call the new paganism. Yet these way stations on the pilgrimage for spirituality have taken thousands beyond the inhospitable doors of their local churches and the Christian churches of their birth and have given them a meaning, a discipline, and a fellowship that most churches in their aping of modernity have been unable or unwilling to provide.

One of the deacons of my home church told me of a visit she made with our pastor a few years ago to one of our shut-ins. The old lady on whom they called was not shut in in the conventional sense of being confined by age or infirmity to her home, but she had not come to church on a regular basis for years, and when asked why, told her church visitors that she got more comfort and consolation, "even fellowship," from watching Dr. Robert Schuller and his Crystal Cathedral services than ever she did from sitting in the pews of our church, where no one seemed to notice her. This was not so much an affirmation of the effective television ministry of the Crystal Cathedral as it was an indictment of the ineffective ministry of the local church. When someone can feel more companionship in front of a television set than in the midst of a congregation, our first response ought not to be to smash the television. It gave our deacons and pastor much to think about, to pray on, and to work for.

When we realize that the Bible is about the formation of a fellowship, a community of men and women who are reminded over and over again that they are not alone, not on their own but part of a communion, a company of both the living and the dead in which is to be found the living presence of a loving God, we find that the Bible's unambiguous answer to the question "Am I on my own?" is a resounding "No!"

In the creation story in Genesis, it is God himself who says, "It is not good for the man to be alone," and in the New Testament it is Jesus who says to his despairing disciples, "I will not leave you comfortless." (John 14:18)

Willa Cather calls that sense of communion "happiness," that sense that we are not on our own but that we belong. She writes in *My Antonia*, in an entirely secular sense, "That is happiness; to be dissolved into something complete and great." We know, however, that it is not about happiness but about belonging that she speaks. The white Baptist sharecropper in the hills of Georgia knew it as well when he sang at his annual camp meeting or revival this hymn of Elisha A. Hoffman:

> *Leaning on Jesus, safe and secure from all alarms;*
> *What a fellowship, what a joy divine,*
> *Leaning on the everlasting arms;*
> *What a blessedness, what a peace is mine,*
> *Leaning on the everlasting arms.*
> *Leaning, leaning, safe and secure from all alarms;*
> *Leaning, leaning, leaning on the everlasting arms.*

Every human being wants to love, to be loved, and to know that he or she is loved, and when one does that and knows that and shares that, then the question "Am I on my own?" is answered in the place where that love is found. That is what the Bible is all about, and the good life to which it points.

Can I Feel Good About Myself?

Answering the telephone in my business can be both a dangerous and a revealing experience. Awhile ago, on a busy Saturday morning in the church office, I picked up the telephone when it was about to ring off the hook. It was one of the many Saturday calls we get from the anonymous public asking who the preacher on Sunday is to be. As it was I, I answered warmly but without identifying myself: "The preacher is the Minister in The Memorial Church and Plummer Professor of Christian Morals." The caller paused, and then asked, "Is that that short, fat, little black man?" In some annoyance I replied curtly, "Yes," and slammed down the receiver.

Now what was wrong? This caller had not insulted me, and in fact had given an objective description of my basic characteristics in the course of asking an honest question. Why should I be upset? These were hardly racist or inflammatory remarks; and that was just the problem. Her description flew in the face of my self-image. Not that I think of myself as tall and blond or as a dead ringer for Denzel

Washington. I usually think of myself, however, as more than the sum total of my physical characteristics, and when I was reduced to them my ego was, perhaps appropriately, rebuffed, as she had come dangerously near to my fragile self-esteem. This is not a problem peculiar to short black men!

The conventional wisdom is that we are all possessed of robust egos, of self-images that will not quit, and that the human sins with which we are most concerned are those of pride and arrogance. Ask the average American what comes to mind when Harvard is mentioned, and you usually get something like "You can always tell a Harvard man, but you can't tell him much." Ask the average non-American what he or she thinks of Americans and usually you will hear some variation on the theme of arrogance: The "ugly" American, as we recall, has nothing to do with appearance and everything to do with attitude.

The conventional wisdom in this as in so many other things is not entirely to be relied upon, however, and my experience of Harvard students, and of Americans as well, is not that they suffer from a surfeit of self-confidence but rather that we all experience, almost to the level of a mania, what the psychologists call "the imposter syndrome." Image building, that activity that engages us from our earliest years onward, is designed not so much to impress others as it is to protect ourselves from the discovery on the part of others that we are not all that we appear to be. The games of the boardroom are the same as those of the athletic field and the battlefield, designed to conceal our weaknesses from an enemy all too eager to seize upon them and destroy us. Thus, in cultivating the art of defensive living we cultivate a good offense. Catch them before they catch us. This does not mean that we believe ourselves to be less fraudulent than we really are, but that we must be inventive and persistent in preventing the fraud from being exposed to our disadvantage. From our earliest days we develop strategies to achieve this, from the way we dress, to our body language, to our speech, and to the acquiring of credentials meant not to certify but to intimidate.

We live in constant fear of exposure. We live all our lives fearing that we are going to be found out, and in a way we are all little Wizards of Oz. We do it all behind the green curtain with smoke and mirrors, terrified that somebody will discover that that big big voice and that clever clever mind, and all that power, are really just a little tape going round and round and round and round.

Well, there is good news, and that is why they call it the gospel. The news is not that we are worse than we think, it is that we are better than we think, and better than we deserve to be. Why? Because at the very bottom of the whole enterprise is the indisputable fact that we are created, made, formed, invented, patented in the image of goodness itself. That is what it means, that is how one translates being created in the image of God: It means to be created in the image of goodness itself. We are cast from a perfect die and the imprint is on us, and it cannot be evaded or avoided. God made us, male and female, in the image of goodness, and goodness itself is who and what we are, and God pronounced it good, and hence it is good, because, as the kid in the ghetto said, "God don't make no junk." What God makes is good.

Self-worth, self-esteem, self-value, these are not essays in mere ego, these are essays in divinity. These are essays in goodness, the stuff of goodness and godliness itself, and it is *that* image that provides security and serenity in the world. People may take everything away from you, they may deprive you of everything you have and value, but they cannot take away from you the fact that you are a child of God and bear the impression of God in your very soul. You cannot be destroyed, and that cannot be denied.

To be in the image of goodness, then, involves the act of imaging, a technique I learned while talking to a very large football player at a House dinner. Sitting next to him, I decided to try to make easy conversation, one of the things I'm very good at, at least that's my image of myself, and so I said to him, "Young man, what do you do?" He said that he worked in sports theory. Well, that's an intriguing answer, as I've heard of people who are theoretical types, and I know people who work in sports, but I thought that sports was anything but theoretical—either you knocked them down or you didn't—

and I thought that that was a very simple sort of thing. So I said, "What is sports theory about?" and he explained it in terms that even I could understand. He said that it was the process of imaging, of getting the brain to play through all of the right plays over and over and over again, to anticipate and to respond in the brain so that the plays and the actions are patterned, and that by the time you actually do a play, on that one time the brain doesn't know that you haven't done it dozens and dozens of times before, and so has perfected your ability to perform. It isn't practice, this kid said to me, it's imaging. "Imaging," I said, "does that mean imagining?" "Yeah, something like that," he answered. "The imagination has everything to do with how you perform. If you imagine yourself going through all of this patterning in the brain, anticipating and responding, then when it comes time for you to actually have to do it you have done it, and you are much better off doing it because you're done it here before you have to do it out there on the field."

I was absolutely astounded by this, and to show how diverse college is, opposite us sat a piano player. She said, "Yeah, that's what I do. When I practice the piano and I'm not at the piano, I practice at my desk, or I practice in my room, or I practice in the library. I first have the music out and I image what I am going to do with it, and then I don't even need the music, and I don't need a piano. I can image it in my head, I know how it is supposed to come out. I know what my fingers are supposed to do, and when it comes time for my fingers actually to do it they are much better able to do it because I have imaged it, I have done it, I have experienced the thing before actually having to do it."

In other words, to see or to image perfection is to strive for it and, indeed, to accomplish much of it. The imagination has more to do with virtue than virtue itself. What an extraordinary thing. A football player doesn't need a field or a team with which to play football, and a piano player doesn't need the music or even a piano to perform the great work. The only equipment we require to live out the image of goodness in the world is what we have, because God has given us by his very creation of us a capacity to image, to imagine what is good, what is true, and what is beautiful. Here the image is not the external result but just the reverse. An image is not fashion, it is the internal change that we call imagination, and if you cultivate a lively moral imagination, that is a considerable improvement over the maintenance of mere fashion and style.

Think of it—the power to be rests within. It requires only what Professor Tillich once called the *courage* to be and to see things not as they are but as they ought to be, so that you can cope with things as they appear to be. To be created in the image of God means that we are in some sense a picture of God. There is that of God in us, there is that of God in the poor and destitute of the world; in them there is something of God. Sin is when that something, that image, is distorted or denied or deprived or twisted. When we deny that image in ourselves and, even worse, deny it in others, that is the point when we have committed the almost unforgivable sin, the point when we demean and demonize others so that we can abuse them and treat them badly.

Slavery was only possible in this country when white Christians denied the humanity of their slaves and suppressed their own humanity in the process, for even they knew that human beings do not treat others in that way, since there is that of God in each and all of us. That is also what happens in racism, and in anti-Semitism. How could the Germans, for example, that most civilized of people, treat the Jews as they did without demeaning or taking away that of God in themselves? How could Americans treat the Native American in the same way, if they did not take that of God which was in them away from them? If the denial of the image of God is the problem, the affirmation of the image of God in self and in others is the solution.

Perhaps the most radical thing for the modern pilgrim to say is "I am a child of God." "I am a child of God" is the mantra of the free woman and the free man of Christ. I am a child of God. In the image of goodness I am created, and so is everyone else, and when we believe that, when we image that, we can act upon that image, we can image that goodness as our mandate in life. We have the power to do this. We don't have to read books, go to college, take a correspondence course. We have the power right now to do this, with everything we have this very instant.

Jesus says in Mark 11, "What things whatsoever you desire when ye pray, believe that ye receive them and ye shall have them." Who are we, to do this? How can it be thought that we can do this? The Bible tells us who we are. I Peter says, "You are a chosen race, a royal priesthood, a dedicated nation of people claimed by God for his own," and that is who we are. We are to proclaim the glorious deeds of him who has called us out of the darkness into his marvelous light. Peter said, "Once you were nobody, not anybody at all. But now you are God's people. Once you were without mercy, but now you have mercy." To work on our image is to realize that our image is the image of God, and that we are better than we are right now. The work on our image is nothing less than the work of God in our lives. In the image of God created he them, male and female he created them. We are made with goodness, for good. Knowing that, and knowing that the Bible is about that, is a good start on the pilgrimage toward the good life. We affirm not ourselves but the God who made us, is in us, and who is with us.

How Can I Face the Future?

Over my years of dealing with students in their last year of college I have learned that what might appear to be an innocent question has hostile implications. I used to ask, "What are you going to do next year?," and as more and more students seemed to know less and less about what the future held for them, I noticed that they were less than happy with the question. They often felt guilty if they could not provide a definitive answer, as if somehow the uncertainty was a moral fault and a defect in their character. Perhaps they were anxious about the question because it was the sort of question their parents had been putting to them with increased urgency, or perhaps they were upset because they had not yet got around to making the necessary plans. Perhaps the plans had fallen through, or perhaps they were feeling more like grasshoppers than ants, and psychic winter was coming on. Whatever the reason, my innocent and in some sense profoundly ignorant question caused more anxiety than it was worth in my young friends, and so I agreed with myself not to ask it in the last term. It seemed a fair question in September, a tender one in January, and downright rude in May. I consoled myself and my young friends with a piety of reassurance: "You have a future, we all have; you just don't know what it is yet."

Anxiety about the future, I discover, is not confined to the college young. Many of my older colleagues, neighbors, and friends face their futures with a sense of apprehension, and of foreboding and dread. The prolonging of life, that miracle of modern science and technology, has turned out to be a mixed blessing for many. The long stretch of postretirement years, the "sunset" or "golden" years, as the euphemists would have them, do not hold out the promise of blessed idleness with time to do all the things that work prevented, or a contemplative and serene old age in which one lives off the well-earned bounty of a well-lived life. Will I have enough money to live on? Will I have my health, in particular my mind? Will I be stuck in a nursing home, or with dutiful but unhappy relatives? Will I have a lingering decline, watching my parts fail in succession until I hope that I lose my mind before I lose everything else? What will happen when all who knew me in my prime are gone and there is no one left to love me, and I am surrounded only by those who are paid to maintain me? Anxiety about the future is not confined to the young.

Polls tell us that most people in a land thought to be mindlessly optimistic are worried about the future. We often hear these anxieties expressed in economic and material terms, and for the first time there is the perception in America that children will not necessarily have a higher standard of living than their parents. The American Dream, upon which so many politicians trade, once thought to be the pursuit of happiness and the blessing of liberty, is seen more and more as more and more and more and more at risk. The dream of upward mobility became first an expectation and then an entitlement, and is now a disappointment, and that disappointment has fueled what can be called the politics of disappointment and bile. Taxes that mortgage the dreams of the middle class to subsidize those perceived as undeserving are more and more resented. Institutions such as colleges, industry, even the government, all once thought to be essential to the solutions of our problems, are now, in this climate of anxiety and recrimination, seen to be the problem.

Anxiety about the future, however, is not obsessed merely with the material and the economic. We know that there is a profound spiritual anxiety about the future. At the height of the Cold War, Robert Jay Lifton and other observers of our social condition thought that the anxiety had to do with the fear of nuclear annihilation and the destruction of life on this planet as we know it. For years we were dominated by doomsday scenarios and the climate of moral angst that they created. I well remember the national frenzy created by the made-for-television movie *The Day After*, a bit of docu-fiction of the early 1980s about the day after a nuclear attack, which was meant to be a nuclear-age version of Orson Welles's famous radio program, *The War of the Worlds*. It was nowhere near as good a piece of writing, but it brought to the national hearth of television the fears and forebodings that attended a culture of soulless science, rampant militarism, and arrogant technologies.

When the Cold War came to an end the anxiety about the future did not vanish and we could see that the Cold War and the nuclear age were not the causes of our fears but merely present-day expressions of them. In some sense these clear and outward manifestations of terror

served us well by focusing our e
deflecting our consciousness from
within. This could lead to despai
existentialist nihilism, a mechani
of the hedonistic, the absurd, and u.
and for many these were the facts of lic
1980s. That period could be captured in c
classic exchange between the optimist who
argued that this was the best of all possible
worlds, and the pessimist who agreed.

Hope is a slippery word and particularly so
when it is used in connection with the future
and as an antidote to anxiety and fear, but it
is just hope that people require in facing their
futures; and hope's greatest power is that it
enables the present by embracing the future.
The essence of the good life for which this age
seeks is that hope is worthwhile, worth living
for, worth waiting and working for. Hope does
not deny the circumstances of the present, and
hope doesn't help us get out of our difficulties.
Hope doesn't get us out, but it does get us
through. Contrary to the street smarts of the
age, hope is not the enterprise of last resort, it
is the quality that transcends both failure and
success, for it substitutes the ultimate for the
temporary. Hope is not stoical endurance,
although it does help us to endure, but whereas
endurance has a certain almost fatalistic quality
to it, hope itself goes beyond that which must
be endured. Hope allows us to transcend
definition by mere circumstances and
appearances.

Job is often cited as an example of unconble hope, and if we remember his story will recall that he did not use his hope to ny the reality of his present pains and circumstances. The hope that was his was of the same essence as confidence, and that confidence was not in himself or in anything that he did, or could do, or was. Hope thus always points away from the one who claims it to the one who is its source. Thus hope is not solipsistic and self-centered, but directed invariably to that which is worthy of confidence. This is what Job 11:18–19 makes clear, thus enabling Job to look beyond himself and his circumstances:

> *And you will have confidence because there is hope; you will be protected and take your rest in safety. You will lie down and none will make you afraid.*

This is also the direction of hope in Psalm 27:13–14:

> *I believe that I shall see the goodness of the Lord in the land of the living! Wait for the Lord; be strong, and let your heart take courage; yea, wait for the Lord.*

And again in Psalm 43:5, we read:

> *Why are you cast down, O my soul, and why are you disquieted within me? Hope in God; for I shall again praise him, my help and my God.*

Hope therefore is what connects the present to the future; it is the mother of courage, confidence, and endurance. The good life is not that for which one hopes; hope is that which makes the good life possible, and thus the good life is not an objective but a consequence. When we are able to see that, and to adopt that reality as our own, we are free from the tyranny of an unredeemed past, a remorseless present, and an unknown future. We are free to become, in the glorious phrase of Zechariah 9:12, "prisoners of hope."

The Bible is the record of God's action of creation, redemption, and sustenance. The hope of those who trust in God is the result, the consequence of these divine demonstrations. Biblical hope is thus not wishful thinking, an extrapolation into the future based upon little more than pious expectations. Hope is certified in the experience of people's relationship to God, to which all scripture gives testimonial: Because of what God has done, the people have hope in what God will do and is in fact doing. Hebrews 6:19 calls this "a sure and steadfast anchor of the soul," and I Peter 1:3–4 thanks God, the father of our Lord Jesus Christ, for the fact that by his mercy "we have been born anew to a living hope through the resurrection of Jesus Christ from the dead, and to an inheritance which is imperishable, undefiled, and unfading."

Such a discussion of hope as this may seem too abstract or even pious to the battered and defeated in a world dedicated to the fast track of success. Such hope is little more than an opiate, a Band-Aid, a palliative that makes inevitable suffering bearable and encourages a form of spineless quietism. Critics of the therapeutic uses of hope allege that the act of hope has been substituted for the content of hope, and that because of that, hope has lost its edge and become dubious, illusory, and little more than a diversion. The act of hoping becomes little more than that which is expressed by the impious and frequently ill-used phrase of modernism, "hopefully." The grammarians have nearly given up reminding Americans of our regular misuse of this word *hopefully* as a synonym for "it is to be hoped," as in "Hopefully, it won't rain on our parade." We know what is meant by this now nearly universal idiom: "It is to be hoped that it won't rain on our parade." The act of hoping in this sense has neither content nor object, and is thus merely wishful. Interestingly enough, *hopefully* in this sense is the secular version of the far more ancient expression of hope, once universal, which had both content and direction, the Latin phrase *Deo volente*, reduced among our literate ancestors to *D.V.*, which of course meant "If God wills, it will not rain on our parade." The age that is hopeless is reduced to the mere act of hoping, which is little more than wishing.

The content of hope consists of the promises of God, promises that give those who hope in those promises the right to expect peace, justice, mercy, equity, joy, and equanimity. God has hallowed or made holy the future just as the past, and indeed, even the present, are hallowed by the presence of God, and thus hope becomes the operative opposite not of experience but of fear. It is customary to speak of the "triumph of hope over experience" as if hope were opposed to experience, but for the believer, hope is based on experience, the experience of what God has done. Hope then is the opposite of both fear and anxiety. It does not operate out of ignorance as is so commonly believed, but out of knowledge: "I know that my Redeemer lives," says Job, and thus he cannot be seduced or overwhelmed even by his dire circumstances or miserable comforters, because he has the knowledge upon which the content of his hope is based.

It was the content of hope and not the mere act of hoping that gave Dietrich Bonhoeffer a confidence in facing death by the Nazis that was more than bravado or romantic courage. Those who take the content of hope seriously see the future not simply as an escape from the difficulties of the present, but as the place in which that for which they are willing to live and to die is to be found. When Martin Luther King, Jr., was in the midst of his campaign to redeem the soul of America, he was sustained over and over again by a clear vision of the content of a future hope in which the promises of God were to be fulfilled. That is what his "dream" speech is about, and in that almost mystical final sermon on the night before he was to be killed, in alluding to Moses, King said, "I have been to the mountaintop." What could he have possibly meant, other than that, like the earlier prophet, he too had "seen" the promises of God fulfilled? The more rational among us will assume that this was just one more preacherly hyperbole, an example of colorful black church-speak. If we understand, however, that King meant what he said, and that what enabled what he did was the content of his hope in a God of justice who provides for the future, we will have got the message. Thus, when in that same sermon he said, "Children, don't be afraid," he was not simply offering a pastoral word of encouragement; he was saying that the God who is and who sustains the future will bring us through this present time, that time that Saint Paul, in Romans, calls "this brief momentary affliction."

I consider that the sufferings of this present time are not worth comparing with the glory that is to be revealed to us. For the creation waits with eager longing for the revealing of the sons of God; for the creation was subjected to futility, not of its own will but by the will of him who subjected it in hope; because the creation itself will be set free from its bondage to decay and obtain the glorious liberty of the children of God.

(Romans 8:18–21)

Despair is the absence of hope. The content of hope banishes despair and empowers in the present, and for the future as well, those who hope.

This conviction is at the heart of one of the best-selling books of these last days of the present millennium. Its very title tells us what we need to hear: *Crossing the Threshold of Hope*, by Pope John Paul II. Speaking of his high regard for the young, and of his hope in them and for them, the pope says in response to his interlocutor's question, "Is there really hope in the young?"

The very day of the inauguration of my papal ministry, on October 22, 1978, at the conclusion of the liturgy I said to the young people gathered in St. Peter's Square, "You are the hope of the Church and of the world. You are my hope." I have often repeated those words.

The pope is convinced that young people are searching for God, for something worthy of placing their hopes in. They want to know what the rich young ruler wanted to know when he asked Jesus, in Luke 10:25, "What must I do to inherit eternal life?" The content of that hope for the pope, and for the rest of us as well, is Christ.

...Christ who walks through the centuries alongside each generation, alongside every generation, alongside every person. He walks alongside each person as a friend. An important day in a young person's life is the day on which he becomes convinced that this is the only Friend who will not disappoint him, on whom he can always count.

As theologian Jürgen Moltmann has reminded us, the Middle Ages developed a theology of love, and the Reformation developed a theology of faith. Now, in these days as modernity's confidence in itself becomes unglued, perhaps the time has come to cultivate a theology of hope and to prepare the people of this age to encounter the content of that "inheritance which is imperishable, undefiled, and unfading." The consequence of such a hope is indeed the good life, and the only life worth living. The question then is not simply what is the good life, but where does the search for it begin, and where does it end? These are the questions with which the Bible is concerned.

CHAPTER 10

THE BIBLE AND SUFFERING

THE church was crowded with the young and the good, those filled with promise and the first flush of achievement. Many of them were in the "industry," the almost oxymoronic euphemism that describes what people in Hollywood do to entertain and divert us, and to make enormous sums of money while doing so. Some observers of Harvard graduates have noted that the three cities to which our brightest and best gravitate are New York, Washington, D.C., and Hollywood. In New York they make money, in Washington they make policy, and in Hollywood they make not only films but fantasy for the whole world. Those who go there in some sense never grow up. They are Peter Pans, and they are in the business of catering to the Peter Pan and Wendy in all of us.

This was such a crowd. I had last seen many of them on Commencement morning fewer than five years before when they were also in church, and among a large crowd; and on that morning the world was bright with promise and waiting for them, the sober black of academic dress neither concealing nor checking their exuberance and expectations. Few if any of them on that glad day had expected to return to Harvard or to The Memorial Church quite so soon, or for the sad and solemn purpose of burying one of their own who had been killed in a senseless, irrational car accident in the prime of life. Here they were, however, black-suited, still fair of face, and looking younger and indeed more vulnerable than when last we had all been together. Death had intruded, and with it a monstrous assault on the human claim to immortality. They wept, and they raged at the loss of their friend. Death was an abstraction about which movies were made, and death happened to grandparents, to the occasional victim of terrible crime, or to participants in war. Death in theory would come to them eventually, but so far down the road of reality that it was hardly real at all. How does one deal with unscripted death? How do the worldly-wise, the hip, the interpreters of life in the fast, or at least in the interesting, lane deal with it?

How do they deal with the irrational and immutable judgments of death unprepared, unexpected, unwelcome?

The Victorians, we are told, loved death and feared sex, and hence their culture embraced a culture of death and mourning, and constructed strong taboos against sex. We, on the other hand, love sex and fear death, and our taboos are of a different sort. We delight in sexuality, we pander to the sensual, and we have made Calvin Klein a very wealthy man. Death is not something we want to understand or to know; death is somehow unfair, and in this country it is culturally unconstitutional, violating our right to life, liberty, and the pursuit of happiness. Thus, when death intrudes, particularly among the young, we respond in terror, anger, and fear.

As I listened to the heartrending eulogies of the young for their young, I heard anger and fear. I heard their love as well, and their pained, pathetic desire to make sense of it all. "What does it mean?" asked one tearful young woman. "We must make it mean something," said another. "It doesn't make sense," said a third. "Will it get easier to understand this as we get older?" a bright young man asked me as the white wine flowed at the reception. "Will I wake up some day and understand why Willie had to die in this way, at this time?" It was not a question that required an answer, at least not then, for he was baying at the moon, not making a theological inquiry.

I think I said most of the right things. One

hopes, in my calling, that one does on occasions like this. Clichés become truths when they are applied to one's own situation, I have discovered, and I reminded these young people that while funeral-going was perhaps a new experience for most of them, it was an all too familiar habit for the rest of us. I reminded them that the context of life is not living, but death, and that it is out of death that life comes. Death is the rule to which life is the exception. It is not how long you live, but how well you live with what you have, and I quoted that lovely and relatively unfamiliar passage from the Apocrypha, which says of early death: "He, being made perfect in a short time, fulfilled a long time; for his soul pleased the Lord: therefore hasted he to take him away from among the wicked." (Wisdom 4:8–14)

I always end memorial services and funerals with the prayer long associated with Cardinal Newman, and I did so on this day. Many were familiar with it, and many more were not, but were interested in it:

> O Lord, support us all the day long of this troublous life, until the shadows lengthen and the evening comes, and the fever of life is over, and our work is done. Then, in thy great mercy, grant us a safe lodging, a holy rest, and peace at the last.

We scattered again, as we always do, back to the demands and diversions of this troublous life, pondering the meaning of suffering, the purpose of life, and trying to make sense of it all as in the making of a living we try to make a life as well. It is for moments such as these that religion was made, and when we confront the unconfrontable, or more to the point, when it confronts us, we are at a religious moment, and for a moment at least we are religious. Contrary to the popular misconception, religion is not an escape from reality but rather a genuine effort to make sense of what passes for reality and all that surrounds it. Religious people are not escape artists; they are not practitioners of evasion or of self-deception. Religion is not the answer to the unknowable or the unfaceable or the unendurable; religion is what we do and what we are in the face of the unknowable, the unfaceable, and the unendurable. It is a constant exercise in the making of sense first, and then of meaning.

"I'm not very religious, but I had to come to this service," said one of my secular young mourners. He was more religious than he thought, not because he professed certain doctrines or behaved in a particular way or performed certain rites and rituals and believed in what they said and did. He was religious because he wanted to make sense of what he was experiencing, pain and all, and on his own and by himself he could not. Legal, medical, physiological, even psychological answers, themselves definitive and helpful, were not sufficient of themselves; somehow something else was wanted and needed.

That something else wanted and needed is what religion is about. "Religion in its simplest terms," says John Habgood, the recently retired Archbishop of York, "is about making sense of life, of this life first of all, and particularly of those aspects of it which challenge and disturb us. This is why suffering and ways of responding to it have always been such central religion." Not only do we have a need to try to make sense of suffering, Dr. Habgood tells us, but we also want to make sense where we can of joy—"undeserved happiness," he calls it—or "blessings," as the devout and pious call it; and of mystery, those close encounters of the transcendent kind that suggest relationships beyond the power of our experience to reckon, but which we know in some fundamental way to be true. Suffering, joy, and mystery are those points where the human and the divine come into the most intimate and profound of proximities. They unite all human experience in all ages and beyond all particulars of place and of circumstance. All religions of the world are and always have been concerned with their substance. It is the common ambition of our common humanity to make sense and meaning of these encounters wherever we can. Religion is the attempt to give some formal record of what we may learn from these experiences, and, for Christians, the Bible is the authoritative record of the human encounter with God at these points.

There is in Celtic mythology the notion of "thin places" in the universe, where the visible and the invisible world come into their closest proximity. To seek such places is the vocation of the wise and the good, and those who find them find the clearest communication between the temporal and the eternal. Monastries and holy places were meant to be founded at such spots to increase the likelihood of a transcendental communication. These thin places were threshold places, from the Latin *limen,* which can mean a border or frontier place where two worlds meet and where one has the possibility of communicating with the other. In Celtic studies the phrase can refer to places that stand at the border between the spiritual and temporal realms, and between people gifted with supernatural gifts in the mundane world and those living on the border.

Perhaps we can adapt the concept of such thin places to the experience that people are likely to have as they encounter suffering, joy, and mystery, and seek in some fashion to make sense of that encounter. If we think of these encounters as the ultimate thin places of human experience, and of religion as a way of talking and thinking about the encounters, we might do very well to think of the Bible as our guide through the thin places, and as providing us with a record of how our ancestors coped with their encounters, and guidance beyond their particular situation which may be useful in ours. Contrary to the efforts and assumptions of many, the Bible is not a systematic book. It is not a doctrinal handbook or a systematic theology, nor is it a comprehensive history or a compendium of morals and ethics. To argue that it is any of these is to make the Bible conform to an extra-biblical set of convictions and assumptions, and to make it pass a test of theological orthodoxy of which it is not capable. Doctrines of inerrancy and infallibility are merely modern human efforts to impose order both on scripture and on those who read it. These are what John Huxtable once called "dogmatic vested interests," designed to preserve as the word of God a particularly partisan way of looking at scripture. Such a way of reading the Bible is designed to support those interests, and they are "found" in the Bible because they are brought to the Bible.

There are principles and ideas that develop over time through the pages of scripture that make it possible for us to detect truths that transcend the contexts in which they are found, principles that go beyond captivity to a given situation, and which stand out like the mountains on the moon. Indeed, it is such normative teaching and such developing ideas and ideals that enable us to judge scriptural situation by scriptural principle, and thus, in order to be biblical, we are able to read scripture freed of the expectation that we must reproduce its every detail and circumstance. If we have learned anything in the last section, I hope it is that this is what being biblical means—not playing "Bibleland," as my old colleague Krister Stendahl used to like to say, but determining what in the Bible transcends the limits of the world in which the Bible was developed. This was the question upon which rested all the debates concerning our so-called hard passages, and, as Roland Bainton argued in his case for total abstinence from alcohol, biblical principle takes precedence over biblical practice.

If we are to think of scripture not so much as we would a book of history, theology, or philosophy, but as the human experience of the divine at the thin places of encounter, then perhaps we may enter into a book that is perhaps less elusive and more accessible than we might have at first been led to believe. If the Bible is understood to be the place where not only others long dead but we ourselves encounter those thin places of suffering, joy, and mystery, and the efforts to make sense and meaning of those encounters, then perhaps we have rescued it from the clutches of the experts and the specialists and placed it where it rightly belongs, namely in the hands of those who find themselves more religious than they thought.

What Dare We Make of Suffering?

I recall reading some years ago of the death of the young son of William Sloan Coffin, in a horrible automobile accident in Boston. At some point, perhaps at the funeral, perhaps later in a sermon, the anguished father discussed his reaction to this terrible experience, saying that frequently people would attempt to comfort him with the Christian cliché, "It is God's will." Coffin thundered, "The hell it is. When my boy was killed, God was the first who cried." If God can be sympathetic and empathetic, why can't God prevent the source of those troubles that require human and divine sympathy? Suffering makes us ask hard questions of God, i.e., where were you when I needed you? Suffering also makes us ask hard questions of ourselves: What have I done to deserve this?

If suffering is, as I suggest that it is, a thin place, indeed a place of proximity to the divine, such proximity has served to alienate many from God rather than draw them nearer. If God is indifferent to suffering—for example, if God really does not care about the manifest human sufferings in Bosnia, or in Rwanda, or in the AIDS wards of the local hospitals, or in the galloping Alzheimer's disease of an old and once-bright friend or spouse—who cares for that kind of God?

If God is merely sympathetic but impotent in the face of such difficulties, then again, of what value is the idea? Sympathy is cheap, and hence abundant. Divine sympathy is no more or less helpful than any other kind.

If God is the source or cause of the suffering, and the suffering is an expression of God's will, then is this not a malevolent, vengeful, even perverse God, who exercises ultimate power in a capricious, or even immoral, way?

Indifferent, sympathetic, arbitrary—somehow God is usually called into our conversations about suffering, for the ultimate suffering is that suffering itself is meaningless and must be endured alone. Misery loves company, we are told.

Well, there is more to it than that, for misery actually requires company. Just as it is really not possible to be happy alone, "the sound of one hand clapping" and all of that, so too it is not really possible to suffer alone. That is why we invoke God, even the godless among us, and that is why we are constantly looking for companionship in suffering, either to share or to blame or at times to do both.

Suffering, we are taught very early on, is a part of life. As the Yankee adage has it, "What can't be cured must be endured," and most of us were brought up with an understanding of that concept. We were taught as well that suffering was redemptive or, at the very least, instructive. When we suffer, we are more apt to learn. Our mothers used to say that suffering was God's way of getting our attention, and that there were lessons to be learned from suffering. We would be the better for it.

Redemptive—dare we even say therapeutic?—suffering is that of which Paul speaks with a beguiling candor when, in writing his second letter to the Corinthians, he speaks of his "thorn in the flesh": "And to keep me from being too elated by the abundance of revelations, a thorn was given me in the flesh, a messenger of Satan, to harass me, to keep me from being too elated."

Paul was not a masochist delighting in this object lesson in humility and suffering, for he asked not once but three times to be rid of this trouble: "Three times I besought the Lord about this, that it should leave me; but he said to me,

'My grace is sufficient for you, for my power is made perfect in weakness.'"

Paul's sufferings were not relieved, and he understood his weakness to be an opportunity to manifest the power of God: "I will all the more gladly boast of my weaknesses, that the power of Christ may rest upon me. For the sake of Christ, then, I am content with weaknesses, insults, hardships, persecutions, and calamities; for when I am weak, then I am strong." (II Corinthians 12:7–10)

Many have speculated upon the nature of Paul's affliction, his "thorn in the flesh," and the speculations range everywhere from physical distemper and psychological disarray to homosexuality. Our purpose here is not to discuss the affliction but rather the response to it, and what it tells us about God and about Paul.

We learn first that the thorn is sent to Paul in the form of a messenger from Satan. The source of his trouble, whatever it is, is not God. The moral of the affliction, however, is that he should not boast or brag—the affliction is an exercise in humility, the purpose of which is to give glory not to Paul but to Christ. This is not suffering for suffering's sake; it is suffering for Christ's sake so that Paul and all who see and learn from him might learn of the strength that Christ supplies. We learn as well that God's role is not to relieve suffering or to spare us from it, but to enable us to bear and endure it so that even our suffering is redemptive for ourselves and others. Thus, God will not interfere despite the three appeals of the apostle. Why not? So that Paul will learn that he can rely upon Christ when he needs him, that is, in his weakness. The sufferings, the persecutions, the calamities, the insults and hardships, all of these are not ends in themselves but means to a greater end, the demonstration that Christ gets us through such things. The only way "out" of suffering is "through" it, and only Christ can get us through. Knowing this, Paul is now able to demonstrate this as an act of faith, not in the redemptive powers of suffering but in the redemptive powers of the redeemer to help him through his weaknesses. "For when I am weak, then I am strong." In other words, when I can no longer rely upon myself to solve the problem or to overcome the weakness, when I acknowledge that in my weakness I cannot "go it alone," then I am strengthened, empowered by the one who gives me strength. To be strong in this sense is to acknowledge the fact of my weakness and the source of my strength.

Writing to the Romans, Paul applies the theme of suffering as a communal and not just a personal virtue. The Christians are to rejoice in their hope of sharing the glory of God, of testifying of their peace with God through Christ, and of the grace in which they stand. As a result of this the Christians are also able to rejoice even in their sufferings, "knowing that suffering produces endurance, and endurance produces character, and character produces hope, and hope does not disappoint us, because God's love has been poured into our hearts through the Holy Spirit which has been given to us." (Romans 5:3–5)

When Paul, therefore, writes of suffering, he is not speaking abstractly either about himself or about the Christian community. His personal sufferings are real and painful, and although we do not know their precise nature, we know enough about Paul to know that these sufferings of mind and spirit were sufficient to cause him stress and trouble. He was not pretending to be afflicted as a kind of moral object lesson. We can identify with his anxiety, and indeed with his frustrations. We can "feel his pain," as they say in today's vernacular, and we know the very real sufferings of the people with whom he worked in the gospel. These too were not abstractions. We get an idea when the persecutions of the Christians are described in the book of Hebrews:

> Some were tortured, refusing to accept release, that they might rise again to a better life. Others suffered mocking and scourging, and even chains and imprisonment. They were stoned, they were sawn in two, they were killed with the sword; they went about in skins of sheep and goats, destitute, afflicted, ill-treated—of whom the world was not worthy— wandering over deserts and mountains, and in dens and caves of the earth.
> (Hebrews 11:35–38)

Suffering, in the New Testament, is real. Paul, and everybody else writing there, wants us to understand this. There is no sympathy with the notion that pain is illusion, that suffering is merely an appearance, or even a deception. There is little room for optimism in the real-world circumstances of the New Testament, and optimism implies either that suffering is unreal or that we can get over it fairly quickly or that if we are very, very good we can avoid it altogether. How anyone can read the New Testament and remain an optimist in this world amazes me. The early Christians seemed to understand that suffering does not come despite one's faith, but rather because of it. In this world virtue and suffering are not opposites, as we would find it so convenient to believe; suffering is the consequence of, not the opposite of, virtue. This is the burden of that difficult verse in I Peter 3:17, which says, "For it is better to suffer for doing right, if that should be God's will, than for doing wrong."

Suffering, therefore, is not an exception to the human condition, it *is* the human condition, and as such it is almost impossible to avoid; and since religion, as we have said, has to do with the human condition, and indeed with the enormous task of trying to make sense and meaning of it, religion by its very nature has an intimacy with suffering. That intimacy is the stuff of which our lives are composed.

Sigmund Freud, no friend of religion, nevertheless gives us a comprehensive sense of suffering, and thus we are enabled to see the scope of religion's intimate relations with it. Says Freud:

We are threatened with suffering from three directions: from our own body, which is doomed to decay and dissolution and which cannot even do that without pain and anxiety as warning signals; from the external world, which may rage against us with overwhelming and merciless forces of destruction; and finally, from our relations to other men. The suffering which comes from this last source is perhaps more painful than any other.

Morality, conflict, and ethics: These sources of our sufferings have always been the business of religion and of the Bible. How do we deal with the fact that inevitably we die, that our life before we die is conflicted and besieged, and that we find it difficult to get along with our fellow creatures? These are not Freudian categories; this is life itself.

The Trouble with Paul

Few women, blacks, homosexuals, or Jews are very fond of Paul, and it is easy to see why on the basis of the reading of the Pauline letters we have discussed in Part Two of this book. Each has a text or two to hold against him, for of all the figures of the New Testament, he is at once the most difficult to evade and the most difficult to embrace. For many he is an example of spiritual arrogance, who, even when he writes about not boasting, boasts that he is not boasting. He is mistrusted, and the basis of that mistrust goes back to scripture itself. In Acts

8, the chapter opens with Saul—the preconversion name of Paul—consenting to the death
of the first Christian martyr, Stephen. After
Stephen's burial, the text says, "But Saul was
ravaging the church, and entering house after
house, he dragged off men and women and
committed them to prison." (Acts 8:3) We know
that Paul was on his way to Damascus, "still
breathing threats and murder against the
disciples of the Lord," having asked for letters
to the synagogues in Damascus that would
empower him to arrest any Christian men or
women and bring them bound for trial to
Jerusalem. This was an ambitious and successful
young zealot; he could have been a Hitler Youth,
an upwardly mobile officer in Oliver Cromwell's
army, a Sandinista, even a young Republican.
We know the sort, and they are not easily cured,
and we are not easily charmed by them. After
his conversion he preached of Jesus in the
synagogue in Damascus, "and all who heard
him were amazed and said, 'Is not this the man
who made havoc in Jerusalem of those who
called on this name? And he has come here for
this purpose, to bring them bound before the
chief priests.'" (Acts 9:21)

We know the hesitation of those in Damascus
who thought that they knew this Paul, and who
were not altogether enthusiastic about his
enthusiasm for them and their gospel, and yet
without Paul there would be no Christian church,
nor would there be a gospel for us. Without Paul
we have very little that is authentically Christian,
and thus the great irony, for many of us at least,

and certainly for women, blacks, homosexuals, and Jews, is that the source of our liberation from this life, and our endurance and perseverance within this life, is the very Paul who has been used in various ways and in various times to oppress us. If suffering is the fate of life in this world, and for Christians in particular, then Paul is our tutor in suffering. The model of Christians holding on and out against overwhelming forces that seek to do them in, that "external world which may rage against us with overwhelming and merciless forces of destruction," according to Freud, is Paul. He teaches us what to do with our sufferings, and what they are for.

Paul teaches us that we are not ruled by our bodies, nor are we prisoners of the flesh. We are not simply material people in a material world. "You are not of the flesh," he writes the Romans, "but of the spirit." We belong therefore to an unconquerable realm, to a place that is immune to the ultimate assaults and ravages of this life. To be liberated from the idea of bondage to the body is to be freed from the fear of death. This is why Paul can laugh at death and say, "O death, where is thy sting? O grave, where is thy victory?" Death's power is in our fear of it. Death's dominion is exercised not after the grave but before the grave. In death no one need fear death; we will know it for what it is, and for what it is not. It is before death that death reigns. Death will take our bodies, and so before we die we live in terror that our bodies will be destroyed. As we grow old and sick we realize that we are waging a losing war against death; death, we say, will win.

There is a profound paradox at work of which Paul is fully aware, however, and that is that death does its work on us before we die. Death holds us hostage to the idea of death and the loss of all that we know and value, and only in life can death rule in such a way. If in life we are attached to more than the mere form and vessel of life, the body, and if we do recognize that the body is merely the temple of the spirit, the dwelling place of that God who is in us, when we really believe that because of this, death is not to be feared and the body not to be worshiped, then we have been given life after death without having to die. Death is real. We do not dispute that. The body is real; it is no mere phantom or illusion. We do not dispute that. The spirit is also real, in fact, more real than death or the body, each of which, when it has done its work, disappears. The spirit lives on, passing through the frontier, the thin place, the border, into a realm that we can speak of only as beyond the grave. It is nothing less than this concept with which Paul arms us to overcome the very world that would in his name do us in. As the old gospel hymn goes: "Faith is the victory that overcomes the world."

There has been much to overcome in this world for those who have been driven to its margins. I am often asked why it is, considering their experiences, that woman, blacks, and homosexuals still cleave to the church and still fight for the Bible and the right to see themselves in it. The evangelists of the Nation of Islam say this to black people all the time, asking if we realize that the Bible is a white man's book, that it was given to our ancestors to oppress them and make them docile, and that even today it requires that we perform mental gymnastics in order not to see ourselves as the inferior slave children of the banished son of Noah. What black man, woman, or child with any integrity, any sense of self-worth and a lick of intelligence, would read a book and stay in a church whose fundamental assumptions were racist and imperialist? The evidence, they argue, is not ancient; it is as contemporary as the nearest white church; and, they argue, "Who needs all that?"

Secular women make much the same case for women, and wonder why women even care to be included in the patriarchal churches of Christendom, whose gospel not only excludes them but defines them as God's afterthought and of no intrinsic worth. How well I remember that before she left, on the Sunday of her exodus from The Memorial Church, Mary Daly had invited women from the Divinity School to read as the scripture lessons for that morning all of the Pauline anti-woman passages they could find in the New Testament. Needless to say, they did not have to look very hard, and as the passages were read many laughed, others hissed, and as one conservative woman said to me years later, in retrospect of that occasion, "We were condemned out of our own book." Many women did take the message and left the church, never to return. I think, however, that more remained than left, and if any group can be said to have fought for the Bible, it is those women who remained and were determined to be included in that from which they had been excluded.

The so-called inclusive language debate, which has exercised so many for so long, is, in my view, but a tiny sign of a much larger, more interesting, and more significant issue of discovering what is, and has always been, in the tradition that liberates principle in such a way that we are not tied to practice and precedent. Woman have had to read Paul and to take Paul very seriously, and to distinguish between the situational and the normative in Paul, and to use the one to combat the other as they lay claim to the gospel that Paul yet proclaims to them. Rewriting hymn texts is not the issue; rereading and rediscovering the gospel in the Bible is. Language, contrary to certain theories of literary criticism, does not define reality, and to be bound to language is in some sense much like being bound to the body and realm of the material. Reality for the Christian is the realm of the spirit, and only there is there sufficient freedom to cope with the lack of freedom in the realm which the world calls reality. That confidence, that strength, is very much of the same substance as that which allows us to live life before death without the fear of death.

Perhaps the hardest group to which to sell Paul and his liberating doctrines is to the gay community. This is understandable, for no group today suffers more from the stigmas made legitimate by centuries of Christian interpretation of scripture. Blacks were always within the church although in separate institutions, and women were always in the church although diminished in expectations and responsibilities, but homosexuals, as such, have not been seen to be either a part of the church or an object of its ministry.

Yet there are millions of homosexuals who have found their sufferings, often at the hands of the church, to be an instrument of freedom and not of bondage. They have seen in Paul's towering images of reconciliation in II Corinthians 5, and of transformation and renewal in Romans 12, a new identity that is based not on their sexuality but on their redeemed nature in Christ. Having been formed once in the image of God, which we read in Genesis, they are now formed again after the likeness of Christ, who, in the words of the ancient church fathers, "elevates their humanity that they might participate in his divinity." Knowing this, and the actions of Christians notwithstanding, the homosexual hears Paul's words in Galatians 5:1, "Stand fast, therefore, in the liberty wherewith Christ hath made us free," as an invitation to liberation and participation in the community of the faithful. The Christian homosexual knows that his sufferings at the hands of Christians have in fact brought him nearer to God, for God is always where suffering is to be found. Who better than the Christian homosexual today can read Romans 5:1–5, and know from personal experience not only what it means, but that it is true?

Therefore, since we are justified by faith, we have peace with God through our Lord Jesus Christ. Through him we have obtained access to this grace in which we stand, and we rejoice in our hope of sharing the glory of God. More than that, we rejoice in our sufferings, knowing that suffering produces endurance, and endurance produces character, and character produces hope, and hope does not disappoint us, because God's love has been poured into our hearts through the Holy Spirit which has been given to us.

There Must Be More to This Than That

Writing in 1919, in the bleak shadow of the "war to end all wars," W. Somerset Maugham said, "It is not true that suffering ennobles the character; happiness does that sometimes, but suffering, for the most part, makes men petty and vindictive." As with most literary pronouncements, there is some truth in this one. We have all read, even the least literate of us, of characters poisoned by suffering, made old and mean-spirited before their time. The petty little scorekeepers who dignify their daily dose of deprivation as "sufferings" are with us on every hand, "whinging away," as the English say, embezzling sympathy, and suffocating all and sundry with their sense of how well they are bearing up under unbearable burdens. The clergy run into this sort of person all the time;

it is, alas, a characteristic of garden-variety Christians, many of whom fill the churches.

Whether suffering ennobles or embitters, most Christians have no idea of what real suffering is. This does not mean that there is not enough tragedy and calamity to go around. We know that there is. It does mean that as a rule most modern Christians in the industrialized West, if they think of suffering at all, think that it happens to other people or, if it happens to them, that it is the exception rather than the rule of their faith, and that it must be a stroke of bad luck which God or the minister needs to explain away in a hurry. In churches whose gospel is success, prosperity, glory here and rapture now, suffering is clearly not in God's game plan for them; it is an aberration.

This is what makes Mother Teresa so disturbing to the modern sensibility. She is so disturbing to the world as we know it, and to the church as we believe in it, that we must get her out of the way as quickly and as thoroughly as possible by making of her a saint, for saints, whether living or dead, as we all know, are virtually harmless.

I met Mother Teresa some years ago when she came to Harvard to speak at Class Day, that great gathering of seniors on the day before Commencement, and then on the next day to receive an honorary degree. I was asked if Mother Teresa and her entourage, which consisted of one nun, could use my office as a place to rest for a few minutes before her speech. I was delighted to offer her my room, and she was duly brought in and I was presented to her. I tried to make small talk, but saints, I discovered, are not very good at small talk. I told her that I and millions of others thought that she was doing a great work in Calcutta. She fiddled with her beads and said, "It is Jesus." I made several other feints at chatter but she was obviously on a different plane, and so I chose the wisest course of all, that of silence. When the university marshal came to collect her and to take her out to be presented to her audience of more than twenty thousand expectant listeners, he turned back to me and said, "I bet that was a deeply moving experience."

In retrospect, I suppose it was. Here was a woman who makes no apologies for the suffering in the world. She doesn't pretend that she is "solving" the matter, nor does she pretend that the suffering she sees does not exist. In fact, if one dared to criticize a living saint, one might say that her quietism simply compounds the problem of the poor by doing nothing to address the social and moral root of the problem. She would not make a very good Gingrich Republican.

My impression of her was that she was tough and crusty, not frail and gentle as she appears. She is, after all, a nun, one of God's infantry, and she has spent her life on the front lines. It was no less a converted cynic than Malcolm Muggeridge, the British journalist and author, who brought Mother Teresa to the attention of a wider public through his book about her of some years ago, *Something Beautiful for God.* When asked what "good" her work of caring for the dying in the streets of Calcutta did, what its lasting social value was, and how she could go on in the face of remorseless suffering, she replied,

> Without our suffering our work would be just social work, very good and helpful, but it would not be the work of Jesus Christ, not part of the Redemption. All the desolation of the poor people, not only their material poverty but their spiritual destitution, must be redeemed. And we must share it, for only by being one with them can we redeem them by bringing God into their lives and bringing them to God.

Unlike Somerset Maugham, Mother Teresa seems to remember that both suffering and redemption have something to do with Jesus Christ, the one in whom, for the Christian, suffering is manifested, redeemed, and transcended. That fact, central to the Christian enterprise and symbolized in the cross upon which Jesus was executed, has been so long undermined by a false gospel of Christian triumph and success that it is almost impossible to recover for the edification of the church. Protestants have long beguiled themselves with the notions that they worship a victorious and risen Christ, and thus an empty cross. Unlike their Catholic and Orthodox brethren, they will not make their devotions to the broken and bruised Jesus hanging down in garish Roman detail from his crucifix, and so the Protestant churches are filled on Easter but empty on Good Friday. The faith that is formed out of such a travesty of the gospel is one that is unfamiliar with suffering, incapable of enduring it, and unable to recognize the work of God in it. Those who worship at the church of the costless cross literally "have their reward," as Jesus says. Literally, what they see is what they get, a convenience-store religion which may provide what one needs in the short run at great price, but which is incapable of sustaining one over the long run at any price.

The reason that the dying ask to see the cross before they die is to be reminded that Jesus has been where they now are, and that by his grace they are now to go where he is. Suffering, of which death is the ultimate expression, they know by the cross is a means, and not an end. They know that death was as real to Jesus as it is now to them. They know that he was not rescued in the nick of time. They know that when his hour was come he had to meet it, and that there was no way out; and they know also that that is true for them.

Knowing this, they also know that in the cross Jesus made it through and that he came out on the other side; their prayer is that what was promised and achieved in Jesus may be achieved for them as well. It is not for nothing that we sing, in the memorable verse from "Abide with Me"...

*Heaven's morning breaks, and earth's
vain shadows flee:
Hold thou thy Cross before my closing
eyes;
Shine through the gloom, and point me to
the skies;
Heaven's morning breaks, and earth's
vain shadows flee:
In life, in death, O Lord, abide with me.*

That cross represents suffering not set aside from life but suffering that springs from life, and is found within life itself. It is the most orthodox of Christian doctrine that the Savior does not save us *from* suffering, but is with us *in* and *through* suffering. It is hard to remember that truth when the cross becomes an empty object of bronze situated between two candlesticks and often obscured by flowers, but we forget it at our peril.

Where in the world, then, does one look for hope? Not for optimism, mind you, but for hope? On the basis of the biblical witness one looks first to the places of suffering and of stress. That means that if we want to see where God is more likely to be found in this world, in these last days of the twentieth century, we look, for example, at South Africa, where for so long suffering was the context of life for both the oppressed and the oppressor. Yet who cannot fail to see in that "beloved country" of Alan Paton's old novel a place alight with the stirrings of hope? Where else might we look? To Northern Ireland, of all places, that place of which the airline pilots used to say, "We are now approaching Belfast; please set your watches back three hundred years." Here, in the place where the Troubles define normality, peace seems to be holding. It is unsteady, to be sure, and a bomb could go off tomorrow and back we would be, but it nevertheless represents the biblical principle that hope is spawned and is only hope in the place that appears to be hopeless. Even in the Middle East, where the peace process was so brutally endangered by the assassination of Yitzhak Rabin, we may look to hope as emerging out of suffering, for I am convinced that it was the fear of peace and the fear of the triumph of hope over bitter experience that caused the assassin to kill both the dreamer and the dream. It didn't work with Joseph. It didn't work with Jesus. It will not, I believe, work with Rabin.

If global politics is not the model in which to try out this principle, where then is hope to be found among the people? Where the sufferings have been the greatest. That means that we look to those who have been excluded and placed on the margins, to those who by the terms of the world are not successful, to those who, in Jesus' words, "suffer and are persecuted." It is not simply that we expect now, as the result of our raised consciousness and improved scholarship, to find a place for blacks, women, and homosexuals within the household of faith, and perhaps even in the Bible. It is that the place for creative hope that arises out of suffering is most likely now to be found among blacks, women, and homosexuals. These outcasts may well be the custodians of those thin places; they may in fact be the watchers at the frontier between what is and what is to be. If, as Martin Luther King, Jr., said, "Unearned suffering is redemptive," then those who have suffered most, particularly at the hands of other Christians, have the most to give to a world of tribulation.

All who know suffering may well stand in their debt, and all who suffer may well have something to give.

CHAPTER 11

THE BIBLE AND JOY

I have never met anyone who has won a big-time lottery, but I have always been fascinated by the television accounts of those who have won millions from such places as the Publishers Clearing House. All I have ever got from the Publishers Clearing House is a lot of magazines, and so I am impressed with those who get that splendid check from Ed McMahon. Invariably the winners are surprised, and who wouldn't be? They usually say something like "I've never won anything in my life!" "It can't be true!" "This can't be happening to me!" "How did this happen to me?" "At first I thought they had made a mistake!" We know the truth of their reactions, even if at times that truth seems to be a little rehearsed or premeditated. One of the great contradictions of our culture is that while on the one hand we can be described as optimistic, on the other most of us do not expect good news, and we almost always assume that real news is bad news. In the days of telegrams few people ever sent good news by wire; that could wait for a letter or even for a visit. When the Western Union boy appeared on his bicycle at your door, you knew that he carried bad news. When today you say to your companions at work that you have just won a million dollars, they laugh uproariously, and then, calming down, they say, "Come on now, get serious!" Serious news could not be as good as that.

Yet the essence of that which Christians both receive and preach, the gospel, is called the "good news." Good news in the Bible nearly always comes up unexpectedly, catching by surprise the individual who is its beneficiary. When Moses encounters the burning bush and the call of God within it to lead his kinsmen out of slavery in Egypt, Moses does not rejoice. He asks how this can be, and he doubts the wisdom of God's choice of him; he further doubts that the people will accept his leadership, and pleads ineloquence as a reason not to accept this commission. Jews look upon the work of Moses as their ultimate act of deliverance, the sign that God was particularly with them, and they keep the remembrance of this deliverance as their holiest day. Christians too recognize the primary agency of God in this act and the election of Moses to perform it, and thus he becomes the first of the prophets. To Moses, however, this word from the Lord does not come to him as good news, at least initially. It is a task, a burden, a responsibility for which he may well be unfit, but God has made an offer that he cannot refuse, and in the remorseless spirit of such offers Moses accepts it, but not with joy.

Moses is in some anticipation of Mary, who also receives rather unexpected tidings—hers from the angel Gabriel. Mary has been so often depicted as weak and submissive, "the handmaiden of the Lord," or, as one angry feminist once put it, "the doormat of God," that we forget the feisty and challenging nature of her initial response. To the salutation of the angel Gabriel, she asks, "What kind of greeting can this possibly be?" To the news that she is to bear a son, Mary, no fool though she may be young, asks, "How can this be, seeing that I do not know a man?" Rather than rushing to anticipate her humility or to make an argument about the doctrine of the Virgin Birth, we might do well to pause and ponder her wariness, her caution, indeed her reluctance to being pushed into joy. We know, as do the Jews with Moses, that this is a great thing, and we imagine that something of our joy must be hers, but she is caught unaware, and when we encounter her in this conversation with Gabriel she is a long way from joy and rapture. It is only after she visits her cousin Elizabeth, as recorded in Luke 1:39, that Mary catches up with the joy that lies before her. Her song, known now as the

Magnificat, begins, "My soul magnifies the Lord, and my spirit rejoices in God my savior."

The examples of Moses and Mary and their slouching toward joy have always been a comforting set of examples for me, teaching me as they do that joy is an elusive consequence of something else, and not a first cause or primary habit of mind. This was important for me to remember, for the evangelical tradition in which I was brought up placed a high premium on joy in principle, whereas in fact the tradition was rather joyless. I can recall rather joyless people reading dutifully Psalm 100, "Make a joyful noise unto the Lord, all ye lands..." and Psalm 98, "Make a joyful noise unto the Lord, all the earth...." Our hymnbook even had a section in the topical index called Joy, but we sang those hymns only at the evening service and at the midweek meeting, never on Sunday morning. It was just as well, for I found it difficult to be joyful on command, and it was all the harder to comply when I learned that the grammatical form of the Hebrew in Psalm 100 was in fact the imperative. When I and others would be asked at evangelistic meetings if we didn't feel the joy of Christ in our hearts, I usually winced, because just then, and on cue, I usually didn't. I am grateful now for the inability to follow that command to be or to feel joyful, for from that inability to be joyful on command I learned a most important lesson: Joy is elusive; it cannot be summoned forth like an actor's tears. Joy is a response and not an initiation, and it comes at those moments of encounter with thin places, when we see more than we have reason to believe. I shall say more about this elusive quality of joy later, but now I wish simply to claim joy as one of the elements of religious experience by which people make sense and meaning out of what John Habgood calls "undeserved happiness bubbling to the surface in thanksgiving."

One does not often think of Presbyterians as a joyful people: decent and orderly, yes, but not given to spontaneous expressions of joy. It is hard to think of them knowing quite what to do with "undeserved happiness bubbling to the surface in thanksgiving," and after all, it was Charles I who said that there was nothing more dangerous in all the world than a Presbyterian fresh off his knees. Charles ought to know. Yet that most Presbyterian of all documents, the Westminster Confession and Catechism, a product of the Westminster Assembly of Calvinistic divines held in London from 1645 to 1652, and the basis for historic Presbyterianism, says that the whole duty of man is "to love God and enjoy him forever." There we have it: joy as a command, joy as a duty. No wonder joy is so elusive. Perhaps we all ought to wear sweatshirts and display bumper stickers that say take joy seriously.

The Meaning of Joy

Mr. Justice Potter Stewart once said of pornography that you may not be able to define it but you know it when you see it. Of joy we might be able to say the same thing. Most of us could not give a definition that would pass muster, but we have all had moments of joy and we know them for what they are when we have them. We remember the occasions of such feelings, not because we are such acute students of observation but because such occasions, despite the commands to be joyful, are remarkably rare. For that reason they stand out from the bulk of our experience and we cherish them, even as they nourish us. The Yankees, among whom I was brought up, used to say that firewood warms twice: first when it is chopped, and then when it is burned. So too is it with joy, in experience and in recollection.

I was a young man on my way to receiving a premature dignity, and in the company of an old man, a dear friend and a great poet. When in 1974 I was about to be appointed to the post I now hold, the Plummer Professorship of Christian Morals at Harvard, I was thirty-two years old, and it was thought by some that I needed more *gravitas*, or "bottom," as the English say, if I was convincingly to fill this venerable post and be taken seriously by both students and faculty. My old friend, the poet and consummate Harvard man, David Thompson Watson McCord, decided to take the matter in hand and to push things along. He was a member of the Class of 1921, and in 1974 was a spritely seventy-seven years old. Out of the blue, or so it seemed, I was offered an honorary degree, a doctorate in divinity, the

D.D., long known to the clergy as Donated Dignity. This generous offer came from a small college in New Hampshire, New England College, which had earlier honored McCord and with which he had had a long and helpful association. I was thrilled at the prospect, such vanities having long meant much to me, and so McCord and I undertook to drive to the college for the Commencement. It was the Memorial Day weekend, and New England was in its glory.

A ride anywhere with David McCord was always an adventure, with the conversation as stimulating as the driving was erratic. We always took the byways and back roads, avoiding going anywhere in a straight line or anywhere that could be reached by more than four paved lanes. This ride was no exception, and as we made our way through the New Hampshire countryside, I filled with anticipation and the poet with recollection, we decided to take a detour that would bring us into the lovely grounds of St. Paul's School, on the perimeter of Concord. As we approached the school we could tell that something was on: Japanese lanterns were strung across the paths, and cars lined the drives. Young people and parents were strolling across the lush grass; it was just before dusk, and in that peculiarly haunting light one could see excitement. We had arrived on the eve of their Prize Day, and no one noticed us. St. Paul's chapel is one of the loveliest nineteenth-century Gothic structures in America, a gem of perpendicular beside the river and against the hills. We went in. It was empty, save for someone playing the organ. Light streamed in through the stained-glass windows, glancing off the brass fittings on the altar and the marble plaques to the dead—the great, the good, and the young.

It was all stillness inside even though we could hear the murmur of young voices on the outside, and as we walked among the memorials, I, at least, thought of the intimate proximity between the living and the dead in that space when it was occupied under compulsion by the present inhabitants of the school. We moved about in the same place, together but alone, at our own pace and without comment. We were there for quite a while—in fact, the organist had long finished and gone—and as we emerged we discovered that it was now night, the sun had gone, the Japanese lanterns were ablaze, and the chapel glowed from inside, its windows giving lovely color to the early darkness. For some time we did not speak, for we were both in tears. Later, I learned from David that he had found a tablet to an old friend he had known in college, a St. Paul's boy who had died early and was commemorated in his old school chapel. I was overcome not by an experience of recollection, for I knew no one there, but by emotions so focused and powerful that they frightened and delighted me at the same time. I do not know what the experience was, but whatever it was neither David nor I wished to ruin it by an explanation, and so we drove on into the night in sympathetic silence. It was a moment of joy, the "feeling of satisfaction and fullness of well-being."

That was now nearly a quarter of a century ago, and there have been many happy moments, even joyful ones, since then, but that one experience stands out in my heart's memory. Dear David McCord is now nearly one hundred years old and resident in a nursing home. When I see him and conversation flags for a even a moment, he will say to me, "Remember that evening in St. Paul's Chapel?" and our eyes fill with tears and we hold hands in silence. I take some pleasure, selfishly, I admit, that this memory of joy, still vivid in his imagination after all these years and in all of his years, was one that I shared with him.

Was this a religious experience? The question itself is almost vulgar, impertinent, filled with the implied suspicion that a religious experience must have an angel visitant, a falling down on one's knees, and a doctrinally correct conversation with God readily reportable to others who can verify the legitimacy of the experience. Who knows? I do know, however, that the Bible is filled with accounts of such encounters. When Jacob, for example, no sentimentalist and not given to holy work, had his dream at Bethel of the angels ascending and descending a ladder from heaven to earth, and got his promise in the bargain, he awoke from his sleep and said, "Surely the Lord is in this place, and I did not know it." Then, recognizing that he was at a thin place between two realms, each of which he had now experienced, he was afraid and said, "How awesome is this place! This is none other than the house of God, and this is the gate of heaven." (Genesis 28:16–17)

I consulted my colleague Charles Dunn, now retired, and long expert in the field of Celtic folklore and mythology, and asked him about thin places. He told me that mountains and rivers were particularly favored as such places, marking as invariably they do the horizontal and perpendicular frontiers; religious experiences are very likely to occur in such places. Two vivid biblical instances come to mind. The first is the experience of the prophet Elijah on Mount Horeb, as recounted in I Kings 19, when the prophet is on the run from Queen Jezebel, who has put a price on his head for the slaughter of her priests of Baal. He is at his lowest moment. Depressed, literally, he takes refuge in a cave or depression on the side of Mount Horeb, and there before his eyes God the Lord passed by. There was a great and mighty wind that broke the mountain in pieces, "...but the Lord was not in the wind." Then there was an earthquake, and after that a fire, but the Lord was not in any of these phenomena of nature. He is described as appearing after the fire, a "still, small voice." (I Kings 19:9–12)

That "still, small voice" has always intrigued preachers and commentators. It is clear that the writer of Kings wishes to contrast the noise and power of nature, with its capacity to terrorize and intimidate, with the real power of the Lord, which is displayed in a quite unexpected, unanticipated way. Nature intimidates but God empowers; that is the burden of I Kings 19. That "still, small voice" doesn't mean a little whisper, or a tiny voice, nor does it mean silence as we understand silence. For years I have tried to figure out just what it does mean, and it finally occurred to me at a concert of the Boston Symphony Orchestra. It was a Good Friday performance of Elgar's *Dream of Gerontius*, conducted by Sir Colin Davis, with Jessye Norman singing. By every measure it was an extraordinary performance and experience, and as the last note ended, there was in that vast hall an incredible silence, and then the place erupted into thunderous applause. It came to me that the silence at the end of the concert was not merely the absence of sound but something more than that. It was an expectant, pregnant silence, nearly overpowering in its effect, so much so, so unbearable, that applause was more than approbation, it was essential psychic relief. That, I think, was what Elijah's "still, small voice" was about, not at all something modest or whispery but something grand, intimate, and portentous all at once.

If Elijah had his moment on the mountain, Jesus, we are told, had his in the river at his baptism. All four of the gospels give an account of the baptism of Jesus in the River Jordan at the hands of John the Baptist, and all of these baptismal accounts mark a transition from one aspect of the life of Jesus to another. His ministry begins with the baptism. Matthew says,

And when Jesus was baptized, he went up immediately from the water, and behold, the heavens were opened and he saw the Spirit of God descending like a dove, and alighting on him; and lo, a voice from heaven, saying, "This is my beloved Son, with whom I am well pleased." (Matthew 3:16–17)

For Christians, life begins not with the natural birth to which all flesh is heir, but with the second birth, of which baptism is the sign. Baptism is not only the sign of the new life, a new identity that calls for a new name—the custom of the baptismal name—but it confers new life as well. It initiates one into a new order of being, whose destiny is not death, the end of the natural order, but new life in which one lives in the world but is not of the world. Baptism seals Christians as essentially foreign and outsiders to the place in which they live, aliens and strangers, not natives but transients, tourists even, for as Paul notes in Philippians 3:20, "our citizenship"—or "commonwealth," as the Revised Standard Version puts it—"is in heaven."

This notion of baptism as initiation into a foreign, even alien, realm, making of the baptized resident an "alien," in the provocative language of immigration appropriated by Stanley Hauerwas and William Willimon in the title of their book of the same name, may well seem strange and alarming to the many who dutifully have their children "done" as a mark of respectable membership in the prevailing culture. Baptism is not standing at the border of one realm and looking across at the other side; it is a renunciation of the citizenship into which we are born. It is a rejection of all that we understand to be real and powerful. It is not "joining the church," as so many institutionally minded Christians mistakenly think; it is taking out citizenship papers in another place, as opposite and far distant from this place as can be imagined. This is given vivid expression in Hebrews, which, in speaking of those who died in faith as "strangers and exiles on the earth," says of them,

> For people who speak thus make it clear that they are seeking a homeland, If they had been thinking of that land from which they had gone out, they would have had opportunity to return. But as it is, they desire a better country, that is, a heavenly one.
>
> (Hebrews 11:13–16)

Twice now I have had the privilege of presiding at public ceremonies of the naturalization of new American citizens. These ceremonies were held in Plymouth, Massachusetts, as part of the Federal District Court's happy custom of swearing in new citizens at places of great historic significance. In Plymouth both of the ceremonies were under the auspices of the Pilgrim Society, of which I was president. At the spiritual shrine of American immigration, Plymouth Rock, I watched in August 1995, when on the occasion of the 375th anniversary of the landing of the Pilgrims, Mr. Justice David Souter of the United

States Supreme Court administered the oath to one hundred and two new citizens. In that oath the citizens were required to give up any allegiance they may have to the lands of their birth, and one of these new citizens, an Englishman and an old friend of mine, said that the hardest part for him was the public renunciation of his allegiance to foreign potentates and sovereigns, in his case, to Queen Elizabeth II. He did so, however, for that was the only way he could become a citizen of this new country.

I had seen such a forswearing before: in the baptismal service in the Book of Common Prayer where the persons to be baptized, or their sponsors, are asked, "Dost thou renounce the devil and all his works, the vain pomp and glory of the world, with all covetous desires of the same, and the sinful desires of the flesh, so that thou wilt not follow, nor be led by them?" The person to be baptized, or the sponsor thereof, must reply, "I renounce them all; and by God's help will endeavour not to follow, nor be led by them." In the old order, affirmation is preceded by a necessary renunciation.

Christians may not be able to follow the experiences of Jacob and his angelic dream, or of Elijah and his still, small voice on Horeb, but in baptism we are meant to follow Jesus across the boundary from one realm into another. Such a realm has as its gift to the faithful the promise of fullness of joy or joy made whole and complete. "If you keep my commandments," says

Jesus in John's gospel, "you will abide in my love, just as I have kept my Father's commandments and abide in his love. These things I have spoken to you, that my joy may be in you, and that your joy may be full." (John 15:10–11)

Perhaps to experience joy, you should go to a black gospel church when first the choir and then the whole congregation "get happy" or carried away in the spirit. It doesn't happen right away, it takes a while. It begins, and it spreads slowly, gathering momentum, and then no one is immune. It is the kind of worship of which James Baldwin and Richard Wright speak. It is what nearly every black country church and urban storefront church knows; and white people now know something of it by virtue of the exported and denatured secular soul of Motown. As everybody who is in the know knows, Aretha Franklin learned to sing in church, and at the knee of her daddy, the Reverend C.L. Franklin.

A white friend of sociological mind once asked me why black people, who had so little to sing about, who knew so little joy in either the wicked South or the brutal North, sang so much? Were they singing simply to drive away dull care? Was this a form of diversion, a self-induced ecstasy to kill the throb of a deadening existence? Was this an opiate or a primal scream, or a religious form of kicking the dog after a bad day or week or life? I concluded that my friend had read too much Joseph Campbell and not enough of the Bible. The brothers and sisters weren't singing to drive dull care away, nor were they irrigating their sorrows or sublimating their fears. Their joy, and that is what it was, in the sense of all three New Testament Greek words, was a consequence of what they had discovered and knew to be true, and this was beyond the level of mere speculation and guesswork. They sang because they knew themselves to be at the thin place between this world and another, and while their daily existence might be bound hand and foot to a world in which there was little about which to be glad, they nevertheless knew that they "had a title to a mansion on high," and that knowledge was so delicious, so absolute, and so paradoxical that they had to sing about it. Such joy did not make sense out of reality; it transcended and overwhelmed what passed for reality. That is what every cook, hairdresser, chauffeur, Pullman porter, mailman, laundress, seamstress, old auntie, and arthritic uncle knew and recognized as true when Mahalia Jackson would begin to sing:

Why should I feel discouraged, and why should the shadows fall,
And why should my heart feel lonely and I dream of a heaven I know

When Jesus is my portal, a constant friend is he:
His eye is on the sparrow, and I know he watches me....

*I sing because I'm happy, I sing because
I'm free,*
  *For his eye is on the sparrow, and I know
he watches me.*

I didn't have to go to the south side of Chicago or to exotic Harlem, or even to Roxbury in Boston to hear this; we had it at home, in our little Bethel AME church, right around the corner from where I lived. There weren't many of us but we knew the gospel when we heard it, and even Mahalia Jackson could not outdo our old neighbor and friend Corrine Walley when *she* sang "His Eye Is on the Sparrow."

Now the great question is this: How did we know that "His eye is on the sparrow"? Where did we get that notion? Where did that idea come from? It came from the Bible, of course, and everybody knew that it did. There were many who may have thought that such a message was not for us, the "colored" people, but we knew that the message of freedom and encouragement in Christ, despite every attempt to pervert and to keep it from us, was meant for us; it had our name on it. That fact, perhaps more than anything else, and certainly more than this world's circumstances in which we found ourselves, gave us cause, without command or a sense of duty, for joy.

The Context for Joy

In his famous little book, *Surprised by Joy,* C.S. Lewis early on is eager to make a sharp and clear distinction about what joy is and what joy is not. Writing about what he calls "the central story of my life," he calls joy "an unsatisfied desire which is itself more desirable than any other satisfaction."

I call it Joy, which is here a technical term and must be sharply distinguished both from Happiness and from Pleasure. Joy (in my sense) has indeed one characteristic, and one only, in common with them: the fact that anyone who has experienced it will want it again.

Pleasure is often in our power to give ourselves but we cannot give ourselves joy, and the pursuit of it is frustrating and fruitless, and in the end, he concludes, irrelevant. What about joy? "To tell you the truth, the subject has lost nearly all interest for me since I became a Christian." As with much of C.S. Lewis I like the analysis but not the conclusion. His discussion of joy is much like the curate's egg. When given a bad egg by the squire and asked how he liked it, the curate is said to have replied, "Parts of it are quite good, my Lord." Joy is not the same as pleasure. Joy cannot be pursued. Joy is elusive. Once you have known joy you will want it again. Joy, however, is not a way to find God. It is not a reward; it may well be result. Joy may be the expression and experience of being the discovered and the discoverer.

To make certain that we understand that joy is not merely pleasure or aesthetics, or self-induced diversion or delusion, we must realize that the context of joy is not delight but deprivation. The experience of joy reminds us, by what we have momentarily gained, of what we did not have before we gained it. It is said that lovers cannot remember when they were not in love. I do not believe that this is true, for how would they know that they were in love if they did not know, that is, did not remember, what not being in love was all about? Joy is akin to holiness, not because of some sense of moral perfection or beauty but because both partake of the sense of the whole, of the complete. When we know joy, for a moment we see everything in its completeness, we have a whole view, and that is what the fullness of joy means. It is an instantaneous and complete glimpse, as it were, of that which ordinarily we see only in part. Remember where, in his most lyrical mood, Paul, speaking of love in I Corinthians 13, that most famous and beloved of all passages from scripture, says, "For now we see in a mirror dimly, but then face to face. Now I know in part; then I shall understand fully, even as I have been fully understood." (I Corinthians 13:12) Joy is both the moment and the response to the moment, when the partial becomes complete, the cloudy clear, and we see even as we are seen, and understand even as we are understood. Joy thus is not an out-of-body or out-of-mind experience contrary to knowledge, reason, and understanding. Just the opposite. Joy is when it all becomes clear, a *Eureka!* moment.

What is the response when you suddenly come upon the clue to a complex problem, thereby solving it? Victory comes to mind, even satisfaction, and a sense of achievement as well, and pleasure is gained. The moment when it all falls together, either because of our efforts or despite our efforts, is that moment we call one of joy; the broken has been made whole. That is what Pentecostalists understand in the ecstasy of their worship. That is what colored folk know when they sing the songs of Zion and see the broken mended and in all its splendor; and when we sing at Christmas, "Joy to the world! The Lord is come...." that is not an invitation to mere merrymaking and mindless happiness, a distraction from earth's gloomy night. Not at all. It means that because the Lord has come to fulfill the promises of God, all that was separated and disparate is now united and whole. Suffering is the context of joy even as darkness is the context for light and silence for hearing. Joy that is complete and full transcends, indeed overcomes, its context, and is not bound by the limitations of the context. Our eyes are opened, and having seen wholeness once we will want to see it again and again. Those who have had this experience are restless for another. This is what Augustine means, in his famous collect, when he prays, "Thou hast made us for thyself, and our hearts are restless until they find their rest in thee."

How Do We Make It Our Own?

We don't. Timothy Leary and the culture of drugs that he spawned tried to manufacture joy and put it into powders, potions, and pills, like the alchemists of old who tried to turn base things into something of beauty and worth. All they succeeded in doing was destroying all those who wanted shortcuts to joy. Joy is not a natural substance to be quarried, mined, or minted, and it doesn't belong to us as we imagine that property or ideas belong to us. That slightly crazed seer-poet William Blake, he who gave us "Jerusalem"—the poem, not the city—reminds us of this:

> *But he who kisses the joy as it flies*
> *He who binds to himself a joy*
> *Does the wingèd life destroy;*
> *But he who kisses the joy as it flies*
> *Lives in eternity's sunrise.*
> *("Eternity," 1793)*

We have known these moments, unbidden, surreptitious, elusive, in which by grace, perhaps in nature or in life, we have seen wholly and fully, if only for an instant, and we have been enraptured by an unexpected discovery, a vision, an incarnation, a manifestation. New fathers tell me that they have had such moments upon sharing the birth of their children with their wives. Women have told me of such moments coming to them as they have held the hand of a dying friend. A young Harvard undergraduate told me in tears of joy commingled with embarrassment that he had seen all heaven and earth in an instant of enlightenment while singing a hymn at the daily service of Morning Prayers in Appleton Chapel. Surely the Lord was in this place, and he knew it not.

I do not have to sell these moments of joy, these exaltations, to anyone, for we have all had them. All I can say is that we ought to recognize and cherish them for what they are: glimpses of holiness at the thin places that remind us that we are neither our own nor on our own. If ever there was a biblical principle for making sense and meaning, this is it.

CHAPTER 12

THE BIBLE AND EVIL

A book about the Bible without a discussion of evil would be about the kind of Bible that most of us would like, but it would bear false witness to the Bible, for the Bible is much about evil. The effective point of communication in the Bible between the divine and the human is that the Bible takes evil seriously and recognizes the reality of evil in the human condition. In the Bible, evil is not an illusion, not a state of mind, not a mere moral inconvenience; evil is real. It must be real if the human lives in which it is found are to be real, and if the redemption from the ultimate domination of evil in that life and in this life is also to be real. There are those who argue that the trouble with religion, with the Bible, and with Christianity in particular is that all of these tend to emphasize the negative, that is, evil, and fail to give emphasis to the positive, which is the gospel of love. Pastoral sensitivities, we are told, should affirm that which is good and negate that which is not. Too much emphasis on sin and evil will drive people away, and besides, now that we know so much more than our primitive ancestors, we know that evil is really a synonym for ignorance. The corollary is that the more we know, the better off we will be because evil and ignorance will disappear or at least be contained, in much the way that modern medicine has conquered such once rampant diseases as tuberculosis and poliomyelitis.

The Bible, however, never speaks of "curing" evil, and nowhere does it speak of "conquering" evil. If the Bible is about anything, it is about the subtle, ruthless, remorseless persistence of evil. The book of Genesis speaks of evil as trouble in paradise, and one cannot diminish the presence of evil in that account of Adam and Eve. It might even be argued that the star of the drama is the serpent, evil incarnate, and that Adam and Eve play significant but secondary supporting roles in a tale that is not really about them but is about the beginning of the siege of the hearts of men and of women. The last book of the Bible, the enigmatic book of Revelation— the interpretation of which engaged the last days and hours of David Koresh and his Branch Davidians, and about which the secular observers of that cataclysmic scene in Waco were so bewildered—that book is about a grand and final confrontation between the forces of good and the forces of evil. Evil, we might say, is the Bible's leitmotif. If the Bible were set to music by a composer of Wagnerian dimensions, one can imagine the constant iteration in dozens of devious but recognizable ways of the evil motif throughout the full expanse of the production; we would recognize that it is always there, ready to burst forth, and even when it is defeated or when it withdraws, it does so only to reinsinuate itself into the very fabric of the composition.

When theologians and religious philosophers talk about evil, the word is usually preceded by such a phrase as "the problem of..." for it is the problem of evil and not evil itself that tends to fascinate the learned. They are intrigued to know where it came from, how it got into the world, how a good and powerful God allows rampant evil and its attendant sufferings and sorrows into the creation. The problem of evil soon becomes the problem of God, and the conversation has become just one more theological tête-à-tête.

When ordinary people speak of evil it is not so much "the problem of..." as it is "the problem with..." for ordinary people are not driven to speculation in the discussion of evil. The apocryphal farmer from Maine, when asked if he believed in original sin, replied, "Believe in it? Why, I seen it." So have we all. Our helping professions, I think, and those of us in the church have done people a grave disservice in underestimating their abilities to recognize and to deal with the reality of evil in the world and in their lives. I have often complained about the revisions of the General Confession of the Episcopal Church in the Book of Common Prayer of 1979, which excised as too penitential and Calvinistic the sharply worded phrase of Archbishop Cranmer that had people declare that as a result of the intolerable burden of their sins they were "miserable offenders," and that there was "no health" in them. I have been told on countless occasions that the ritual repetition of these phrases on the part of the penitent diminished both themselves and the work that had been done for them in the atoning work of Jesus. Furthermore, this public sense of sin created "pastoral problems" in matters of spiritual self-esteem.

I am all for matters of spiritual self-esteem. If we are to love our neighbors as ourselves, which is the second commandment in Jesus' summary of the law, we must first and also love ourselves. We must remember and rejoice in the fact that we are created in the image of God and that we share in the full dignity of creation. I believe that. I affirm that. I also believe, however, that most of us are "miserable offenders." We are made miserable by the offenses we commit and by their consequences. Sin and evil make us miserable. That does not deny the dignity of creation; that simply affirms the reality of sin, and that there is no health in us; which does not mean that we are unhealthy. It means that on our own, of our own, by ourselves, there is nothing within us to cure the malady of sin and of evil. The cure of sin is not simply a matter of mind over matter; it is not pure willing that leads to goodness. No orthodox Christian can possibly believe that. To say that there is no health in us means both that we are sick and that we cannot cure ourselves. We need help. We do not tell the physically ill that they can get better by denying that they are sick. The physician tells them what is wrong, most of them can take it, and then the physician prescribes what is best to cure the illness. We expect nothing less.

Ordinary people know something of evil; they are not strangers to it, and they know that evil flourishes in the world, and, alas, even within themselves. When a terrible disaster occurs, such as the explosion of the airplane over Lockerbie, Scotland, some few years ago with the terrible loss of innocent life; or when the Federal Building in Oklahoma is bombed, again with hundreds of innocent people killed; or when Prime Minister Yitzak Rabin of Israel is assassinated in the name of God, we know that something terrible, and not only terrible but wrong, and not only wrong but evil, has occurred. We don't have to be instructed or tutored in this; we know it to be so.

We know as well when we see a schoolyard bully beating up a defenseless younger child that that is wrong, and that evil is at work. When parents abandon or do violence to their children, and when children murder their parents, when a deranged gunman opens fire aboard a crowded commuter train, and when, as happened in England a few years ago, two children under the age of ten kidnap a baby and maim and murder the young child as if for sport, we know that for the evil it is.

These are in some sense easy cases, which by the sheer scale and audacity of their wickedness we can recognize on sight as manifestations of evil. There are, for instance, very few people in the world today, with the exception of some white supremacists and Holocaust deniers, who do not recognize Adolf Hitler as an evil man. It used to be one of the favorite moral lessons of literature and history, in the days when literature and history were thought to be able to teach moral lessons, that "man's inhumanity to man" was the theme we could not escape. When Cain slew his brother Abel and asked the rhetorical question, "Am I my brother's keeper?," we knew that we were seeing but the first act of the continuing human drama. Saint Augustine declared that the earthly city, as opposed to the city of God, was descended from the violence of Cain, that society was founded upon fratricide, envy, deceit, and violence, and that in such a society, under the patronage of the first murderer, Cain, there never would be real or lasting peace. Life under these circumstances was one endless Balkan civil war, with the dead in constant conflict with the living.

Few centuries are better witnesses to this sad truth than our own, now mercifully drawing to a close. Two world wars, one cold war, and now numerous bitter skirmishes remind us that we have not learned very much, and that Augustine in this respect is still very much a contemporary social scientist. "All our progress," Bertrand

Russell once said, "is but improved means to unimproved ends." Amid the shambles and shame of the Battle of Dunkirk in May 1940, Herbert Read wrote with more bitterness than sweetness this ode:

Happy are those who can relieve
suffering with prayer
Happy are those who can rely on God
to see them through.

They can wait patiently for the end.

But we who have put our faith
in the goodness of man
And now see man's image debased
lower than the wolf or the hog—

Where can we turn for consolation?

Dunkirk, we may be quick to note, was before America entered the Second World War, and hence was not really an "American experience." We might call it a catastrophe, a bit of very bad luck and worse planning, but in 1940 this was hardly "our" problem, and the evil of Hitler had not yet fully dawned upon us. Evil in America tends to fall into two apparently mutually exclusive categories, under the common rubric of moral evil: social sins and societal sins or, if you prefer, sins of the flesh and sins of the system.

Once upon a time we were much more intimately acquainted with the seven deadly sins than we are today; that is simply to say that we knew their names and could list them as Pride, Lust, Gluttony, Anger, Sloth, Envy, and Greed. Literary critics and the historians of theology know the evolution of these "diseases of the soul," as eighteenth-century mystic William Blake called them, but while the sins themselves can be found represented in various ways in the Bible, no list of the seven deadlies will be found in scripture. This doesn't mean that because they are not in the Bible they are not biblical; the list is a convenient form of shorthand in which to discuss the moral human condition.

For most of us the sins of the flesh have to do with pleasure and indulgence, giving rise to the old canard that everything we want to do is either immoral, illicit, or fattening. Pleasure and the flesh are condemned as a result of the fall from grace in the Garden of Eden. The sins of the flesh are troublesome and therefore condemned because their pleasure diverts us from virtue and makes us want to satisfy ourselves rather than God or others. Such pleasures become ends in themselves, which easily leads to idolatry, which establishes an unacceptable rivalry between what is created and the Creator. It is wrong, but easily understood, to think of pleasure as in itself evil.

It is not. Its consequences, however, are understood to be dangerous because they draw us away from our proper destiny, which is the service of God, and from the control of our reason, which would remind us of that duty and keep us faithful to it.

It is to Augustine, and not to the Bible, that we must turn if we want to talk about the sins of the flesh for, unlike the Bible, Augustine was much concerned with the topic. For better or for worse, it is the convert from a self-indulgent worldly urbanity, Augustine, who is responsible for the Western moral teachings on sex. It is lust in the explicitly sexual sense that he writes about in *The City of God*: "The lust that excites the indecent parts of the body" is dangerous because it "assumes power not only over the whole body, and not only from the outside, but also internally; it disturbs the whole man, when the mental emotion combines and mingles with the physical craving," resulting in so intense a sensation of pleasure "that when it reaches its climax there is an almost total extinction of mental alertness; the intellectual sentries, as it were, are overwhelmed." Since such a lust is not subject to rational or physical control but is itself master of all, it is both to be feared and controlled. "It is right, therefore," he writes in the very next chapter, "to be ashamed of this lust," and the organs that serve this lust should be called *pudenda*, or "parts of shame." The trouble with arousal for Augustine is that it does not operate at the behest of the mind, but literally has a mind of its own. The corrective to lust is shame, and shame itself is not a virtue, like modesty, but a punishment for lust. Thus lust, of which sex is the manifestation, is to be punished by shame not because it is pleasurable but because it is irrational.

Most Baptists and Methodists have not spent much time in consideration of the moral philosophy of Saint Augustine, but their anxieties about the sins of the flesh could not be better expressed than his. They threw off much of Roman Catholicism's moral theology, but they retained the notion that somehow the sins of the flesh got between the sinner and God. Such sins, however, were not sinful because they offended reason but rather because they gave pleasure, which in the refracted Calvinism to which they were all heirs, was itself an unacceptable end. Thus sex was only for the begetting of children, shameful for the man, painful for the woman, both part of a divine plan; and sex for any other purpose simply confounded pain and shame, especially if any pleasure without penalty was involved. Women were thus vessels of shame who, like Eve, Jezebel, and Delilah, led their men to disastrous ends. Masturbation was forbidden because it wasted valuable and necessary seed for an endangered species, the holy community, and because it gave pleasure without a compensatory pain. Hence prices of masturbation had to be invented: hair on the palms, blindness, insanity, and impotence by reducing the finite supply of sperm.

From these anxieties come many of the other social inhibitions of the flesh. Drinking, for

357

instance, like sex, contributes to the "almost total extinction of mental alertness; the intellectual sentries, as it were, are overwhelmed." Dancing was also forbidden for its similitude to the sexual act. The old Southern Baptist joke has the young man say to the young woman with whom he is about to have illicit sex, "We'd better do it on the sofa so they won't think we're dancing."

Although it is fair to say that biblical morality encompassed a much wider spectrum of virtues, including those of the Commandments, and those to be aspired to in the Beatitudes and the Sermon on the Mount, when most Christians think of morality they think first of the sins of the flesh, and then most explicitly of sex. Thus, one whole strand of Christian ethics contributed to the dangerous *reductio ad absurdum* that sin is simply sex and thus sex is evil. There is more to sex than sin, and more to sin than sex. Augustine has much to teach us, but even he cannot possibly teach us all that we now need to know.

Sins of the System

Until Jimmy Swaggart's highly publicized infidelities and the increasing public consciousness of the AIDS epidemic renewed their newsworthiness, sins of the flesh were for most citizens of modernity rather old-fashioned and left behind in the sexual revolution of the 1960s and 1970s. In fact, Carl Menninger would write a briefly popular book in 1973, with the catchy title *Whatever Happened to Sin?* It seems that nobody knew. What was clear was that very few people were any longer responsible for anything at all. The comic Anna Russell put the sentiment of the age in her "Psychiatric Folksong":

> *At three I had a feeling of*
> *Ambivalence toward my brothers,*
> *And so it follows naturally*
> *I poison all my lovers,*
> *But I am happy now I've learned*
> *The lesson this has taught:*
> *That everything I do that's wrong*
> *Is someone else's fault!*

One of the great acts of transference in modern times is the transference of the responsibility for evil and sin from individuals to institutions and to society at large. It is not altogether clear when this began. In the period of American revivalism and reform in the first half of the nineteenth century, preachers and the reformed condemned the sins of drink and the drunkard, both. When the slave trade was condemned, so too were those who participated in it. The revival of society, it was understood, began with the revival of the individual, the redemption of society with the redemption of the individual. "Lord, send a revival," was the old cry, "and let it begin with me." John and Charles Wesley preached for the revival of the world through the sanctification of the individuals in it. They understood, as did Saint Paul and the patristic doctors of the early church, that as through a human being, the man Adam, sin entered into the world, only through the renovation of human beings, a work accomplished in the atonement of Jesus Christ in his human form, would the price of sin be paid and the fallen society redeemed from sin through the redemption of its members. "As in Adam all die," says Paul, "even so in Christ shall all be made alive." Soul winning, as the process of conversion and evangelization was once called, was also world saving, producing even within the fallen city of man, as Augustine put it, the City of God.

Social sin, or what I am calling sins of the system, is understood to be the sinful, fallen nature of the institutions and social systems that are created, managed, and manipulated by sinful men and women. When Reinhold Niebuhr spoke of *Moral Man and Immoral Society*, the title of one of his most penetrating and influential books, he addressed the conundrum of how "good people" could participate in and perpetuate sinful, wicked, and destructive systems. Part of this had to do with a rather sophisticated analysis of how people who were good, but not good enough, could not in aggregate avoid social sin, which tended to negate whatever individual and private virtues the individual might possess. Theologians describe this as the consequence of a corrupt or wounded will. When Saint Paul says that the good he would do he cannot do, and the evil he would not and wills not to do he does, that is an illustration, personal and powerful, of the inadequacy of the unaided will on its own to be, to do, or to know good.

The manifestation of this dilemma is not simply the personal discomfort that individuals feel between their intentions and their deeds. That itself is quite significant, but the sins of the system, or social sin, has to do with the active participation of good people in deeds and systems that are themselves not good. The classic examples are clear and terrifying. Most of the evils in the world have been performed and perpetuated by individuals who, convinced that they are doing good, even doing God's will, participate corporately in wickedness. We can call upon ancient historical examples to make our point. Surely, those Spanish Christians who fueled the fires of the Spanish Inquisition with their unspeakable tortures and maimings did what they did, and felt that they could do no other, because they believed ever so firmly that they were doing good and doing God's will. The Puritans of Salem, Massachusetts, in the summer and autumn of 1692 were convinced that they were doing God's will by hanging those whom they believed to be witches. In moral retrospect we like to think that such people themselves were deranged or lacking in virtue or in cultural sophistication.

When we look at Nazi Germany, however, we are dealing with the heirs of one of the world's most sophisticated and gifted peoples, the land of Bach and of Beethoven, of Kant and of Hegel, of Luther and of Brahms. These were not

361

barbarians but men and women learned in the arts and sciences, with an appetite for the beautiful and for the life of the mind. When they raped, robbed, and pillaged Europe, they saw to it that the finest art treasures of the lands they conquered were preserved for their own pleasure. Nazi Germany was by no means all thugs and Brownshirts and Bavarian drunkards, and the great moral problem was how so great a civilization could perpetrate and tolerate such immense evil.

For many of us that moral dilemma had its more immediate demonstration in the United States in the very same period. When I taught at Tuskegee Institute, I discovered that the institute's archives held the world's largest single collection of documents having to do with lynching. I remember an exhibition on lynching in America in the period between the First and Second World Wars, in which were displayed photograph after photograph of lynch scenes taken, in many cases, by participants. What was so horrifying in these pictures was not the obscene display of the lynched and often otherwise mutilated Negroes, but the faces of the white mob, faces not frenzied in anger but filled with pleasure as at a sporting event. Women and children featured prominently in these photographs, together with the men, and one knew that these mobs were composed almost exclusively of Christian men and women, Baptists and Methodists, who knew and read their Bibles, who said their prayers, who took sins of the flesh very seriously, and who saw themselves as God-loving and God-fearing. One could imagine these people lynching on Saturday and worshiping on Sunday, with no hint of the slightest moral discontinuity. These were not merely the hooded white knights of the Ku Klux Klan. These people had no shame to cover up in the bedsheets; their unconcealed faces revealed an almost grotesque pride in the perverse pleasures of their violence. They would condemn dancing, drinking, and sex; they opposed legislation opposed to lynching. Lynching was sport masquerading as justice. At the last judgment these Christians in particular will have much to answer for.

In the 1960s and 1970s, movements for social justice would speak out against the sins of those systems that perpetuated violence and injustice in the world. Thus racism was not only the collective acts of violence on the part of racists but the system that encouraged and supported a culture of violence and discrimination. Individuals might repent and change their ways, but no real change would happen until the systems themselves were changed. Racism was such a system. So too were naked capitalism, militarism, and sexism, and the institutional structures that gave them aid and cover; and one of the great ironies of the developing consciousness of institutional sin is that it developed in a culture when it was becoming increasingly fashionable to denigrate the notion of personal responsibility for sin and evil. Thus many of those who in the 1960s and 1970s were leading the crusades against structural and institutional sin were themselves increasingly indifferent to the notion of personal sin. Thus there developed a great divide between those whose priority was the reform and repentance of the individual for whom sin for so long had been defined almost exclusively in terms of sins of the flesh, and those who, having abandoned the personal piety that took sin and repentance seriously, embraced the wholesale reform of society and its system.

Sins of the system, while real, have a way of becoming so abstract, so structural and analytic, that it becomes very difficult to clothe them in the moral authority they require to convince and convict those who participate in them of the need for change. The antiwar movement of the 1960s and early 1970s tried to do this, and if war cannot be addressed in moral terms, few other phenomena can. The antiwar movement was frustrated by a countervailing morality that combined patriotism and pride with profoundly secular cultural values wrapped in the odor of sanctity. A paradox not often commented upon is that the rhetoric of the antiwar movement often was far more religious, indeed, moral, and was waged with a higher sense of the consciousness of sin than the one that favored the war. That rhetoric tended to indulge in the unexamined shibboleths of national pride, mindless anticommunism, and a profound distrust of any change in what was in essence a secular status quo. The war ended, as we know, not because of the moral weight of the arguments against it but because of the unbearable social costs of proceeding. We have only to read the memoirs of Robert McNamara to confirm this anxious-making analysis.

Social justice issues, at the hands of their most articulate advocates, suffered in the communication of their values because those values seemed so abstracted from any sense of sin and concerned themselves almost exclusively in the realm of rights, policy, and strategies. This secularization of virtue has long inhibited the movements in favor of women, homosexuals, and the environment. Having yielded up the notion of sin to those who claim it in opposition to all threatening change, those who are advocates for rights are seen simply as well-orchestrated lobbyists for selfish interests and special considerations, and thus are deprived of the moral high ground. They see themselves as the heirs of the civil rights movement, and wonder in frustration why they do not reap the moral capital of that movement's success. What so many fail to understand in these comparisons with the civil rights movement is that at its origins and heart that movement was not merely political or social, but fundamentally religious and moral, and in particular animated by a Christian perception of the biblical notions of sin and redemption. From this conviction, drawing upon the great moral substratum of American piety, came the energy of the marches, the confrontations with conscience and guilt, and even the legal and strategic maneuvers.

To be deprived of these resources is to disadvantage any significant movement for moral and social change, and that is why all marches in Washington, D.C., since Dr. King's famous address at the Lincoln Memorial tend to be pale imitations, lacking not simply the vital spark of so compelling an orator as Dr. King but the moral urgency and sense of sin and rehabilitation that turned that 1963 gathering from a protest into a sacrament. Mere displays of numbers on the Mall, as women and homosexuals have discovered, do not guarantee that the moral imagination of the nation will be engaged. The surprising, and, to some, disturbing, success of the 1995 Million Man March, despite the controversial and distasteful views of its leader, Louis Farrakhan, was achieved because it embraced the discourse of sin, atonement, and redemption.

In what I hope is not too esoteric a theological footnote, I would argue that the Million Man March gave public display to the theological principle conveyed in the Latin phrase *Ex opere operato,* "Through the performance of the work," which in the teachings of the Roman Catholic Church means that the efficacy of a sacramental action depends upon Christ's promise and not upon the character or merits of the person performing the work. Thus, a "whiskey priest" does not make invalid by his questionable character the validity of a proper work properly done. Louis Farrakhan was to many a whiskey priest, whose character invalidated an otherwise good idea. The good idea and its merits could be said to have prevailed despite the character of its chief proponent, and it did so, I think, because it appealed to conscience.

Good People and Bad Things

Any of us who has ever wanted to write a book hopes to enjoy the phenomenal success of Rabbi Harold Kushner, whose book *When Bad Things Happen to Good People* has become a legendary success story in the literature of American popular piety. It ranks with Russell Conwell's *Acres of Diamonds*, Bruce Barton's *The Man Nobody Knows*, Charles Sheldon's *In His Steps*, and Norman Vincent Peale's *The Power of Positive Thinking*, not to mention that second-only-to-the-Bible perennial best-seller, *The Prophet*, by Kahlil Gibran, as an example of the right book at the right time. Every pastor has dealt with those of the flock upon whom some disaster or tragedy has been visited, who, in a combination of anger and anguish together with an acute moral curiosity, ask, "What have I done to deserve this?" Rabbi Kushner, as good an expositor as he is a pastor, has done us all a tremendous service in his straightforward and useful book, and he and it deserve every success.

Perhaps it is the people with whom I have ministered over the years, but I have often given thought to another book that would deal with an equally profound and pervasive pastoral problem. I would call this book, with due apologies but with no royalties to Rabbi Kushner,

Why Good People Do Bad Things. That is what we have been talking about all along, and it is no small subject of the Bible as well. The people I see want to know why it is that they cannot restrain themselves from hateful, hurtful attitudes and actions; they are not in a moral quandary; that is to say, they are not ignorant of what the good is, or of the consequences of the wrong. They are not morally obtuse or ethically challenged. They have not inverted wrong into right; they have not deluded themselves into thinking that what they are and what they do is virtuous. These people have a ruthless honesty about themselves. "I have behaved badly toward my wife, my husband, my lover, my children; I have been a terrible colleague, a less than responsible employer. I have not been a good neighbor." They recognize themselves in those memorable phrases of self-indictment from the General Confession of Archbishop Cranmer's Book of Common Prayer: "We have left undone those things which we ought to have done, and we have done those things which we ought not to have done."

Whether, as the old TV comic Flip Wilson used to say, "The devil made me do it," or whether one sees oneself as a victim of circumstances that compel one to choose between the lesser of two well-known evils, the sinner recognizes a no-win situation and is thus miserable, indeed a miserable offender. Would that we could take comfort in the lines attributed to Mae West, who said, "Between the two evils I always choose the one I haven't tried before," but even such hedonism after a while becomes boring. Ignorance is not an excuse for sin, but it is a bliss. The misery of the sinner is the knowledge both of the wrong and of its inevitability.

It is often suggested that we do not know what the good is, and as Pontius Pilate asked half sincerely, half sardonically of Jesus, "What is truth?," we ask "What is good?" Those who do wrong in the Bible more often than not know perfectly well what they are doing; they do not act out of ignorance. They act out of what is called in theology a corrupted will, what we might call a twisted, partial, imperfect vision of what goodness is. The Bible is filled with vivid images of people caught between the knowledge of what is good and what is evil, and the inability to avoid the easy wrong and to affirm the difficult right.

Such knowledge is both good and bad. In the creation story Eve is seduced by the serpent into eating of the forbidden fruit of the tree that contains the knowledge of good and evil, and when she and her husband do so, the first knowledge they gain is of their own nakedness. Not only do they see that they are naked, which is nothing new, but they realize that they shouldn't be, and experience shame, and thus hasten to cover themselves with fig leaves, or "aprons," as one of the earliest English translations puts it. Augustine, and those who take their moral philosophy from him, think that this all has to do with sex and their awareness of their genitals, what he calls the "parts of shame." He assumed that nakedness was *ipso facto* a cause of shame because it provided the occasion for lust, and we know his views on lust. It is hard, however, to take seriously the implication that the story of that first disobedience is simply a tale of prudery and a genealogy of shame. The story is not about sex or lust or "parts of shame," no matter how titillated Augustine was by the conviction that it was. It is about limitations, indeed, about the ambiguity of knowledge. The fact that they knew that they were naked means that they saw themselves for the first time as they were, and that knowledge, contrary to the modern notion that "knowledge is power," made them realize with their first infusion of knowledge just how weak and vulnerable they now were and had been. It was not knowledge that had protected them from the blandishments of the serpent, but ignorance that had preserved their innocence. Now they knew all, but their knowledge was not a blessing, it was a curse; and hence, as John Habgood says, "All knowledge is ambiguous."

Cain knew that he should neither be envious of his brother Abel, nor should he murder him. He was not in doubt about what was right, yet he did wrong. Joseph's brothers knew that it was wrong to sell their younger brother into slavery, but they could not prevent themselves from acting on their passions even despite their knowledge. Jacob knew that he should not have cheated his brother Esau of his birthright, nor should he have deceived his old father in doing so, but he did it anyway. King David knew that it was wrong to lust after Bathsheba and to send her husband Uriah into the heat of battle to die so he could marry his widow, but he acted despite his knowledge. The cynical preacher of Ecclesiastes says, "For in much wisdom is much grief; and he that increaseth knowledge increaseth sorrow." (Ecclesiastes 1:18) Saint Paul writes, "Knowledge puffeth up, but charity edifieth. And if any man think that he knoweth anything, he knoweth nothing yet as he ought to know." (I Corinthians 8:1–2)

Ignorance is not why good people do bad things, and knowledge itself does not prevent good people from doing bad things. Good people do bad things because by themselves they are not able to manipulate their knowledge of what is good in behalf of goodness and over against what is bad. The first and most basic reason the good do bad is that the good are weak and are not fully in control of themselves or of their circumstances. This sounds like a ready-made alibi, and the now all too familiar moral escape of the perpetrator as victim. We want people to take responsibility for their actions and not to blame the devil, or voices, or circumstances, or victims. The moral chaos of our time is deepened by the sense of evasion and scapegoating that this concession to moral weakness would seem to condone, but we have no choice. We must begin here with the fact that our knowledge and our will, even our good intentions, are not sufficent to prevent the good from doing bad.

This is not a concession to victimology, but rather a concession to the reality of evil. The only way to answer the question is to acknowledge that the good are not in control, and are usually outwitted and outsmarted by the forces of evil that surround them on every hand. To put it more plainly:

1. Evil is real.
2. The good are not as smart as they think they are.
3. The good need all the help they can get; one cannot be good on one's own.

Let us look again at the lynch mob. Every faceless mob is composed of the faces of individual people, many of whom have much good in them. They do not see themselves or their neighbors as evil; they do not contemplate evil acts. In fact, under certain circumstances they are driven to their actions by a sense of offended righteousness. They would argue that it was a sense of justice that motivated them to join with their neighbors in dispensing rough justice. Where others see what they are doing and what they have begun as evil, they themselves literally see no evil, and would deny its power. If you do not recognize the reality of evil, and your own capacity for evil and its artful designs, then you are ripe to be overtaken by that which you deny exists. The first thing the good need to recognize is that they are at one with evil. The reason the church on earth is called the church militant is because it understands itself to be in a state of constant warfare with a real antagonist whose troops are legion and whose resources are without limit. To deny that reality is the first step toward moral defeat.

Second, evil has a brain. Someone has said that cancer is not simply a medical condition that results in death but a disease with a brain and a strategy of death. It works to wear down the body, to outwit the physicians, outmaneuver the therapies, strategies, and potions. It almost seems as it if has a will of its own, and it can never be underestimated. Evil is like cancer; it has a brain and a strategy, and millennia of experience. As we have said before, evil is so smart that it will not attack our weak points, knowing that we have those guarded. Rather, it attacks those places in which we feel confident, hence places that we neglect. Thus, the morally superior person is vulnerable to evil at those points where the moral strength is felt to be sufficiently strong that he can afford to neglect it.

This may perhaps explain the phenomenon of the abuse of moral trust by such people as physicians and psychiatrists and priests and clergy. Secure in the identity of their calling, confident in the honor others accord them, and unwilling to think themselves vulnerable in the work they do so well, they are prime targets for the power of evil over them. They think that they are in control, when in fact they are controlled. Roman Catholic priests charged with pedophilia often tell their victims that nothing is wrong because "I'm a priest: I can't do wrong." Protestant clergymen like Jimmy

Swaggart say some variation on the same theme, and add, "and I can't get caught." The mousy bank clerk who embezzles millions from the accounts in his charge knows that embezzling is wrong, but his actions stem either from vengeance against an unjust employer—a form of radical redistribution of the undeserved wealth of patrons—or from meeting virtuous needs such as the support of an invalid relative who requires the money. These good often think themselves smarter than the evil they perform, and they are always mistaken.

Finally, one cannot combat evil, especially the evil within, on one's own. You cannot be good by yourself. One of the first defenses against evil is to acknowledge that one needs help against it. Confession is good for the soul not only because it performs a therapeutic cleansing of the impurities that clog the spiritual bloodstream but because to address it in confession immediately objectifies the evil and places one in a community outside of oneself. Evil's greatest ally is solitary silence. The Roman Catholic Church long understood this in its rites of auricular confession. The sinner had to name the sin to a priest and to accept responsibility for the thought, word, or deed. The sinner then had to accept a penance as an act of expiation and contrition, and then the sinner had to promise an amendment of life. This was not "private," in the sense of a psychiatrist's conversation with a client, but an exercise done in the name of the community of the faithful.

Public liturgical confession helps to accomplish the same goals. It is a point worth making that those religious traditions within which acts of confession both private and public are minimized or nonexistent are those traditions in which a wise and necessary restraint to evil masquerading as moral zealousness is missing. Confession of sins helps articulate what the sins are and acknowledges the trespass, it calls upon God and the community to witness the confession and to assist in the amendment of life, and it reassures the penitent that he or she is not alone either in the sin or in the redemption from it.

Now indeed one could take the self-righteous prayer of the biblical Pharisee as one's own: "I thank thee, Lord, that I am not as others are," and one could argue, "I am confessing on behalf of those other people who need it." If I am right that the person who seeks after righteousness and is anxious to know and to do the good knows his or her sin and recognizes that sin as a reality and not an abstraction in his or her life, that tinny moral boasting of the Pharisee will be seen for the whistling in the dark that it really is.

Good people do bad things because good people are not good enough. They have to fight and to outwit a superior enemy, and they need all the help they can get to do it, all the time. The Bible reminds us over and over again that Satan, the personification of evil, is not interested in the wicked, but in the righteous. Therefore those who would be righteous, or hunger or thirst after it, are and always have been

Satan's prime targets. It is to amplify this fact for the sake of our spiritual welfare that the gospels make the first encounter Jesus has after his baptism an encounter with Satan himself. We are meant both to take notice and to take what we notice very seriously indeed. With evil working overtime, virtue cannot be a hobby.

CHAPTER 13

THE BIBLE AND TEMPTATION

WHOEVER could devise a cure for temptation would be richer even than the discoverer of the cure for the common cold, or the successful alchemist who is able to turn base metals into gold. People for whom abstract theories of sin and evil are just that can easily observe a daily existential experience of the moral combat called temptation—the would-be dieter. She knows that it is in her absolute best interest to maintain the healthy regimen upon which she and her advisers have embarked; she knows what is good and what is bad for her in this regard. She is not ignorant of the facts, and perhaps indeed knows more than is necessary for her to know about nutrition, for all food and drink have been reduced to grams, ounces, calories, and carbohydrates; and the aesthetics of eating are subordinated to the rational process of achieving and maintaining an ideal weight. Moral self-interestedness is not only clear but easily measured and monitored, and yet no day passes, not even an hour of it, when visions of chocolate indulgence or the imagined smell of hot buttered popcorn, or some other forbidden delight fails to initiate moral warfare. To resist the diet buster is understood to be a short-term sacrifice for a long-term gain, and deprivation becomes the moral substitute for gratification. To yield and eat is an exercise of the will, but the instant gratification is instantly overcome by a sense of guilt and a renewed resolve not to do so again, thus raising the stakes for the next level of encounter.

Substitute the keeping of a diet for fidelity in marriage, honesty in finance, truth telling in conversation, responsibility in conduct, and we have the wretched pathology of human moral ambition and human moral failure. We can call the act, whatever it is when we betray our moral ambition, "sin." We can call the interior reaction to our own knowledge of that failure, "shame," and we know that the phenomenon that ignites this seemingly ineluctable transaction is called "temptation."

Temptation is older than sin and the mother of shame. More than sex, with which from ancient times it has been most intimately associated, temptation is the single greatest source of human anxiety. In the thousands of people with whom I have counseled over the years of my ministry, I have found the problem of temptation to be at the heart of their personal anxiety. Very few people have come to me lacking knowledge of what is good for them or bad for them. People generally are not ignorant, and to suggest that they are generally sells them short. If people were truly ignorant or uninformed there would be neither wrong nor sin, and certainly no shame, for all of these require a sense of transgression, a knowledge of error, and hence a sense of right: You don't know *it's* wrong if you don't know *what's* wrong. So, the young man who cheats on an examination in order to better his chances for admission to the graduate school of his choice knows that he has done a wrong thing. He knows that the desirable end does not justify his wrong deed, and he feels appropriate shame, although not yet enough to risk his ill-gained advantage by repudiating his actions and facing the music. When I asked a certain young man why he did it, his answer was simple: "I wanted what I could get, and I knew of no other way of getting it." It is as pure an answer under the circumstances as that which Willie Sutton, the famous bank robber of a generation ago, gave when asked why he robbed banks: "Because that's where the money is."

My young man's situation, however, was more complicated than that of Willie Sutton. My young friend did not act out of mere expedience. He cheated, he said, because he felt powerless to do otherwise. He knew what the choices were but he had no choice, so he felt. He was under the power of a force beyond the scope of his moral compass. He was, in short, tempted, and like those before and after him, he yielded. He was not fundamentally wicked, evil, perverse, or a moral cripple; he was human, and where temptation is concerned, that is good, or bad, enough. Of course he is not alone. He has lots of company in the Bible, and the Bible, if it is anything at all, is an essay in the genealogy of temptation. We will look at three heroic instances of temptation, and the struggle with it, in the Bible. The first of these is the story with which the Bible begins its narrative of the human condition, the account of Adam and Eve and the temptation in the Garden of Eden. The second is the account of Jesus' temptation, not in a garden but in the wilderness, at the beginning of his ministry, an account that takes pride of place in the gospels of Matthew, Mark, and Luke. The third instance is the account in I Corinthians 10 of Saint Paul's struggle with what he calls his "thorn in the flesh," an allegory, I suggest, of the great apostle's temptations.

In the Beginning Was Temptation

We do not think of Oscar Wilde as either a theologian or a biblical scholar, but in the aphorism he puts into the mouth of Lord Darlington, in *Lady Windermere's Fan*, he proves himself insightful in both callings: "I can resist everything except temptation." This is, of course, the trouble in paradise, the trouble with Adam and Eve. The problem, contra Augustine, is not sex, nor is it obedience, and it isn't even evil as such. It is temptation, and the inability of men and women to resist it.

Temptation as an abstraction does not work very well, and that is why the writers of Genesis are at very great pains to give temptation a personality, a *persona*, a character. It is a sort of incarnation, and the first in the Bible. When orthodox Christians think of an incarnation they tend to think, and rightly so, of *the* Incarnation, that divine Word made flesh in Jesus and described in the glorious prologue to the gospel of Saint John, "and the Word became flesh and dwelt among us." That is the manifestation or the enfleshment of God in terms that human beings can begin to understand. The incarnation in Genesis of which I speak is also an enfleshment—not of the divine will or person but of the opposite force which temptation represents in its invitation to evil. Thus, temptation is given the form of the serpent; a name, the Tempter; and qualities we will recognize and even appreciate: He is called the subtlest of all the creatures. Adam and Eve are thus far morally neutral. They have no personalities, no characters, and no distinguishing characteristics other than that they should be companions to each other and serve as caretakers of the Garden. They are not even instructed to worship God, or to be good and kind to one another. They are, of course, forbidden to eat of the fruit of the tree, but that commandment tells us more about the anxieties of God than it does about the characters or personalities of Adam and Eve.

Thus it is that the serpent has all the best lines, and we are meant to understand that the serpent is the actor and that Adam and Eve are acted upon. There is neither any one nor any thing to shield them from the impact of this, the mother of all temptations. It reminds one of the Victor Borge set piece where the Danish comic recalls a conversation between Adam and Eve before the Fall, where Eve, in a fit of unanticipated jealousy, asks Adam, "Do you really love me?" And Adam replies, "Who else?" It is the intention of Genesis to give us as clear and uncluttered a view of the moral stage as possible, so that we will not fail to get it.

What is "it"? First, that temptation is as old as creation itself and is not an exception to the created order but inherent in it. Those who look to the environment as the cause of social and moral ills will find little comfort here. Eden is no corrupt urban environment filled with evil and moral ambiguity. It is the smallest unit of human society, a suburban paradise without children or neighbors, and those who argue that the dilemma of Eden is to be found in the failure of character in Adam and Eve, that somehow they should have "known better," or "done something," want to turn them into plaster moralists or rationalists, willfully and ignorantly participating in their own destruction. Such an analysis gets "it" wrong. Historically, Christian doctrine since Augustine has been so eager to foist responsibility for the original sin upon Adam and Eve without blaming God for the problem of evil, that it has tended to risk the minimalization of the naked, coercive, subtle power of the tempter and his temptation.

Hebrew readings of the Adam and Eve story,

not burdened with making the case for the doctrine of original sin, and confident of God's role in the enterprise, tend to focus on the irresistibility of the tempter's blandishments. The first moral decision is impossible to make in the absence of evil and the temptation that leads to it. Thus, in trying to explain both the origins of the human race and its inescapable dilemmas, those who constructed the story of Adam and Eve placed emphasis neither upon the virtue nor upon the vice of these ancestral figures, but upon the sophistication, attractiveness, and subtlety of the tempting force with which they in their moral ignorance must now contend. The tempter does have the best lines; they are natural and reasonable, and thus make it very clear from the beginning that nature and what is natural, and rationality and what is reasonable, are suspect, and part of the problem rather than the solution to the human dilemma. In paradise nature and reason may be seen to be morally neutral, but as the drama is constructed, it is clear that these neutral means are easily put to bad uses, with disastrous consequences for those who do not know better.

The proximity of temptation to creation, and the overwhelming success of that first temptation within earshot of God, as it were, is meant to remind those who hear and read this story that temptation is a primal force to be reckoned with, never to be underestimated, and is forever a part of the human condition. If our foreparents, uncorrupted by a world not yet old enough to have gone sour, lost their innocence to the beguiler, the old deluder, the tempter, what reason have we as their descendants to expect that we will be spared their trouble? Neither temptation nor its agent, the tempter, have been banished from the created order. The punishment accorded Adam and Eve for their disobedience, their yielding to temptation, is not simply exile from Eden and innocence; it is exile to live forever with the very source of their trouble in their midst. In the moral household of the human being after Eden, temptation is the man who came to dinner and remains a permanent though unwelcome guest. To be human, therefore, is to live in daily proximity to temptation.

Temptations and the Sensible Soul

Temptations to evil and wickedness are understandable. Faustian bargains with their Baroque entreaties and Gothic deals are the stuff of which moral melodrama is composed. Familiarity with the idiom tempts us to believe that we will recognize such dangers when we see them, and that we will also take appropriate measures. We sympathize with the remark of Mae West, who said, "I was pure as the driven snow until I drifted." We smile because we think we know better, but what about those temptations that seduce on behalf not of evil but of good? What about those temptations that do not, at first, tempt our self-indulgence but rather our sensibility for the good? I suggest that more people are subject to temptation in an effort to do good than they are in pursuit of pure evil or pleasure. Temptation masquerades most cleverly in areas of moral ambiguity where good people can be tempted either to do good things for the wrong reason, or bad things for a good and high purpose. Self-deception, pride, and moral ambition are the means whereby temptation engages the soul, and in the name of virtue vice is given aid and comfort. Thus temptation appeals most particularly to those who would think of themselves as good, and who pursue the good as a goal they themselves are capable of bringing to pass.

Temptation thus appeals to moral vanity. Goodness is inevitably the host for the parasitical temptation, and thus goodness must be constantly addressed and challenged. When people ask why preachers waste their time on the people in their pews, "preaching to the converted" or "preaching to the choir," they fail to understand that it is those who aspire to goodness who most need to be reminded of and protected against the dangers of the moral ambiguity that is the seed of temptation. Those who are in church are like those who are in a hospital; they are not there because they are specimens of virtue or health. They are there because they know their needs. Hospitals are not healthier places than other places, but in the hospital the weapons to fight the illness are ready to hand. So too is it with the church.

This is the context and these are the considerations that compel our attention when we look at the famous series of temptations with which Jesus is confronted at the beginning of his ministry, encounters recorded in the gospels of Matthew, Mark, and Luke. The prominence given to these temptation stories suggests that their themes and concerns are of high value to the communities of believers in Jesus. These encounters with temptation at the start of the public ministry are also meant to describe the persistence and perversity of temptation in the life of Jesus, and in the life of all those who would aspire to godliness and the good life. The nearer one lives in proximity to God, contrary to our expectations, the greater is the influence of temptation.

This paradox is driven home by the placement of Jesus' temptation in the wilderness to his baptism. Baptism is seen as the high point of one's spiritual life, the cleansing of the stain of sin, the washing away of the claims of the lower life upon the higher. Some even think of baptism as an innoculation against sin and temptation. Thus it is something of an irony that Jesus is tempted immediately after baptism and not before it. The temptations are not a form of hazing before he is allowed to enter the fraternity of the holy and good life. Quite the contrary. The temptations in some very real sense are the consequences of a life set apart for goodness and God's will. That is why they follow directly upon that moment of consecration and dedication; there is no one more desirable to Satan, more susceptible to Satan, than the one who has just given his or her life to God. Jesus and his temptations remind us that the good life is the context of the ultimate struggle with evil. I am convinced that this construction of these episodes in the early ministry of Jesus is no accident, no mere formal chronology. The gospel writers have an acute instinct for those situations that help animate Jesus' investment in the realities of the moral life in the real world. No Olympian recluse, Jesus must be seen to be engaged with the real forces of this world that argue for evil and that appeal to the best in people in order to seduce them into bondage to that very evil.

It is not only proximity that makes this case, however, but the very nature of the temptations themselves that reveals the subtlety of those forces for evil that would lay siege to the soul. We recall that subtlety was the chief characteristic of the serpent in the account of Adam and Eve, and the uncanny ability to appeal to the desire and curiosity of the human being; and we get it wrong again if we focus all our attention in the temptation story of Jesus on his ability to withstand and overcome Satan. We like moral winners, and we expect Jesus to win, and applaud when he does, but the point here is not so much the victory of Jesus, real as it is. The point ought to be the reasonableness of the temptations themselves and the craft with which they are offered. It is no longer Jesus who will be subjected to these blandishments but his followers and successors, among whom are to be counted ourselves. We have much more in common with hapless Adam and Eve than with Jesus, in coping with the artful deceptions of that chief deluder, Satan. Thus we should pay attention to the Satanic strategy, the appeal to our better instincts, the manipulations of what the Book of Common Prayer calls "the devices and desires of our own hearts," which alone are not sufficient to wage moral combat against temptation.

The three temptations that Satan places before Jesus in the wilderness appeal to three ideals of the good life to which Jesus and all who would follow him in holiness would ordinarily be attracted. These ideals are spirituality, power, and faith. What religious person would be immune to the divine possibilities for good and goodness inherent in each of these qualities? Who has not yearned after one or all of them? Who could not use any or all of these to enormous benefit for the well-being of the world? The religious aspirant, the soul-sensitive man or woman, is not easily bought with silver or gold, or the glittering prizes of earthly success, but who can resist the moral allure of spirituality, power, and faith, all to be used, of course, in the service of God and in the help of the people of God? We must give Satan the highest possible marks for recognizing these admirable qualities as our points of vulnerability rather than of strength. Appealing to these demonstrates that Satan knows us better than we know ourselves, and certainly better than we know him. It is this point, I believe, that the gospel writers are at pains to demonstrate to us for our good, and the temptation of Jesus at each of these points is their means to do it.

Is it fair to regard the first temptation, the invitation to turn stones into bread, as an exercise in spiritual pride? I think that it is, but we must consider the context of that temptation in order to make the case. Luke sets the stage: "Jesus, full of the Holy Spirit, returned from the Jordan and was led by the Spirit for forty days in the wilderness, tempted by the devil. And he ate nothing in those days; and when they were ended, he was hungry." (Luke 4:1–2) Jesus is on a spiritual retreat, disciplining his soul, mortifying the flesh so that the spirit housed within it can flourish. His first temptation occurs at the conclusion of this season of acute loneliness, physical hunger, and spiritual tension. All of the senses are on edge; Jesus is a moral athlete at the height of his training, and as all who have ever attempted a season of intense training—physical, spiritual, or intellectual—realize, the demons that one attempts to monitor, control, and indeed overcome do not diminish in their ferocity as one develops more skills to cope with them. No. Like a deadly cancer they develop new resources to combat our vaccines and develop new and frightening resistances to our cures. Evil, like cancer, does have a mind, a will, and a strategy, and temptation is the maneuvering device that doesn't stay still or in the same place long enough for our cumulative resistance to have any useful effect. Thus, at the end of his temptation—and the gospel is clear that these temptations occur at the end rather than at the beginning of the fast—Jesus is more rather than less susceptible to the wiles of the Tempter.

Spiritual pride suggests that if we practice and study, and keep steady in our moral diet and regimen, we will be equal to any force that comes our way. Infected as we are by the doctrine that more is better, and by the athletic metaphors that suggest that when a ninety-pound weakling pumps up and beefs out, he will then be able to whip the bully who had heretofore intimidated and humiliated him, we think that when we are strong spirtually and physically we are invulnerable to attack. It is that very conceit that Satan uses against us, like the tactic of using your enemy's superior weight against him in a wrestling match.

Satan invites Jesus, in his physical hunger, to turn stones into bread. The first level of inquiry would suggest that this is little more than asking Jesus to satisfy his own need for nourishment by performing a harmless and useful trick. Satan is asking Jesus to prove that he has attained the spiritual wherewithal to solve a simple problem: "If you are the Son of God" is the taunting bait that Satan uses here. In other words, if you are who you say you are, and if your God is really who you say he is, and if your spiritual exercises have had any effect, prove it by this simple demonstration.

Spiritual pride would easily tempt us to respond in kind; it would be to the honor of God, a demonstration of spiritual superiority, and an appropriate rebuke to an audacious doubter who by the performance of this action should be won over to the faith. Christians are always eager to prove that "my God is bigger than yours," and spirituality, that benighted buzzword of the late twentieth century, tempts us so often to play such games. The amateur martial-arts student is always susceptible to the vanity of smashing a plank or a pile of bricks to prove to doubting onlookers that his years of practice and discipline have paid off, and that his deprivations have been rewarded by a new and terrifying skill. The onlookers will be impressed by such a display of power, and the reputation of the would-be Karate Kid will be forever established by a single blow or kick. Scholars of the martial arts, however, remind us that the skills of karate and the other disciplines are not meant to be displayed as parlor tricks or mere entertainment. These skills are only to be employed when necessary, and in fact, their greatest power lies in their potential. Those who are powerful in these dangerous arts are so because of their capacity for deterrence rather than for their mere demonstration.

Spirituality is an attitude, not a set of actions designed to impress the otherwise unedified, but the spiritually immature are those who are easily tempted to "prove" their new skills and to test them out, "kicking the tires" of the soul, so to speak. It is in those moments that spirituality can so easily be abused and manipulated. Jesus is not prepared to squander the spiritual gifts he has cultivated in the wilderness simply to impress Satan or to prove the validity of that gift to his skeptical antagonist. He is unwilling to play the game of "Gotcha!" just for the momentary satisfaction of winning, for to do so is to play Satan's game by Satan's rules.

Most of us would not be able to resist that offer, however, and for the best of reasons—"our" God is on our side, and we can prove it. Then, while giving God the glory, we take what really counts in the game, the credit; and people will see our piety, our morality, and our superior spirituality, and admire us for it. This first temptation is meant to remind us that spirituality is a matter of substance and not of signs. Satan and the world require signs, proofs, incontestable evidence that we and our God can deliver the goods, and we are sorely tempted to provide these proofs and signs to confound the bullies of this world.

If Only I Had the Power, Then I Would Do Good

Religious people in general, and Christians in particular, feel powerless in their religion because they do not feel that they have a power that the world takes seriously. Thus, religious people want to be taken seriously by the world and so they seek after power, and it is in this ambition for power in the world that Satan makes use of religious people. The second temptation of Jesus is an exercise in the temptation of power wrapped in the chameleon desire to do good and on such a massive scale that the world will have to take notice.

"And the devil took him up, and showed him

all the kingdoms of the world in a moment of time, and said to him, 'To you I will give all this authority and their glory; for it has been delivered to me, and I give it to whom I will. If you, then, shall worship me, it shall all be yours.'" (Luke 4:5–7) This is how the second temptation is introduced. Classical commentators have often seized upon the Devil's presumption in claiming the kingdoms of this world as his own. He is promising to give away that which does not belong to him, and so his promise is based upon a lie. That is true, but that is also the easy way out. The kingdoms of this world may in fact not belong to Satan, but it is an ancient principle of the common law that possession is nine tenths of the law, and to all intents and purposes the Devil seems much in possession of the kingdoms of this world. He may not be the lawful owner or the landlord, but he is a very effective squatter, and there is little realistic doubt of his ability to deliver worldly power to whom he will. He has had remarkable success in this transaction to date, and so appeals to legal pieties are neither helpful nor persuasive.

What this really is about is trafficking in the tempting power of power, which in the minds of the faithful in all places and in all ages would be a preemptive strike for virtue and goodness. Think about how much time and effort would be saved on the part of the righteous if they could command goodness and orchestrate secular power in its behalf. We should remember the irony of Satan's proposition here in Luke's gospel. Those who first read it, the dispersed and defeated followers of a Lord whose kingdom was not of and not intended for this world, would have found the notion of a powerful religious state, Christian or Jewish, laughable. What Satan was offering Jesus was nothing that any follower of Jesus would want. It is only after the formation of a stable cultural and political force in a world not yet dissolved in favor of the kingdom of heaven that this second temptation in fact becomes tempting.

The record is not encouraging. The Holy Roman Empire was never a good example of either statecraft or of Christianity, and the modern efforts at theocracy, whether in Calvin's Geneva or in Oliver Cromwell's England, proved equally venial. The Puritan oligarchs of New England gave it a good try in the seventeenth century, but it became pretty clear that religion and power do not mix well, particularly when religion has the power. In contemporary America, despite the Bible's chary attitude toward the state, many Christians cultivate civil and political power in order to exercise a biblical rule over the state. Power to do good and thereby to compel a more just and moral society is the kind of theocratic illusion that has always proved such a tempting ambition to religious fundamentalists who, in the name of God, would seize power to compel others to righteousness. The English and New English Puritans of the seventeenth century, the Islamic fundamentalists, and the American Christian Coalition, among other religious constituencies, have all flirted with the seductions of power, all for very good and high-sounding reasons, and all with questionable, even dangerous consequences not simply for the secular order but for the proponents of this power themselves. Lord Acton's famous dictum on power's capacity to corrupt is absolutely true, and when such power is compounded with a sense of moral purity and absolutism, the corrosive force on those who possess and wield such power is utterly corrupting, because virtue and the capacity to compel are neither the same thing nor necessarily complementary. Not to know that is to be subject to the one who does, and that is Satan. This is the lesson that Jesus teaches when he rejects the power Satan so wantonly offers him in the second temptation. The temptation to do good with that power simply is not good enough.

To Tempt God Is Not Faith, but Sin

The third temptation is little more than a naked abuse of faith, turning a virtue into a vice. To believe that God can do anything is one thing; to ask God to do something to see if God can do anything is an abuse of belief, a testing of God. That is not faith, that is sin. Satan wants two things here: He wants Jesus to prove his own belief in God, and he wants God to prove that God is God. Thus, he invites Jesus to throw himself down from the tower of the Temple. If Jesus believes in the goodness of God he will not be afraid to risk his own life in this seemingly suicidal act; and if God is good, the good God will not allow Jesus in his swan dive from the tower to come to any harm. From Satan's point of view, the added incentive to this heroic gesture would be to witness to Satan the ultimacy of one's faith in God. Like the appeal to power, and the earlier one to spirituality, this appeal to faith encourages a dramatic shortcut in the tedious journey of moral perfection. Satan offers these racy, bottom-line opportunities, and they are tempting because they offer in an instant what it would take a lifetime to accomplish through preaching and teaching disciplined evangelism and slow, steady spiritual growth. That is the lure of the get-rich-quick schemes, and that is why the unwary are so susceptible to them.

To tempt God, for this is what Jesus rightly charges Satan with attempting to do, is not an exercise in faith but rather in doubt. It is to put God to the test, and to make God satisfy our need for satisfaction and reassurance, thus subordinating God to a human agenda. For any believer in God this is an unacceptable consideration. This makes the Creator the agent of the creature, when faith maintains that it is just the other way around. Faith thus manipulated by a subtle tempter and a needy believer becomes an abuse of confidence in the divine rather than an expression of it, and the abuser is revealed to be a creature of anxiety rather than of faith. Tempting God then is to try to get God to act in such a way as to satisfy our agenda. Certain Christians in the mountains of Tennessee who practice the rites of snake handling do so as a testimonial to the power of their faith in God, God's faith in them, and their faith in the Bible. Acting upon their reading of Mark 16:18, "They will pick up serpents, and if they drink any deadly thing, it will not hurt them," they incorporate into their worship the handling of poisonous snakes. The theory is that God will not allow them to be bitten. The fact of the matter is that many of them *are* bitten, and die from their wounds. To many, the handling of snakes in such a fashion, due respect to cultural diversity and sensitivity notwithstanding, is more foolishness than faith, and is the sort of thing against which Jesus rebuked Satan when in this third temptation to manipulate faith, he said, "Thou shalt not tempt the Lord thy God."

Beware Your Strong Points;
They Are Spiritual Land Mines

One of Saint Paul's consistent themes is the danger of spiritual overconfidence, a form of moral arrogance that overestimates one's own abilities and underestimates those of Satan. No moral shrinking violet himself, Paul certainly could speak with existential authority about the dangers of moral and spiritual self-confidence. He thought he knew all he needed to know and was beyond learning in piety and knowledge, a moral aristocrat; yet it was he who in his spiritual blindness was the zealous persecutor of the church of God. Saul, as he was before his conversion, was not just a spear carrier in the movement against the Christians; he was a self-promoting, ambitious agent of persecutions. He reminds one of those fanatical Jewish settlers in modern Israel who, so attuned to the righteousness of their cause, hear God's instructions in their ears to murder those who stand in the way of their particular vision. Nothing less than a colossal clout on the head on the Damascus Road and a confrontation with the risen Christ was sufficient to get Saul's attention, and to turn him from the persecutor of the church into the Apostle to the Gentiles.

We are therefore to take his counsels on overconfidence and spiritual arrogance, the greatest temptations for all believers, seriously. In I Corinthians 10:12, he writes, "Therefore let any one who thinks that he stands take heed lest he fall." He then goes on to a discussion of temptation, encouraging the faithful not to believe that they have been tempted any more than anyone else, for such a belief would itself be another form of spiritual pride. He then reminds them that God is faithful, and "he will not let you be tempted beyond your strength, but with the temptation will also provide the way to escape, that you may be able to endure it." (I Corinthians 10:13)

Paul does not demonstrate his observation by citing the gospel accounts of Jesus' temptation, but we know how Jesus in fact both escaped and endured the subtle snares of the tempter. He recalled in every instance the instruction of scripture, the teachings of an inherited faith to which he subordinated himself in his debates with the tempter. He didn't outfox or even outmaneuver Satan; he simply relied on those things he knew to be trustworthy and true, and therefore, because he had the big picture, he could not be intimidated by the tempting little scenario. Adam and Eve had nothing to fall back upon but their own ignorance and desires. Jesus is the model for addressing temptation, and Paul, by implication, supplies the formula for those who must every day deal with temptations that seem designed to move them farther and farther from God.

It is Paul's conviction that we are enabled to endure what we must bear, or, as our grandparents might have said, "God gives us burdens, and the strength to bear them." This is a view out of fashion in our contemporary vision of ourselves as put-upon victims. We have been promised the pursuit of happiness, and yet these burdens and temptations come to taunt us and to slow us down. They are more punishment than opportunity, and unless we are masochists, it is hard to see temptation or any other burden as a spiritually edifying exercise.

The Bible, however, is not a product of the culture of happiness and personal satisfaction. Biblical religion is not an exercise in self-improvement and private therapy. The Bible is an account of people who in their sinful pride are confronted with a vision of holiness to which they then aspire and to which they are assisted by a holy and gracious God who spares nothing in the morally ambitious exercise of re-creating his own people in his own image by any means necessary. One of those means, implicit throughout all of scripture, and made explicit both in the accounts of the temptations of Jesus and in this discourse on temptation by Saint Paul, is the right and creative use of temptation itself.

Yes, there is a right and creative use of temptation, for temptation is designed to show us what and whom we are up against, and what we can do about it. Like all testing, temptation is meant to strengthen us and build up our endurance; we are not meant to yield but to endure, and, indeed, to overcome. To remind us of this, Paul tells us that God does not and will not tempt us beyond our endurance. So, if we feel we are tempted beyond what we can do or know, we are to explore beyond what we do or know to discover that about ourselves which God already knows and is calling into active service. The adventure of temptation is the adventure now of self-discovery, of learning more about self, and of learning more about God.

Beating the Odds of Temptation

In the gospel meetings of our youth, many of us used to sing an old hymn called "Yield Not to Temptation":

Yield not to temptation, for yielding is sin;
Each vict'ry will help you some other to win;
Fight manfully onward; dark passions subdue;

399

Look ever to Jesus—He will carry you
through.
Ask the Saviour to help you, comfort,
strengthen, and keep you;
He is willing to aid you, He will carry you
through.

Most of us of a certain age associate that hymn with those rambunctiously hormonal years of our adolescence when our bodies were telling us things of which our Sunday school teachers and parents never dared speak. I think we thought it was all about sex and the subduing of those "dark passions," for what else could temptation be about? After all, it was sex that got Adam and Eve into trouble in the first place, was it not? It is, I think, a sign of real spiritual maturity when one comes to the realization that temptation is about more than sex. Realizing that liberates the old hymn for a wider purpose than simply the preservation of teenaged evangelical chastity—itself, however, an admirable purpose—and we are able to realize that in the matter of temptation, as Saint Paul reminds us, God is faithful and does not allow us to be tempted beyond our endurance.

From this I take four points to help us in our temptations, all of which are derived from biblical principles and examples. These are:

1. Name the temptation.
2. Name the tempter.
3. Practice resistance.
4. Call for help.

In naming the temptation we identify what it is that we are tempted to do; we are morally explicit so that we know exactly what it is we are talking about. When contemplating evil, it is always better to contemplate evil in particular rather than in general. When we find ourselves caught in a moral dilemma, we should give that dilemma a name. Naming it gives both it and our attempts to deal with it a reality and a focus.

When we name the tempter we are also giving reality to the temptation, and we are making it clear that there is a force, a personality, a will outside and beyond us that is making an illegitimate claim upon us. So, if the temptation is infidelity to a spouse or partner, name the "other person" so that you realize that you are not consorting with an abstraction. Perhaps a better way of putting this is a call to unmask the delusion under which you are operating. You may justify your petty embezzlement from your thankless job because you are using the money to pay the medical bills of your sick mother, or you are putting your child through college, or you are even contributing to charity. The delusion is your good end. To unmask it is to realize that you are stealing. The naked delusion may in fact help you to come to your senses.

To practice resistance may seem so obvious as not to be worthy of inclusion in a discussion of how to overcome temptation, but because it is so obvious it is often overlooked, and its therapeutic values are lost. In the recovery of moral education that has been sweeping the country in recent years, we have discovered what the ancients always knew, and that is that virtue is a habit. It is not just a series of admonitions, exhortations, and a code of conduct. Virtue is all of that, but it is much, much more. It is a habit, the accumulated and consistent practice of certain behaviors based upon certain beliefs. The chief of these beliefs is that the practice of virtue is a series of actions that, while unnatural at first, become, like brushing the teeth, what one does as a matter of course. Eventually the habit is so ingrained and established that it becomes not only what one does, but indivisible from who one is. Moral training, like any other form of training—we can think of music and of athletics, for example—takes discipline to acquire. That discipline is designed to be experienced, tested, in the exceptions and not the routines. Temptation is the exception in which the moral disciplines are designed to operate. The practice of resistance to that which is likely to tempt not only wards off that particular temptation but provides the means with which to resist other temptations as well.

Finally, in the matter of temptation, again as Saint Paul reminds us, do not rely upon your own resources. "Therefore, let anyone who thinks that he stands take heed lest he fall." This is the New Testament version of Proverbs 16:18, "Pride goeth before destruction, and a haughty spirit before a fall," which is, of course, the ancestor of the secular aphorism, "Pride goeth before a fall." Relying on one's own strength and understanding in the matter of temptation, no matter how spiritually alert one is, is a recipe for disaster. So call for help. Talk about your temptation with one in whom you can confide—a friend, a colleague, your confessor, priest, pastor, or spiritual director. Most important, call on God for help, knowing that God has not sent you this temptation to taunt you but to strengthen you. Lay claim upon that promised strength. Practice the art of divine dependence while exercising all of your graces and gifts. You will discover, as the ancients knew, that temptation is not simply the devil's recreation, it is also for the faithful a school for the soul. Perhaps in this age obsessed with physical exercise and the cult of the health club, we should say that temptation is the gym of the soul, and the faithful take its benefits: dexterity, agility, strength, endurance, and the developing confidence of one who is now more and more able to give the devil a run for his money.

CHAPTER 14

THE BIBLE AND WEALTH

Drama in the Church

ASK any group of people who has ever attended a Sunday service in a Protestant church what it considers to be the most exciting or dynamic part of that service, and while a few will say it is the sermon, most will answer, "The offering." This is not because people generally like the offering or are inclined to natural generosity, but rather because in the structure of most public worship the offering appears to be the point of focus and dramatic intensity. Think about it. Except for the hymns, and in liturgical churches, the kneeling, the offering is the first time the people are actually asked to participate, or invited to do something. There is movement in the aisles as ushers pass the plates, always an exciting diversion to children, and the liturgical tension is relaxed as people shift about. Often there is music accompanying the process, and then comes the climax: The music comes to a great crescendo before making a glitzy transition into a doxology, the congregation leaps up, and down the center aisle marches a procession of men and women carrying plates of cash. The ushers arrive at the front of the church—which has now become a theater—and with the audience on its feet, and at the crescendo, the plates are handed over to the minister, who in many traditions raises them up high over his head in the most dramatic posture of the service, and then places them with great reverence on the altar or holy table. Music, minister, and people then settle down for whatever is to follow—sermon, prayers, or benediction, but it is clear to anyone with the slightest hint of show biz that the climactic moment has come and gone, and invariably will come again; and that it is all about money.

Given the primacy of the ceremonial act of the offertory, one would think that money and worship, among Protestants at least, is a congenial relationship, but we all know that is not necessarily the case. Money, in fact, among Christians is a bit like sex. We know we need it but we don't like to make too much of it in public. Protestants have guilt complexes for every condition, and here is one that involves a conflict between the allegedly spiritual dimensions of worship on the one hand and the unambiguously material dimensions of money on the other. There is the old aphorism that a too spiritual religion is of no earthly good, but there remains among middle-class Protestants the distinct sense of bad form as far as money and religion are concerned.

This has never been a problem among black Christians. I remember very well the excitement of the offering in the little Bethel African Methodist Episcopal Church in Plymouth, Massachusetts, where I worshiped as a child fifty years ago. The custom of long standing in Bethel Church, and still in use in many rural African-American churches today, was for the congregation to take their gifts to the table at the front of the church, and thus there was even more movement and excitement than in those churches where the plate was passed among the people. Here the people got up while singing rousing hymns and made their way up front with their gifts in hand, and, wonder of wonders, the stewards counted it as the process continued. At the end of that procession, if the day's financial goal had not been achieved, the congregation would be asked to pass up front again, and so on until the desired goal was reached. The minister would say, "We need only fifteen more dollars. Who will stand up for Jesus and give him fifteen dollars?" The congregation would sing some more, the stewards would count some more, and only when it was settled would the doxology be sung and the prayer of thanksgiving offered. It was high theater for a child, with the whole congregation on view and in motion, the murmuring of the stewards as they counted, the relentless rhythm of the singing, and the anxious moments while awaiting the result.

It was also the perfect example of what one of America's most famous black preachers, Father Divine, called "the art of tangibilitation." From his Harlem "Heaven" in the 1930s, Father Divine would urge the throngs who attended his services to make their faith real by the reality of their gifts: "You got to learn how to tangibilitate!" he would thunder, and the people would bring their tangible gifts and lay them, New Testament style, at his feet. The black church has never had a problem with the problem of the material, and it may be because the black church has had so little of the material goods of this world with which to have a problem. White Christians who visit black churches are often surprised and not a little shocked at the number of offerings given, and with the fine art of encouraging the people to generosity. It takes them some time to realize that in the black church the giving of money is not a necessary concession to the material needs of the people of God, but that rather it is the central drama in the act of worship.

It is a question of what is nicely called stewardship, which in the church means the wise and prudent use of one's resources. In theory, stewardship implies that one's money is not really one's own; one holds it in trust from God and for the benefit of others. As we used to sing in Sunday school:

> *We give thee but thine own,*
> *Whate'er the gift may be;*
> *All that we have is thine alone,*
> *A trust, O Lord, from thee.*

Though we may sing it, however, very few modern Christians actually believe it. Francis Ridley Havergal wrote the hymn much beloved of Episcopalians, "Take My Life, and Let It Be," the fourth verse of which reads, "Take my silver and my gold, not a mite would I withhold," and the thought of J.P. Morgan or August Belmont—or any other of the "Episcocrats," as Kit and Frederica Konolige call them in their book on the Episcopalians as America's ruling class—giving up their precious metal is enough to generate an undecorous guffaw. "God gave me my money" is the famous remark of John D. Rockefeller, the wealthiest man in the country; and even those who might not have as much as he would have some sympathy with his point.

The theory of stewardship has sound biblical foundations, as we shall see, but theory often runs afoul of practice and raises the irksome questions of the relationship between money and virtue, between money and religion, between the material and the spiritual, and between faith and wealth. Every minister who has ever had to preach a stewardship sermon, or run an every-member canvass, or solicit funds for benevolences, missions, or building campaigns, knows the dis-ease in relationships with parishoners that comes when he or she must get down to cases and talk to the individual about questions of money; and every person who has ever endured one of these efforts knows the clammy feeling that comes at the prospect of having to face these money questions. Our inhibitions in talking about money stem in part from the fear that we will somehow be manipulated into doing something we would rather not do or cannot afford to do, or that we will be made somehow to feel guilty because we are unable or unwilling to respond at the level that we are asked.

This is Benjamin Franklin's famous experience, of which he speaks in his autobiography, when he went to hear the famous evangelist George Whitefield preach in Philadelphia. It was said that Whitefield could make grown men cry with the mere pronunciation of the word *Mesopotamia,* and Whitefield on this occasion was soliciting funds for his orphanage in Georgia. Franklin was determined to resist his appeals. In Franklin's words,

I happened soon after to attend one of his sermons, in the course of which I perceived he intended to finish with a collection, and I silently resolved he should get nothing from me. I had in my pocket a handful of copper money, three or four silver dollars, and five pistoles in gold. As he proceeded I began to soften and concluded to give the coppers. Another stroke of his oratory made me ashamed of that and determined me to give the silver; and he finished so admirably that I emptied my pocket wholly into the collector's dish, gold and all.

Would that all sermons had that effect but they do not, and the problem of wealth, and the appropriate obligations of the believer in regard to faith and money, is one of the persistent problems of the age, which, in this most materialistic of times and with most spiritually ambitious people, is a problem that really ought to be addressed. Quite rightly we may ask whether in the Bible there is any guidance on the question of wealth and faith.

What Does the Bible Say About Wealth?

Perhaps this question should have been taken up in the previous section on hard texts, for much of what the Bible has to say about wealth, riches, money, or earthly treasure is not what many Christians, no matter how kindly disposed to charity and philanthropy, want to hear. A case in point is an invitation that I accepted some years ago, to spend a weekend with some very wealthy Christian businessmen in Texas. They wished to discuss the relationship between faith and wealth, and they asked me to take up with them some of the passages in the New Testament where the subject of wealth is considered. They were particularly interested in the views of Jesus.

I could have taken up with them the story of Zacchaeus, in Luke 19:1–10. He was the chief tax collector, he was short, and he was rich, and Jesus dined with him and received much criticism for doing so. Zacchaeus repented of his sins and offered fourfold restitution to those whom he had cheated, and half of his estate he determined to give to the poor. Jesus celebrates his change of heart and life, and, most important, allows him to keep half of his fortune.

I could have pointed out, also, that it was a wealthy man, Joseph of Arimathea, who provided Jesus with his tomb and in the gospels is justly praised for this act of charity. We read of him in Luke 23:50–56. Then, of course, there is the instance in which Jesus does not rebuke the woman who anoints him with a very costly ointment, seeming to approve of such extravagance despite the objections of the disciples. In Matthew 26:6–13, he not only declines to rebuke her but commends her gesture with the memorable words, "Truly I say to you, wherever this gospel is preached in the whole world, what she has done will be told in memory of her." The parallel passage in Mark

14:3–9 tells the same tale. The economic dimension of the anointing, of which much is made in Mark and in Matthew, is absent from Luke's account (7:36–50), where the woman anoints Jesus' feet with her tears and dries them with her hair. Her sins are forgiven her.

A Perfect Candidate

What the Texas businessmen wanted to hear about, however, was the rich young ruler found in Luke 18:18–30, with parallel stories in Matthew 19:16–30 and in Mark 10:17–27. The elements of the story are painfully clear: The rich ruler asks Jesus what he must do to inherit eternal life. The question is interesting, but even more interesting is the one who asks it. Here is a man—he would have to be a man in order to be described as a ruler—who is a member of the establishment or ruling class. He has position and authority, and he is quite a change from the usual rag-tag sort of follower whom Jesus attracted. He is just the sort of person that any modern church would seek out and grab at the coffee hour, somebody who is somebody and who can possibly make a difference. And he is rich. This is not just a metaphor. He is, as they say, really rich. He, in short, has much to offer.

He is interested as well in spiritual things. He asks the ultimate question of Jesus: What shall I do to inherit eternal life? In Matthew the request is made more specific when he asks, "What good deed must I *do*?" Here is a man eager for righteousness. We learn more of this rich ruler when Jesus asks him if he knows and has kept the commandments, the whole moral law. The answer is as pleasing as everything else about this man: "I have observed them from my youth." (Mark 10:20). This is not someone looking for an easy ride into heaven; he knows and has lived the good life, the virtuous life, if you will. He knows the rules and he has lived his life by them, and Jesus approved. How do we know this? Because Mark says, "And Jesus looking upon him loved him." Only Mark contains this phrase of love, and it places the stamp of Jesus' affection upon an already very impressive man.

"One thing you lack; go, sell what you have, and give to the poor, and you will have treasure in heaven; and come, follow me." Here is the answer to rich young ruler's question, which comes in the form of an invitation to discipleship. As we know, the young man declined the invitation. "At that saying," Mark writes, "his countenance fell, and he went away sorrowful; for he had great possessions." (Mark 10:22) After a moment of silence, two questions nearly always follow the hearing of this story. The first is "Why didn't Jesus take him just as he was, which was very good indeed by the usual standards of discipleship?" The second is "Why did the young man fail to accept the invitation of an eternal lifetime, which he had so earnestly sought?" If this rich and righteous ruler isn't good enough for the kingdom of heaven, then who is? The disciples themselves ask that question, knowing that they do not compare so well with the one who got away.

The temptation is always strong to seek out some moral flaw, some hitherto concealed blemish on the character of the rich ruler, but the text does not permit us this conclusion. Both he and Jesus knew that he was good, and we are meant to know that as well. He was good, but not good enough. This doesn't mean necessarily that he lacked faith in Jesus; we assume that he placed sufficient faith in Jesus at the outset to ask the fundamental question that begins the conversation. We can only conclude that he lacked sufficient faith in himself to contemplate a life without those things by which he has been sustained in his life: his riches. "His countenance fell," we are told, upon hearing Jesus' expectation that he would divest himself of all that he had, and that he would follow Jesus as a disciple. He recognized what was being asked, he calculated the expectation, and he didn't dare take the risk. He may even have known that he had made the wrong choice, but he also knew that it was the only choice that he could make. Perhaps it was that moment of enlightened realization of his own limitations, that freeze-frame moment of self-truth, that caused his face to fall. He went away sorrowful, Mark goes on; and the explanation given for why he was sorrowful, is "for he had great possessions."

Why didn't Jesus take him? Possibly because Jesus knew that the possessions would get in the way, that in some sense the rich young ruler was possessed by his possessions, not in an obsessive way but in a way that would be difficult to disentangle. Jesus does not condemn the man's wealth. He does not deny his legitimate possession of it. The wealth in the story is morally neutral. The test of the man's loyalty and sincerity is his willingness to give up even his legitimate wealth, not ill-gotten gains like those of Zacchaeus, in order to take up with Jesus. Indeed, it may well have been that the man's virtues and wealth were in some sense hindrances to accepting Jesus' invitation, for moral security at times can be like financial security in that it can contribute to a sense of smugness and self-satisfaction. Although we must take the rich ruler's question of Jesus at face value and respond to it as Jesus did, as a genuine interest in eternal life, the ultimate test of virtue is to have it challenged and risk the loss of it. To give up moral and social security to follow Jesus is a risk less likely the more virtuous you desire to be. Jesus perhaps knew this, and gave the ruler a way out by making it impossible for him to come in.

We really cannot speculate about the motivations of Jesus or of the rich ruler, but in the following verses we do not need to speculate, for in explaining to the disciples what has just happened, Jesus makes it fairly clear: "How hard it will be for those with riches to enter the kingdom of God." (Mark 10:24). If that were not clear enough, he offers one of the most vivid figures in all of the Bible: "It is easier for a camel to go through the eye of a needle than

for a rich man to enter the kingdom of God."
(Mark 10:25) The impediment is clear: riches.
In case my Texas friends hadn't yet quite caught
it, which was possible, as I doubted that this
text had been much expounded upon from the
pulpits of many of their churches, I put it this
way: *Wealth is not a sin, but it is a problem.*

It is not a problem only in this particularly
vivid story, but it is problematic throughout all
of scripture. Here is where one of W.C. Fields's
loopholes would come in handy, for it is not
very easy to avoid the problematic relationship
in the Bible between faith and wealth. It is not
as if there is a biblical view on wealth; there
really could not be a systematized philosophy
of economy in the Bible, for this is after all a
collection of books written over the course of a
thousand years under widely diverging social
and economic circumstances. The problem of
wealth is common to them all, but the variety
of ways in which wealth is addressed requires
more than the simpleminded statement that the
Bible either is for it or against it. In certain parts
of the Bible, for example, wealth and riches are
signs of God's approval and blessing: "You shall
remember the Lord your God, for it is he who
gives you power to get wealth." (Deuteronomy
8:18) In I Chronicles 29:12, "Both riches and
honor come from thee, and thou rulest over all."
In Ecclesiastes 10:19, we read that "bread is
made for laughter, and wine gladdens life, and
money answers everything." Among the blessings
God bestowed upon Solomon, in addition to
his reputation for wisdom, was the great wealth

that made him so easily admired. In Psalm 112: 1, 3, we read, "Blessed is the man who fears the Lord, who greatly delights in his commandments...Wealth and riches are in his house; and his righteousness endures for ever."

In the New Testament Jesus himself teaches a hard lesson in the advantages of investments over savings when, in the parable of the talents in Matthew 25:14–30, he excoriates the man who hid his talent in the ground and did not put it out to collect interest. "So take the talent from him and give it to him who has the ten talents." Then, in probably one of the most frightening verses in the Bible, he says, "For to every one who has will more be given, and he will have abundance; but from him who has not, even what he has will be taken away." (Matthew 25:29) This is certainly an exercise in the redistribution of wealth, but not in quite the way we have come to expect, or to expect of Jesus.

These verses of course do not tell the whole story, and one of the least likely places to look in the search for verses sharply critical of wealth is Psalms, that collection of hymns and poems which to many is the most loved book in the Bible because it appears to be so free of doctrine. The tone of many of the psalms, however, is sharply critical of establishments, the combination of the wealthy and the powerful, those syndicates who prosper in their wicked ways while the faithful remain poor and have a hard time of it. There is a high degree of economic envy, even anger, in these psalms, and high hopes of spiritual vengeance and turning of the tables. Psalm 73 is perhaps the most vivid example of this kind of economic class warfare, and it is in the "sanctuary of God," at verse 17, that the pious worm begins to turn. At verse 3, the condition of the psalmist is made very clear: "For I was envious of the arrogant, when I saw the prosperity of the wicked." A familiar theme is introduced in this particular psalm which occurs again and again throughout both the Psalter and the Old Testament: the association of prosperity with wickedness. The virtuous are by definition under this rubric virtuous, and the wicked prosper because they have cheated the poor and have no conscience to convict them. They thus enjoy their ill-gotten gains without guilt. "For they have no pangs; their bodies are round and sleek. They are not in trouble as other men are; they are not stricken like other men." (Psalm 73:4–5). "Other men," of course, meaning the likes of the virtuous psalmist. As if to make the case for moral compensation in the face of material deprivation, Psalm 37:16 says, "Better is a little that the righteous has than the abundance of many wicked." The same theme appears again in Psalm 49:5–6, where the psalmist asks, "Why should I fear in times of trouble, when the iniquity of my persecutors surrounds me, men who trust in their wealth and boast of the abundance of their riches?"

In a rebuke to the mighty man who would boast, Psalm 52: 1,5–7 asks, "Why do you boast, O mighty man, of mischief done against the godly?…God will break you down forever; he will snatch and tear you from your tent; he will uproot you from the land of the living. The righteous shall see, and fear, and shall laugh at him, saying, 'See the man who would not make God his refuge, but trusted in the abundance of his riches, and sought refuge in his wealth!'"

The psalms may be full of consolation, but the consolation is often recompense against the sense of injustice often expressed in terms of justice and power, and couched in the language of anger and violent vengence.

In the New Testament we have the revolutionary line in the Magnificat, where gentle Mary, overwhelmed by the Holy Spirit's news that she will have a child, sings to the Lord, who among many other things "has filled the hungry with good things, and the rich he has sent empty away." (Luke 1:53.) There can be no question about the redistribution of wealth here. Those who have it will lose it; those who have it not will get it. Jesus says that you cannot serve God and Mammon, meaning that the spiritual and the material are mutually exclusive (Matthew 6:24), and his parable about Dives and Lazarus—the rich man who had everything on earth and nothing in the next life, and the poor man who on earth suffered and in heaven feasted—is well known, and it is clear that the story favors earthly deprivation over earthly wealth.

The epistles are no less reassuring, and from the First Epistle to Timothy comes perhaps the most famous verse on money in the Bible, although it is frequently misquoted: "Those who desire to be rich fall into temptation, into a snare, into many senseless and hurtful desires that plunge men into ruin and destruction. *For the love of money is the root of all evil*; it is through this craving that some have wandered away from the faith and pierced their hearts with many pangs." (I Timothy 6:9–10)

In case the rich don't get it, Martin Luther's least favorite epistle, that of James, which Luther called a "gospel of straw" and inferior to the rest of the New Testament, reads: "Come now, you rich, weep and howl for the miseries that are coming upon you. Your riches have rotted and your garments are motheaten. Your gold and silver have rusted, and their rust will be evidence against you and will eat your flesh like fire. You have laid up treasure for the last days." (James 5:1–3) This last verse also applies to the scene outside the place in which the last rites of the church were said for the fabulously wealthy Aristotle Onassis. His super-rich friends all gathered about after the funeral, and the chief speculation was how much he had and who had got it. One exchange went like this: "How much did he leave?" The anwer? "Everything; he left everything." Wealth is not a sin, but for the living Christian who is interested in wealth, it is a problem.

What Does Jesus Have to Say?

In many churches at the time of the offering, it is the custom of the minister to read "offertory sentences," phrases from scripture that lay upon the people the sanction of the Bible as encouragement in their giving. While it is very important liturgically to remember that in eucharistically centered churches the offertory is the time in which the gifts of bread and wine are offered as gifts from God to the people, it has become a habit of long standing, particularly in American churches, to see the offertory as the offerings of the people for the work of God. These gifts were originally the "alms and oblations" for the relief of the poor, based on the theory that those who receive the gifts of God in the Eucharist have an obligation also to give support to the worldly necessities of their less well-off brothers and sisters. In certain branches of Protestantism, such as the so-called free churches with strong congregational low-church traditions, this practice on those Sundays where Communion was a part of the morning service resulted in two offerings. This was the case in my Baptist church, where the regular offering consisted of tithes and pledges for the support of the work of the church, and at the Communion a separate offering was received for the support of the poor and the needy. The first offering was administered by the trustees, the business side, as it were, while the second was administered by the deacons, who with the pastor saw to the spiritual side of the church. Today, however, most churches make do with one offering, which may be put to various uses.

The offertory sentences in the Book of Common Prayer (1979) include these words of Jesus from Matthew 6:19–21, "Do not lay up for yourselves treasures on earth, where moth and rust consume and where thieves break in and steal, but lay up for yourselves treasures in heaven, where neither moth nor rust consumes and where thieves do not break in and steal. For where your treasure is, there will your heart be also." This teaching on the futility of earthly materialism occurs early in Jesus' Sermon on the Mount, his most systematic teaching, where it comes shortly after the Lord's Prayer and is painfully explicit. Neither a parable nor an aphorism, it is a clear and direct command: Do not accumulate earthly wealth, which is subject to the vagaries of the human experience and is at best only temporary. Invest in heaven, which is eternal.

The burden of this text, however, rests not simply on the comparison between the temporary and the permanent, the instability of earth compared to the utter reliability of heaven, but rather on the place of human affection: "For where your treasure is, there will your heart be also." Jesus is not necessarily against earthly treasure, but he is against the seductions and illusions by which humans are tempted to worship only that which they can see and quantify. This is perhaps the ultimate problem with the rich ruler—not that he is wicked but that he is subject to the tyranny of that which he sees and knows. For Jesus, if you have the right kind of treasure, spiritual treasure, your heart will follow. Riches deceive and seduce fallible human beings. Riches themselves are neutral, but the effect they have is destructive on those who have them or who seek after them. If Jesus can be said to have a policy on wealth, this is it. Those who do not believe this are already lost to the kingdom of heaven; a painful example of this is the rich, but sorrowful, young ruler.

It is possible to gather from the gospels what may be regarded as Jesus' principles concerning wealth. Nowhere are these listed as such, but taking into account the social circumstances of the healing stories, the miracles, and the parables, and the explicit teachings ascribed to Jesus in the synoptic gospels and the gospel of John, it is possible to construct a view of wealth that is consistent with the implications of the story of the rich ruler, and with the explicit instruction not to gather up worldly wealth.

Rich Is Not Necessarily Bad

First, Jesus does not regard the possession of wealth as in itself unlawful. Those who have wealth are not by definition sinful, and he does not, as do some of the psalmists, assume that prosperity equals wickedness. In fact, he employs the wise use of money to make moral points, as with the parable of the talents in Matthew 25:14–30, the parable of the pounds in Luke 19:12–27, and the parable of the unjust steward in Luke 16:1–8. In the story of his encounter with the rich tax collector in Luke 19:2, Jesus does not condemn the wealth of Zacchaeus, even though it is ill-gotten. He does not command that Zacchaeus divest himself of his fortune, and when Zacchaeus does so in an act of repentance and restitution, Jesus does not require that he give up such wealth as may still be left to him.

Wealth Is a Gift and Not a Reward

Second, for Jesus, as for much of the Old Testament, wealth is a gift of God, not necessarily a reward but a gift nevertheless. Indeed, it may even be said that the wealth *is* God's, and is only loaned to the one who takes its benefit on earth. "What we need the Lord will provide" is the substance of this particular view of wealth. The provisions of God are surety against the anxiety of human beings. In Luke 12:22–31, Jesus invokes the famous invitation to "consider the lilies of the field, how they grow; they toil not neither do they spin," which is usually used as a text against materialism. I have used it frequently in this way myself, and such use is of course justified by the invitation that appears a few verses following, to "sell your possessions and give alms," a version of laying up treasure in heaven rather than on earth. As far as earth is concerned, however, the reason that the faithful are not to worry is that the Lord will provide what they need. Do not be anxious for food, drink, or clothing. Seek the kingdom, Jesus says, and "these things shall be yours as well." (Luke 12:31)

Wealth Is a Means and Not an End

Wealth, for Jesus, is a subordinate good, a means rather than an end. The trick to moral, faithful living is not to confuse means with ends and not to be deluded by the tangible as a substitute for the imperishable. Upon those who have wealth there is a burden of responsibility to use it wisely and not only for themselves. In fact, how one uses wealth in this life will have significant consequences in the life to come, and that is important because the life to come lasts longer than this one. Thus in the parable of Dives and Lazarus in Luke 16:19–21, Dives, the rich man who feasted sumptuously and arrayed himself in purple, had no sense of philanthropy to the poor man at his gates, Lazarus. He, in assuming that his earthly riches and power were his and permanent, failed to exercise a just stewardship of that which God had only loaned him. When he died he went to Hades, and Lazarus, miserable in this life, went to heaven. Dives from Hades asks Abraham, in whose bosom Lazarus now rejoices, to help him out of his torment. The answer is chilling: "Son," says Abraham, speaking to Dives, "remember that you in your lifetime received your good things, and Lazarus in like manner evil things; but now he is comforted here, and you are in anguish." As if that were not enough, Abraham goes on to say, "And besides all this, between us and you a great chasm has been fixed, in order that those who would pass from here to you may not be able, and none may cross from there to us." (Luke 16:24–26) Of Dives, who was rich in the things of this world but did not use them wisely or acknowledge from whom they came, we can summarize in the words of an old storefront preacher: "He had it, he 'bused it, he lost it, and he won't never get it back."

Wealth Is an Obligation to the Law

Wealth, for Jesus, imposes an obligation upon its use, and a moral responsibility in acquiring and maintaining it. The one who is wealthy is all the more subordinate to the summary of the law that in Matthew 22:37–39 speaks of love of God and love of neighbor. The wealthy must be generous in proportion to their wealth. This is the basis of the negative comparison between the poor widow in Luke 21:1–4 and the rich. The widow's mite represented all that she had, and thus her two copper coins represented infinitely more of a sacrifice than the alms of the rich who "contributed out of their abundance." The principle of stewardship always to be applied is the familiar one: to whom much is given much is expected. Giving in this sense of expectation is not optional, it is the requirement of wealth. Such giving, however, is not to be ostentatious nor is it to be done to warrant praise or earthly pleasure. "Beware of practicing your piety before men in order to be seen by them; for then you will have no reward from your Father who is in heaven." This requirement of modest generosity certainly goes against all of the principles of modern philanthropy, but this is, after all, yet another hard text. What follows is even harder: "Thus when you give alms, sound no trumpet before you, as the hypocrites do in the synagogues and in the streets, that they may be praised by men....But when you give alms, do not let your left hand know what your right hand is doing, so that your alms may be in secret; and your Father who sees in secret will reward you." (Matthew 6:1–4)

What You See Is All You Get

Jesus is not opposed to wealth. He does not regard wealth in and of itself as a sin, but it is a problem both for those who have it and for those who want it. In Luke 6:24–25 Jesus says, "But woe to you that are rich, for you have received your consolation. Woe to you that are full now, for you shall hunger." These "woes," or curses, are not pronounced because the rich are rich, but because the rich have been deluded by the notion that what they have makes them rich. They have been overwhelmed by the illusory power of their possessions, and doubtless in their efforts to gain their wealth, keep their wealth, exercise their wealth, and add to their wealth, they have been tempted much in sin by taking moral shortcuts and by neglecting their obligations to neighbor, to family, and to God. Their wealth has given them temporary advantage in this life but in their heart of hearts, with the example of rich man Dives before them, they realize that it is all temporary and they seek to devise more and more clever ways of securing their wealth against the dreadful days when they must leave it.

They seek its immortality through ingenious economic devices and in earthly monuments and institutions, as well as in the imposed burden of gratitude upon their heirs and beneficiaries. Meanwhile, in this life, their wealth gives them much power, some pleasure, and a great deal of anxiety. Their reward or "consolation," as Jesus puts it, is also their punishment: What they see and have is all they can see or will ever get. In the language of business they have mortgaged the future for the present, the invisible for the visible, and the spiritual for the material. In summary, Jesus is harsh with the rich because they could have so much more if they made better, that is, spiritual, use of what they have. Jesus does not so much condemn as pity the rich, and the only way to be sure they will not be deluded by their riches is to invite them to give the riches up and follow him. Any other way is fraught with moral risk.

Are the Poor Morally Superior to the Rich?

One certainly could come to the conclusion upon reading the Bible, particularly the Psalms and the New Testament, that God in general and Jesus in particular prefer the poor to the rich. Not only does it appear that the gospel has "a preferential option for the poor," in the language of Roman Catholic social theory, but that God has a negative disposition toward the rich. This is indeed a hard conclusion for a Western Christianity whose chief evidence of its existence in the world is its wealth and the seeming devotion to wealth on the part of its adherents. Why this is so is explained in Max Weber's *The Protestant Ethic and the Spirit of Capitalism,* first published in German in 1905, and translated into English in 1930 by Talcott Parsons. In seeking to know why capitalism flourished in the West and not in other parts of the world where there were also large resources and educated classes, Weber became fascinated with Protestantism, and particularly with Calvinism with its sense of an earthly calling as a divine enterprise in which industry would be visibly rewarded by God as material success. The harder one worked, the more one achieved; the more one achieved, the more were revealed the blessings and the approval of God.

Thus, in an extraordinary reversal of the social implications of the teachings of Jesus as revealed in the New Testament, wealth became the sign of holiness, and holiness the reward of wealth. Somehow the "plain sense of scripture," so beloved by the Protestants of the reformed tradition, was, at least in economic matters, turned on its head, with spectacular results in the West, at least for this life. The dilemma, of course, is how Christians—the poorest of whom are, for example, in a country like the United States certainly rich by the standards of the world, and have a keen interest in becoming richer, or as rich as possible—read the Bible, with its generally censorious tone about riches. If there is, as Abraham says in the story of Dives and Lazarus, "a wide gulf fixed" between those poor who are rich spiritually and those earthly rich who are spiritually poor, where is the good news to be found?

Anxiety and Charity

Historically, most Protestants in the West, particularly in the United States but certainly also in England, have simply refused to accept that what Jesus and the New Testament have to say about wealth has anything to do with them. So thoroughly have they adopted as their own the "wealth as blessing" concept as an inheritance from Calvinism, and so difficult is it to account for earthly success as anything other than God's direct blessing upon the individual, the church, and the state, that to suggest otherwise is either heresy or treason, or both. It should hardly surprise anyone that the only successful heresy trial in the Episcopal Church in the United States occurred in the 1920s when a priest in Holy Orders suggested with the specter of Bolshevik Russia clearly in mind, that world socialism would render the church irrelevant because it was a closer approximation to the teachings of Jesus and the New Testament. He was promptly defrocked from a church that was horrified to think of Jesus as a socialist.

One of the leading laymen of that church, George F. Baer, president of the Philadelphia & Reading Coal Company, in defending God's interests in capitalism against the claims of labor during a strike in 1901, said, "The rights and interests of the laboring man will be protected and cared for—not by the labor agitators, but by men to whom God in his infinite wisdom has given the control of the property interests of the country, and upon the successful management of which so much depends." A few years later, in 1907, Bishop Robert L. Paddock, an "Episcocrat" bishop in no danger of defrocking because of socialist tendencies, preached in New York on the gospel of wealth: "He calls some men to make money, a million it may be in one case, a thousand in another. Whatever the difference may be between the men who make these sums is God-given, and the million men should realize that fact and live accordingly."

Squaring these views with those of the New Testament, a problem, I might add, not peculiar to Episcopalians but very much a part of the religious Faith=Wealth culture of much of American Protestantism, takes a great deal of hermenutical energy, and it is very hard for many to accept Jesus' premise that the good life is not this life. As Thomas Linacre (1460–1524) is reported to have said upon first reading the gospels in an early vernacular translation at a late age in life, "Either this is not the gospel, or we are not Christians."

In his book *English Philanthropy, 1660–1960*, the late historian David Owen traces the origins of modern philanthropy to the biblical injunctions to charity and works of mercy incumbent upon all Christians, but particularly upon those of means. By the period under Owen's consideration, philanthropy could claim as its motivating factors civic, humanitarian, and personal satisfaction and the desire to improve and to "leave something behind." For many Christians, however, the motivation to good works lay in the desire not only to improve the lot of one's fellows but to alleviate somewhat at least the burden of wealth of which Jesus spoke in the gospels with such unambiguous clarity. One such eighteenth-century Christian cited by Owen, Robert Nelson, in "An Address to Persons of Quality and Estate," defined charity as "sort of restoring that proportion of wealth which does not belong to you. If in fact you do not do good with your riches you use them contrary to the intention of God who is the absolute master of them."

Medieval charity often involved good works toward the poor by means of hospitals, almshouses, charity schools, and the provision of food and drink at certain seasons of the year by the rich benefactor, through means of what we would today call a charitable trust, provided that the beneficiaries would offer a certain number of prayers for the repose of the dead benefactor's soul, in the belief that God was more partial to the prayers of the poor than to those of the rich. Charity and anxiety thus are linked, as we know from the Victorian hymn beloved at Epiphany, "Brightest and Best of the Sons of the Morning," in which the rich gifts of the Magi are denigrated in favor of the prayers of the poor:

> *Vainly we offer each ample oblation,*
> *Vainly with gifts would his favor secure;*

Richer by far is the heart's adoration,
Dearer to God are the prayers of the poor.

Not everyone, of course, shares this view. Lady Thatcher, while prime minister and in the heyday of her fame as the Iron Lady at war with the decaying welfare state that was socialist Britain in the early 1980s, gave one of her rare sermons, during a noontime Lenten series in a London church. She preached on the Good Samaritan, and remarked that while everybody pays much attention to the charity of the Samaritan toward the man beaten on the Jericho Road, she thought that some attention should be paid to the fact that the Samaritan had the means to pay the charges at the inn for the man, and did not expect that he should be put up for nothing. The ability and the obligation to pay should not be minimized in a story that can easily get treacly with sentiment.

The impulse to charity is not necessarily a direct line to anxiety or to guilt. Isabella Stewart Gardner, of Boston, Massachusetts, when asked at the turn of the century to contribute to the Boston Charitable Eye and Ear Infirmary, declined to do so on the grounds that there was neither a charitable eye nor a charitable ear in the city, which regarded her as something of a femme fatale.

Despite Lady Thatcher and Mrs. Gardner, however, the problem of wealth for Christians who seek to take the Bible seriously and yet take responsibility for life in the material world seriously as well may be addressed by giving consideration to the concepts of charity, philanthropy, and stewardship.

Money Talks

Money talks, and we as Christians must talk about it, overcoming that unbecoming squeamishness that only gets in the way. Neither money nor talk about it is vulgar; what is vulgar is that artificial gentility that suggests that it is. The word *charity*, alas, has both an old-fashioned and condescending ring to it. Its secure place in the English Bible, where it is most memorably found in Saint Paul's hymn in I Corinthians 13, was displaced by the more modern substitution of *love*. So, where since 1611 English Christians heard, "Though I speak in the tongues of men and of angels and have not charity..." they have for most of the twentieth century heard "love" in its place. This change, meant more accurately to portray Paul's meaning in his use of the Greek word *agape* in I Corinthians 1, suffers in the late twentieth century's confusion of the English word *love* with sentimentality and sexual feeling. People glaze over when they hear the "love" chapter as part of the liturgical decor of endless wedding ceremonies, and to recapture their attention I often revert to the older "charity," which of course means work that proceeds from the heart, the seat not only of the emotions but of rational and responsible feeling. Acts of charity thus are those that proceed from the responsible heart. They are actions that proceed from an attitude.

They are, as we could say, outward and visible signs of an inward and spiritual dimension.

Charity is what is done for others because of what has been done for us. Because the Christian has been from creation onward the object of God's charity, the Christian is obliged to translate that into a care and concern for the neighbor, the orphan, the alien, the stranger, and all those in need. Charity is an obligation on the part of the Christian, but charity cannot be "earned" by those who receive it, and thus the Victorian concept of the "deserving poor" is contrary to the spirit of Christian charity, as, in its first impulse, charity is not a response to the condition of the neighbor, but to what God has done for us. Charity is enjoined upon each of us, not simply upon the rich, or upon those who can be said to be able to afford it. The widow's mite is a telling moral of Jesus' that charity does not proceed from abundance or from surplus giving but rather from one's proportionate ability to respond to the need. Just as God does not restrict divine charity to the rich but blesses rich and poor alike, neither are the poor exempted from acts of charity; and it is certainly expected of the rich. It is to this responsibility for good works that Paul speaks when in II Corinthians he writes:

Each one must do as he has made up his mind, not reluctantly or under compulsion, for God loves a cheerful giver. And God is able to provide you with every blessing in abundance, so that you may always have enough of everything and may provide an abundance for every good work.

(II Corinthians 9:7–8)

The concept of philanthropy is closely akin to that of charity, and means "the spirit of active goodwill toward others as demonstrated in efforts to promote their welfare." Alas, while charity has retained something of its private, interpersonal character, philanthropy has assumed an almost exclusively institutional personality, and is often confused with "fund-raising" or "development" or "institutional advancement." The word, however, means "love to mankind," and works of philanthropy proceed not from necessity but from love. Personal philanthropy is so easily lost in the large corporate culture of philanthropy, in the large foundations, social service agencies, and the government, that the personal investment in good works is often lost. Or worse, the view obtains that only the rich can be philanthropists, thus absolving most ordinary people from their charitable responsibilities and depriving them along the way of their philanthropic opportunity.

At the 1996 Harvard Commencement this lost dimension of philanthropy was recovered in the awarding of an honorary degree to Oseola McCarty, a black laundress from Mississippi who scrimped and saved from always meager resources to provide a scholarship of $300,000 to the local historically black college, so that she might help someone. Honored just before Miss McCarty was perhaps America's most generous philanthropist, Walter Annenberg, whose benefactions to American higher and secondary education are the largest ever given by one individual. When it came time to present the honorary degree to Miss McCarty in the wake of Ambassador Annenberg's, the university marshal began, "Mr. President, we have with us today another philanthropist..." The choice of words was deliberate; and more than her gift, Oseola McCarty has given new life to the notion that philanthropy proceeds not from great resources, or in response to great need, but out of great love.

Stewardship is the word these days with which the Christian community speaks of charity and philanthropy. It is an important word and concept, for the very word *steward* makes it clear that we are but temporary custodians of that which is another's, and that because it is not ours but another's we must therefore be prudent and responsible in its administration. Stewardship then is an action of trust that becomes the means by which philanthropy is practiced upon the impulse of love. Christian stewardship has long adopted the Hebrew notion of the tithe as the basis for its allocation of resources to the works of charity and the church. Ten percent of what one has "belongs to the Lord," and is therefore meant to be returned. The first mention of the concept of the tithe or tenth occurs in Genesis 14:17–20, and the next reference is found in Genesis 28:18–22, where Jacob promises to God "...of all that thou givest me I will give the tenth to thee." Early in

Christian times the tithe was extended to include all income including money, and by Augustine's time the tithe was understood to be an acceptable though minimum standard of giving for Christians, mindful that Jesus had told the rich ruler to give "all," and that Ananias and Sapphira, the less-than-forthcoming Christian couple in the communal church, had been struck down by God for lying about the amount of money they had to give to the apostles.

A New Concept of Wealth

Wealth is usually understood to be necessary for the undisputed possession of material things, which in turn give advantage and security in the world. Among other things, wealth also confers status and power, with even its symbols having the power to confer status. Hence, in the Greedy Eighties, such status symbols as Rolex watches, Lexus automobiles, second and third homes, cellular telephones, and the right schools for the kids were all taken to be symbols of wealth. Wealth was also necessary to acquire and maintain those symbols, and getting and spending was decreed to be simply the expression of the American dream. When Gordon Gekko in *Wall Street* said that "greed was good," audiences didn't hiss: they cheered with approval.

The Greedy Eighties have yielded to the Needy Nineties, and materialism is not all that it is cracked up to be. "There's an overemphasis on material goods. Like home computers. You're always having to add things to them. Or furniture. You buy things just because of how they will look when people come to your house. It's easy to allow money to corrupt you." Sociologist Robert Wuthnow reports this and many other anxieties about materialism and the modern concept of wealth in his article "Pious Materialism: How Americans View Faith and Money," in *The Christian Century*, March 3, 1993. The good life for so many for so long meant having everything one wanted, whether one needed it or could afford it. Those wealthy by that standard tended to regard any act of charity, philanthropy, or stewardship as an invasion of their resources, and thus lived upon the principle "I've got mine, you get yours."

This good life, as people are discovering more and more, is simply not good enough. When virtue is divorced from value, everyone suffers, but they suffer most who thought that possession would lead to pleasure and to security. They require a new concept of wealth, and there is one ready and waiting for them in the Bible. Wealth is not what you have; wealth is what you have been given that enables you to give to others. This is what the Bible calls "being rich toward God," from the story of the foolish man in Luke 12 who thought himself so prosperous that he pulled down his old barns in order to build bigger ones: "God said to him, 'Fool! This night your soul is required of you; and the things you have prepared, whose will they be?' So is he who lays up treasure for himself, and is not rich toward God." (Luke 12:20–21) The Christian's wealth consists primarily of his or her "creation, preservation, and all the blessings of this life," as The Book of Common Prayer's General Thanksgiving has it, "...but above all...for the redemption of the world by our Lord Jesus Christ, for the means of grace, and for the hope of glory." To be "rich toward God" is to realize that this is the only wealth that counts. Wealth is thus neither having nor getting. Wealth for the Christian begins with receiving that which God is generous enough to give, and from that wealth all charity proceeds.

Receiving in Order to Give

I learned this lesson the hard and vivid way. When I was a young teacher at Tuskegee Institute in Alabama, from 1968 to 1970, I was often invited to preach in the pulpits of small, rural, black Baptist churches in Macon County—tiny, hard-scrabble places that rejoiced in such mellifluous names as Mount Pisgah, Zion's Hill, St. John of Patmos, and Ebenezer. In these places they paid the preacher by taking up a "love offering" for him immediately after the sermon, and it became something of a referendum on preacher and sermon alike. The people were usually generous-hearted, and grateful for the attentions and efforts of a young man new to the ministry and to them. Early on, I refused these offerings on the grounds that these poor people and their poor church needed the money more than I did since I had a decent salary from the institute, after all, and it was my pleasure to give. In fact, it made me feel quite morally superior to decline these gifts, and to give them back. I knew even then that giving was essentially an expression of power, and that it was power perhaps more than charity, philanthropy, or stewardship that caused me to refuse the offerings of the people.

In the nicest possible way I boasted of my practice to the formidable dean of women at Tuskegee, who had become a friend and mentor, and was herself a preacher's widow. She was not impressed. In fact she upbraided me without mercy for my arrogance. "Who are you," she thundered, "to refuse to accept the gift of these humble people? You have given insult by refusing to let them do what they can for you." I, for a change, was speechless. She then concluded with a phrase that will remain with me all of my days: "You will never be able to give until you learn how to be a generous receiver." Jesus himself could not have put it better, and he was perhaps easier on the rich ruler than Dean Hattie Mae West Kelly was on me. Never again did I refuse to accept a love offering, and it was then, I think, that I first got an inkling as to what wealth was about.

You may wonder what happened with my rich Texans? They didn't like a word I had to say, but I certainly got their attention with a little help from Jesus' words on wealth in the New Testament; and when one talks about money and faith, that is no small beginning.

CHAPTER 15

THE BIBLE AND SCIENCE

THE name of William Wisner Adams is not much of a name to conjure with these days. No theological system bears his name, and he left no literary legacy, but at the turn of this century in the prosperous mill city of Fall River, Massachusetts, hometown of Lizzie Borden, the most famous non-murderer before O.J. Simpson, the Reverend Dr. Adams achieved a modest fame by preaching an annual sermon on the latest developments in astronomy. When asked why he went to such extravagant efforts to lay the most sophisticated study of the stars before his congregation of mill hands and bourgeois swamp Yankees who could pretend to neither an understanding of nor interest in the subject, Dr. Adams is said to have replied that he did it because it enlarged his view of God. He probably took as his text Psalm 19, whose opening verses are the most comprehensive and capacious in all of scripture:

> *The heavens declare the glory of God;*
> *and the firmament sheweth his handiwork.*
> *Day unto day uttereth speech, and night*
> *unto night sheweth knowledge.*

There is no speech nor language, where their voice is not heard.
Their line is gone out through all the earth, and their words to the end of the world.
In them hath he set a tabernacle for the sun...

For Dr. Adams, and Christians like him, there could be nothing in science unsettling to religion or to the Bible if one understood that the Bible was merely an effort, and a metaphorical effort at that, to cram into the human imagination the unimaginable immensity of God. In Psalm 8:3–4, the Psalmist asks the great question,

When I consider thy heavens, the work of thy fingers,
the moon and the stars, which thou hast ordained;
What is man, that thou art mindful of him?

The human place in the divine creation, the cosmic scheme of things, is "a little lower than the angels." In the book of Job it is the thundering voice of God himself who puts Job, and hence all humanity, in proper perspective to the divine immensity. To Job's whimpering claims of upright victimization, God speaks out of a whirlwind and asks, "Who is this that darkens counsel by words without knowledge?" Then God asks the great question, "Where were you when I laid the foundations of the earth? Tell me if you have understanding." (Job 38:2, 4) For four thundering chapters God describes his divine prowess, and the inability of a mere human creature to comprehend it. It is an awesome display of power, an intimidation that should warn off the pretentious and the arrogant. It is fire from the nostrils of a dragon aroused, and Job, suitably chastened, knows when to back off:

> I know that thou canst do all things, and that no purpose of thine can be thwarted.... Therefore I have uttered what I did not understand, things too wonderful for me, which I did not know....I had heard of thee by the hearing of the ear, but now my eye sees thee; therefore I despise myself, and repent in dust and ashes. (Job 42:2–4)

It seems, and it is, an unequal match; the anthropomorphic deity of Hebrew scripture is no cozy Creator who dotes on creatures who flatter him with their questions and attentions. This is a force beyond nature itself, a force to be reckoned with, remote, powerful, capricious, revealing only that which he wishes to reveal. This is no cozy universe, no user-friendly creation, no situation in which the Creator is created in the image of the creature. To consider such a God does indeed require an enlarged imagination, and the language of that imagination is an ironic combination of science and poetry. It is not metaphysics but metaphor that opens the finite mind to the infinite God. These old Hebrew prophets seem to have an instinct for understanding this and expressing it, an instinct that seems often to have eluded perceptually challenged Christians who are always trying to "make sense" of things, and who risk the devastation of their faith when they cannot do so.

The Culprit Science

The conventional wisdom is that modern science has rendered the Bible, and hence the religion based upon it, obsolete. Before we really knew what we really know, so the argument goes, religion in general and the Bible in particular filled in the gaps and provided necessary answers for needy people; but now we know more and we know better. Science and its ability to determine what we know, its capacity to organize and test what we know, even the scientific basis of how we know what we know, are all seen not simply as threats to the authority of religion, the church, and the Bible, but to all intents and purposes as successors to them. At the center of all of that knowledge, of course, is no longer "god," but man, who has in fact now become God. That knowledge which was forbidden Adam and Eve and got them expelled from the Garden of Eden is now ours, and we have become as gods, realizing God's first and worst nightmare.

It is little short of amazing how widespread and virtually unchallenged is this theory of the supersession of secular knowledge, that the Bible and nearly all that comes from it is left only for those who do not know any better. Over the years of my ministry at the center of a great research university, the most frequent topic of conversation with people on their way into or out of organized religion is the credibility of the Bible in the light of modern science. Those considering the Christian faith wonder if they have to suspend their intellectual faculties in order to take the Bible seriously, and those on the way out often say that they can no longer sustain a biblical faith that seems antithetical to science and a scientific worldview in which biblical faith, if examined, seems unable to withstand the scrutiny. Most of my Roman Catholic friends are embarrassed by their church's historic hostility to the scientific revolutions of the modern age, and when Pope John Paul II allowed the possibility of error in the church's condemnation of Galileo, that gesture, long overdue, simply reanimated one of the darkest chapters in the church's long history. Liberal Protestants, nearly an endangered species, continually worry that Descartes was right and the secular world no longer has need of the divine hypothesis, and evangelicals either ignore the issue altogether, or are still retrying the Scopes trial, this time with better "scientific" evidence for William Jennings Bryan. The whole enterprise of so-called "creation science" or "creationism," fundamentalism's answer to Darwin, by its very nature still concedes that science is the only game in town. The Bible's credibility has been destroyed by science, so goes the argument; therefore, only science can restore the Bible's credibility.

A secular friend, in the spring of 1996, asked me if my religious view of the world could possibly be the same after *Time* magazine reported the discovery of new planets, and the possibilities of life in the cosmos. She was not a scientist, I should add, but an informed humanist, and she was impressed with the cover story of February 5, where *Time* asked, "Is Anybody Out There? How the discovery of two planets brings us closer to solving the most profound mystery in the cosmos." What a silly question, I thought, but when I read the "thought piece" by Paul Davies, "The Harmony of the Spheres," I saw, as they say, where she was coming from. "These issues," says Davies, on the possibility of the discovery of extraterrestrial life, "cut right across traditional religious dogma. Many people cling to the belief that the origin of life required a unique divine act. But if life on earth is not unique, the case for a miraculous origin would be undermined." He then goes on to deal with the damage this discovery could do to Christianity's central doctrine of the Incarnation. Was this event unique in the universe, as offical doctrine insists, or did God take on alien flesh too? Is Christ the Savior of humans alone, or of all intelligent beings in our galaxy and beyond?

Nervous Christians

These are the kinds of questions that have always made Christians nervous. Rather than rejoicing in the possibility of the discovery of God's handiwork beyond our previous knowledge or imagination, Christians historically have worried, literally, about losing our alleged pride of place in the sun. Science has consistently managed to unmask one fundamental Christian heresy: Rather than placing God at the center of our universe, we have placed ourselves at the center of God's universe and determined that we are the objects of his existence rather than the subjects. Every effort to expand the orbit of creation at the expense of our central and unique place in it has been resisted tooth and nail by Christians. Modernity can be described as a series of guerrilla wars between an egocentric Christianity and an arrogant secular science, neither of which is prepared to concede to the other, neither of which can achieve an absolute and unambiguous victory, and neither of which is prepared to take any prisoners.

Even the beginning student of the history of science knows that it all started when Copernicus determined, contrary to received dogma, that the earth rotated around the sun, and not the sun around the earth. This new astronomical discovery demanded a new physics to go with it, and that was readily supplied by Galileo. The result was at first consternation: "'Tis all in pieces, all coherence gone," wrote the poet-preacher John Donne. Consternation was succeeded by condemnation, and Galileo was forced by the Inquisition to recant his theories. As an undergraduate in college, I recall the mounting anxiety as we were taken through "The Scientific Revolutions" in our required course in Western civilization. Each discovery and theory of Copernicus, Galileo, Descartes, Bacon, and Newton seemed a mortal blow to the faith once delivered to the saints; and this was only the beginning, for Darwin, Freud, and Einstein were just over the horizon. Our professor shared in the observation of Herbert Butterfield, which ran in italics at the top of the chapter on "The Scientific Revolution" in one of our texts:

> The so-called scientific revolution... outshines everything since the rise of Christianity, and reduces the Renaissance and Reformation to the rank of mere episodes, mere displacements within the system of medieval Christendom....It looms so large as the real origin both of the modern world and of the modern mentality that our customary periodisation of European history has become an anachronism and an encumbrance.

This was in the days when we still studied Western civilization and European history and engaged in the intellectual conceit of periodization, but the substance of the point is well taken, and has been a continuing source of anxiety to Christians who are determined not to be excluded from the modern world and wish at the same time to maintain their place of privilege within it. Biblical scholarship and much theological energy since the eighteenth century have been devoted to a reconciliation of these tender issues, and the struggle is by no means concluded, as any contemporary school board with creationism on its agenda for curricular review will testify.

What Does the Bible Say About Science?

Nothing. That is the simple answer. If science is, as Harvard's chemist-president James Bryant Conant once wrote, "an interconnected series of concepts and conceptual schemes that have developed as a result of experimentation and observation and are fruitful of further experimentation and observations," the Bible has nothing at all to say about such a thing. The very concept is alien to it. Despite the pretensions made for it and the claims made in behalf of it by its devoted partisans, the Bible itself has no such pretensions and makes no such claims. Nowhere in scripture are the faithful enjoined to take as scientific and observable fact the Bible's description of phenomena: the accounts of creation, the sun standing still at the battle of Jericho, the fish swallowing Jonah; these are not presented as articles of fact or of faith, essential to belief and salvation. It is not that the Bible has "good" science or "bad" science. It has no science, for that is neither the language in which it was written nor the mind with which until fairly modern times it was read. To impose the constraints of science upon the Bible is to force it into a role for which it was never intended, and to which without violence to author, text, and reader, it cannot be adapted.

This has not prevented the devout from trying, however, and in the name of preserving the authority of scripture and orthodox truth, scripture was made to fit the facts of science, and the facts of science were required to conform to the facts of scripture. When the evolving science of geology challenged the belief that the earth was created in six days of twenty-four hours each, the concept of "day" had to be reconsidered, and the length of the creation process extended. The simple-minded argument was this: If science is right, then God and the account of creation in Genesis must be rendered irrelevant, if not dead wrong; and if this portion of the scripture is unreliable, what is there to reassure the faithful of the reliability of other parts of scripture—those parts, like the moral law, for example, which are normative? The church was really not interested in defending its views on the age of rocks and fossils with geologists and paleontologists, but if it conceded to science the unreliability of scripture in these areas, it also risked conceding areas of doctrine and morals in which it most definitely had an interest. To defend the scientific credibility of scripture was to defend the substance of the faith. Thus a biblical scholar at Cambridge in the seventeenth century, Dr. John Lightfoot, could argue on the basis of scriptural exegesis that it was possible to date the creation as having occurred on October 23, 4004 b.c., at 9:00 a.m. Such an effort, while herculean, was also laughable, and did nothing for the scientific credibility of the Bible. The great irony is that despite all of these efforts, the Bible requires no such credibility.

Does Science Threaten the Bible or the Believer?

If the believer's faith in the Bible depends upon the Bible's conformity to the norms of modern science, then that faith is very likely to be threatened, for the Bible is not a book of science and cannot, in light of modern science, be made to perform like one. Biology, chemistry, astronomy, physics, and geology are only at odds with the Bible when the Bible is expected to speak with authority in the language of these topics, and its writings to confirm the discoveries and postulates of these sciences. If this test of science is applied to scripture, scripture will always fail.

But having said that, we have said really nothing at all, for scripture does not pretend to be science any more than science pretends to be scripture. The canons of one simply do not apply to the other, and neither is challenged or diminished by being simply what it is. To say this is to take nothing away from scripture except those cultural assumptions that have been added to it from beyond scripture itself. To ask scripture to do what it can do and not to do what it cannot do does not make scripture any less true than science. Is music any less "true" because it does not do the work of fiction, or correspond to the rules of science? Of course not. But some will be quick to say that an aesthetic example does not work, because there is nothing normative about aesthetics and there is everything normative about scripture. This is why believers of a certain stripe delight in finding a compatibility between scripture and science; in both they seek normative and absolute descriptions, upon which they can rely, of things that are fixed and immutable and, unlike fickle humors and mores and fashions, do not change but in fact define reality for all time. Scientific religion, not to be confused with Christian Science, is an effort to provide a science of belief and morality, a system so divinely rational that it operates according to a moral architecture, like the stars in their courses, and is readily accessible to human intelligence. The appeal of science, even in matters of faith and morals, is that it provides the illusion of order out of chaos, and permits thereby the creation of orderly structures with clear rules, fines, punishments, and rewards, easily and fairly administered. This kind of scientific religion reminds one of T.S. Eliot's lines, in which people dream of systems so perfect "that no one need ever be good."

Science, or science as we have come to understand it, has taught us to think this way, and it is thus with these lenses that we read the Bible. To be scientific, we believe, is to worship the sovereignty of fact, and facts alone make truth. Do not confuse us with theories, and surely not with metaphors, similes, symbols, allegories, tropes, and signs. We want a thing to mean what it says and to say what it means in unambiguous and easily accessible English. It is this poor parody of science that we are tempted to impose on the Bible, and this caricature of science is a threat to the Bible greater than anything that Descartes or Darwin or Freud could possibly have imagined or concocted.

"Science" Is Not What We Think It Is

I have always had a healthy aversion to science. I think it began when I discovered that I was no good at glassblowing in high school chemistry. I had already suffered for years from what is now called math phobia: I was terrified by numbers and simply was no good at them. Even today, a computer innumerate, I do my necessary calculations with not much more skill than I had after a miserable year of plane geometry. I chose my college in part because it did not require mathematics and one could substitute geology for a "real" lab science. Science intimidates me.

In my Cambridge years, however, I have spent a great deal of time around scientists, and in a community such as this one, many of these are among the greatest scientists in the world. What has amazed me over these years, in addition to their sheer erudition and the laurels that sit lightly on their shoulders, is the fact that most of them have an intellectual humility that is at the heart of both great competence and great curiosity. By no means are all of these scientists religious believers. In fact, few profess any faith. None, however, possesses the kind of ar-

453

rogant anti-faith that one so easily associates with the image of rampant science. Rather than raging village atheists, most of my colleagues are mildly agnostic, yet strangely sympathetic to the larger dimension and implications of their work. When I listen to Dudley Herschbach or Stephen Jay Gould or Owen Gingerich, each speaking with differing degrees of reverence and awe toward their work and the world within and beyond it, I am reminded that the demonization of science and the scientist is largely the work of humanists. I am further reminded that my colleagues in the humanities and the social sciences are much more the victims of professional hubris than the scientists I know. It is often the humanists and the social scientists who wrap up their scholarly insecurities in what they believe to be the impregnable armor of science, and impose the sovereignty of facts upon their all too elusive disciplines. In professional life these are equaled in immodesty only by doctors.

The disparity between the behavior of my colleagues in the sciences and the reputations of their disciplines caused me to ask if I and others were laboring under a misperception of what science really was, and of how people who took science seriously really behaved. I remember, in my early days of teaching at Tuskegee Institute in Alabama, reading of an interview with the school's most famous teacher and researcher, George Washington Carver. Dr. Carver, late in life, was asked by some writer what he thought was the most indispensable thing for science in the modern age, and Carver replied, "The capacity for awe." What a strange thing for a citizen of the kingdom of facts to say. In my limited readings in the history of science I was to learn that such a view was not unusual: Newton and Darwin stood in mute adoration before the wonders revealed to them by their discoveries in science. That sense of reverence and awe produced a piety all of its own in the Newtonian universe of the eighteenth century, and Christians still sing Joseph Addison's eighteenth-century paraphrase of Psalm 19, "The Spacious Firmament on High," a hymn not untypical of the age of reason.

In our own expanding age of science, with newly discovered planets on the nightly news, and more to come, science just may be the means to rekindle the embers of piety and devotion, and indeed to rehabilitate the doctrine of God, which has suffered heretofore at the hands of a seemingly constricted universe. If indeed the heavens are expanding, so too must now our doctrine, our vision of God, for more implies not less but more of God. This is not quite the conclusion to which Paul Davies comes in his "The Harmony of the Spheres," but the implications of what he does write in his final paragraph suggest an opening rather than a closing in the dialogue between science and the Bible:

But what if, in spite of the second law of thermodynamics, there can be systematic progress alongside decay? For those who hope

455

for a deeper meaning or purpose beneath the physical existence, the presence of extraterrestrial life-forms would provide a spectacular boost, implying that we live in a universe that is in some sense getting better and better rather than worse and worse.

Efficiency and Appreciation

Can a thoughtful believer take both science and the Bible seriously? Is there a way out of the rivalry between two supposedly opposed systems of truth and, as well, a way out of the unhelpful argument that says if one is right, then the other must be false? In the nineteenth century those Christians who tried to accommodate their faith to science were regarded with suspicion by the more orthodox; they gave way too much to science and were left, so it was supposed, with a denatured faith. Those opposed to them either resisted science altogether in the name of defending orthodoxy, or forced science to conform to the ideologies of religion. Religious modernism and fundamentalism are the continuing heirs of that struggle, and science as such goes on its way without them.

Henry Nelson Wieman, in the heat of the science versus religion debates in the 1920s, proposed a division of function and thereby the establishing of a new and healthy relationship between science and religion. He argued that it was the function or task of science to be "efficient," to pursue and organize knowledge, and to come to the appropriate conclusions on the basis of what one learned. Appreciation, on the other hand, was the province of religion and had to do with values, virtues, and judgments. Both efficiency and appreciation were necessary to live responsibly in the world. To many, mere efficiency sounds too mechanistic, too functional, and deprives science of the sense of awe that George Washington Carver and other scientists have found so fundamental to the work of good science. To assign appreciation as the province of religion appears to make religion too passive, a thing to be admired rather than a living faith to be practiced. Concerning the Bible, for it simply to be appreciated and admired rather than believed and obeyed is an unacceptable circumscribing of its role. As one critic of contemporary American theology has put it, rather than throwing the baby out with the bathwater, the baby has been thrown out, and the bathwater kept.

Thoughtful scientists of the later twentieth century, such as Arthur Eddington and J. Arthur Thompson, have argued that the conflict between science and the Bible is a pseudo-conflict and ought to stop. It is an unproductive debate. For the religious mind, science is as much a gift of God as the creation itself and the creation of the mind. While it is bad religion and worse science to suggest that whatever science cannot or has not yet explained is religious, the theory known as the "God of the Gaps," it can be maintained that what science pursues and what science reveals, and indeed the very methods by which it does so, are a godly, religious enterprise. In paraphrase of a wonderful aphorism of Krister Stendahl, science is not religion minus, and religion is poetry plus. In other words, religion requires both science and poetry, both truth and meaning. That the Bible is not a book of science does not make it any less religious, nor does it make it hostile or indifferent to science. The thoughtful believer still requires both poetry and science to enlarge the thought of God.

Chaos, Light, and the Image of God

There is a point of view that science is the new theology, and that like the old theology that many think it has supplanted, it stands fixed and immutable, its laws beautiful and unchanging. The security that men once found in religion and in the Bible they now find in science. Perhaps it started with Pope's lines on Newton two centuries ago:

> Nature and Nature's Laws lay hid in night;
> God said, "Let Newton be," and all was light.

Modern science, however, endures its own scientific revolutions and the stable, knowable, mechanical view of reality is being turned upside down. Frederick Burnham calls this chaos a new theology. "Chaos theory" understands that "randomness is not just a subatomic feature

458

of the world but pervades dynamic systems everywhere in nature." Chaos theory reveals not only that there is unpredictability and that nature is open in its process, but that there is also in this randomness a certain ordered freedom, and that the order and the freedom are bound in a relationship. As Burnham puts it, "Everything in creation is free and yet simultaneously and paradoxically bound by its relationship to everything else that is." A Christian, Burnham is used to seeing the paradox between freedom and relationship, and calling it love. Could such an insight not only help in the ever-unfolding study of the cosmos, but help as well in the understanding of those metaphors that the biblical writers exercised in an attempt to create meaning and value out of the mystery that was and is God?

My colleague Owen Gingerich, professor of the history of science and of astronomy, preached a lay sermon in Washington National Cathedral on the First Sunday of Advent, 1995. In "Journey into Darkness" Gingerich addressed the phenomenon of the winter solstice and the mystical movement into darkness and beyond it, the liturgical journey that the church begins on its long way to Easter. Gingerich does not see himself as a bifurcated soul, one part of which is sound scientist, and the other sound Christian. He uses all of his gifts of soul, mind, and imagination, the skills of science and the insight of faith, to discover in the most efficient way possible what can be learned about the marvelous creation in which God has set us, and of which we occupy such a tiny part. Taking as one of his texts what he calls "the most quintessential verse in the Genesis creation account," the creation of humanity, male and female, in the image of God, he argues that it is this creation in God's image, the *imago dei,* that gives us our self-consciousness and our qualities of creativity, conscience, and consciousness. "One consequence of this self-consciousness," he says, "is that we ponder our place in the universe, and we seek to find meaning and to find God. The search for God is subtle, but perhaps it is this long journey, this search more than anything else, that makes us human. We are the thinking part of this vast and sometimes very intimidating universe, and our quest could well be the purpose of it all."

My Ample Creed

The thought that science could somehow box in the majesty of the Bible, that science had an answer that would of necessity supplant the sense of mystery and awe that the author of Job puts into the mouth of the thundering God, that geology, or biology, or astronomy would hold hostage the teachings of the law and the prophets, the poetry of the psalms, the passion of Jesus, and the revelations of the saints—all of that seems hard to imagine and difficult to credit, as if, for example, we should not have Homer, Virgil, or Shakespeare because they are all prescientific. Secular arrogance and religious ego and anxiety have not served us well, but what remains to stimulate and provoke beyond the capacity of the human mind or imagination is indeed the thought of God, the enlargement of which was the reason for an obscure minister's annual sermon on the latest developments in astronomy. Perhaps old Dr. Adams had his people sing this hymn of Frederick Lucian Hosmer:

> One thought I have, my ample creed,
> So deep it is, and broad,
> And equal to my every need—
> It is the thought of God.

We were meant for such thoughts, created for them, in fact, and the Bible, if we understand it rightly, is a book not about limits but about infinity, and visions, not history minus but poetry plus. The Bible represents the longing of the human imagination to find expression for itself in infinity. The mind is the gift of God with which the Bible is both written and read. Former Harvard president A. Lawrence Lowell once wrote:

> Man cannot set a limit to this thought. Man cannot conceive of a boundary to space, or a time that began and will end because he cannot fetter the processes of his own mind. He was made for infinite conceptions of which he is to partake. Only at infinity can the vision be finished and the end complete.

Lowell was neither biblical scholar nor scientist, but he understood something of the medieval notion that the mind was the soul's road to God: "He was made for infinite conceptions." The Bible has nothing to fear from science, and science, with its sense of wonder and awe and infinity, has much to learn from the Bible. The believer need not be afraid.

CHAPTER 16

THE BIBLE AND MYSTERY

MYSTERY is not an argument for the existence of God; mystery is an experience of the existence of God. Very much like suffering and joy, mystery can often be that place in which we come to know better who God is, and who we are. The Bible is valuable to us because it is the record of those for whom mystery and meaning are not antithetical but a life's work in the growing knowledge of self and of God. It is my impression that this biblical ambition for humankind is perhaps more urgent and vital now than at any previous point in history.

Before we make the case for mystery as one of those thin places in which the human and the divine encounter one another, we must in some sense demystify mystery. I am not trying to be clever. Mystery has a bad reputation in religious language as an all-pervading, argument-proof cop-out when something cannot be explained; when there is a problem to which there appears to be no answer, the temptation is to call the entire thing a mystery. To the impious, or just to the garden-variety secularist, such a device is merely clothing naked ignorance in the fig leaf of mystery, and to the pious and the generally reverent, mystery is not the opposite of knowledge but the opposite of pride or of hubris. Mystery in this sense is the frontier between what we know and can explain and what we experience and cannot explain. Mystery can be seen in the American sense of a frontier, a place or space that remains to be settled or conquered. Mystery here is merely unfinished or unaddressed business, which in the fullness of time and with the inevitable improvements in skills and technologies will be solved. As might be easily said, a mystery is merely an unsolved problem, and unsolved problems do not provoke awe or devotion but merely irritation, intrigue, and persistence.

Some years ago I took up Princeton theologian Diogenes Allen's little book on temptation for my Lenten reading, and through it I learned a lot about temptation, but surprisingly and unexpectedly, I learned more about mystery; and what I learned there has helped me ever since in the appreciation of mystery. Speaking of the greatest mystery of the human experience, the relationship between good and evil or, as Saint Paul says, the conundrum we experience when we want to do good but persist in doing evil and seemingly cannot separate good intentions from bad effects, Allen says, "Mysteries to be known must be entered into." He then goes on:

"For we do not solve mysteries; we enter into them. The deeper we enter into them, the more illumination we get. Still greater depths are revealed to us the further we go."

It is not so with problems. "When a problem is solved, it is over and done with. We go on to other problems....But a mystery once recognized is something we are never finished with. It is never exhausted. Instead, we return to it again and again and it unfolds new levels to us....We live in a universe permeated by a divine reality whose hem we touch when we encounter mysteries."

Such a useful distinction between a problem and a mystery set me off on a consideration of one of my favorite forms of literary diversion, the mystery novel; and I began to take some liberties with Allen's characterization and to apply them to the genre by which so many of us have been so well entertained for so long. When I think, for example, of the Queen of Mystery, Dame Agatha Christie, I am reminded that invariably she sets up the police, the professionals in the murder business, as problem solvers. Somebody is dead, somebody has killed him, and the problem is to find out who as quickly as possible. This problem must be solved so that one can get on to the other problems awaiting solutions; thus Agatha Christie's policemen are usually in a hurry, eager to follow obvious leads, anxious to jump to conclusions because of the very reasonable desire to conclude. Thus, her policemen are made to look impatient, superficial, even careless in their pursuit—not of the truth but of proof toward a solution. The problem-oriented police are what we might call tidy-minded.

Miss Christie's stable of amateur detectives, on the other hand, Miss Marple and the annoyingly fastidious Hercule Poirot, look upon their murders not as problems to be solved but as phenomena to be entered into. They seem to understand, as Allen does and the police in general do not, that "we do not solve mysteries; we enter into them," and they also understand that "the deeper we enter into them, the more illumination we get. Still greater depths are revealed to us the further we go." Thus Miss Christie's detectives are neither distracted by the apparent nor impatient with the apparently obscure. They are usually not in a hurry, and unlike the harried police, they have time to pursue in a fashion that appears to be leisurely but is actually thorough, unraveling the whole skein of relationships, motives, personalities, and the like. True, both the detectives and the police share one objective: the solution of the crime. In that sense they are each problem-oriented, but as with so many things in life, it is not the end that counts so much as the perspective.

An essential ingredient in that perspective is imagination, a characteristic the police are frequently described as lacking in the mystery/detective story genre, and it is to the greatest of all detectives, Sherlock Holmes, that we must turn for the definitive word on the use of imagination in mystery. In "Silver Blaze," the Sir Arthur Conan Doyle mystery story in which the dog did *not* bark in the night, Holmes and Dr. Watson have an encounter with a very competent, aggressive, and self-satisfied young policeman named Gregory. Taking the clues and evidence fully into account, Gregory comes to a conclusion as to the circumstances and culprit, and rules out the inexplicable in favor of a solution. Holmes, however, as we know, is always fascinated more by the inexplicable than by explanations, particularly by those drawn from clues that often stifle the imagination. Basing his investigation upon what isn't there, the absence of the explainable, Holmes goes on to solve the mystery and to get his man— or, in this case, his horse. In characteristically modest triumph, he explains to Dr. Watson: "See the value of imagination. It is the one quality which Gregory lacks. We imagined what might have happened, acted upon that supposition, and find ourselves justified. Let us proceed."

Through the sympathetic but informed eyes of Dr. Watson, the man of science and of rational sympathies, we are led over and over again to marvel at the triumphs of instinct, intuition, intelligence, and the passion for imagination with which the amateur sleuth enters into his mysteries, and thereby manages, in fulfillment of the expectation of the genre, to solve not a few problems.

Two Problems and a Mystery

The two days of the year upon which the churches of Christendom are filled to capacity with the eager, the curious, and the devout are of course Easter and Christmas. There remains, even in these secular and sophisticated times of near barbarous proportions, a primal, almost homing instinct to go to church on the part of even the most casual and remote of Christians; and any of us who has ever been in church on one or both of these days knows this experience. While Easter continues to generate the larger of the two very large crowds, Christmas, I have always found, is by far the most vivid example of the phenomenon, perhaps because the world has been so saturated with the secular banalities and vulgarities of the Christmas season since mid-October that it is a wonder that there is anything left to behold on Christmas Eve or on Christmas Day. Yet I have done duty in churches on Christmas Eve where a capacity congregation with standing room only has been in place for two hours before the service is due to begin, while enormous crowds of disappointed would-be worshipers, many of whom have just risen from Lucullan dinners, are left outside in the cold, literally banging on the doors and demanding admittance. I recently heard one very angry excluded person harass an usher at the door, screaming at him and saying, "This is Christmas Eve! You've got to let me in! I've got my rights; you can't keep me outta church on Christmas Eve!" He represented the same kind of disappointed crowd as that left out of a rock concert or a sporting event.

Inside, the scene was remarkable, made up of the good, the great, and the smart—those who had arrived early—surrounded by those who had been drawn in either again or for the first time, and who knew that this was where they wished to be on this night. The vast crowd knew the hymns for they were the great carols and songs of Christmas, hardly ruined by their tinny overorchestration and exposure at the hands of crooners, TV specials, and Luciano Pavarotti, and the roar of their glad tidings was overwhelming. The secret delight of the clergy is that we live all year for a night like this.

Then the great paradox of the evening began to unfold. The liturgy was unfamiliar to this vast throng and they didn't know when to stand or when to kneel or when to respond or to join in. Every effort was made to make the liturgy user-friendly in an attempt to reduce the unnecessary distinctions between those who knew what they were doing in the service of worship and those who did not; yet what unfolded before us was a tableau of what might be called a "speaking aristocracy in the face of a silent democracy."

They loved the music. They liked the familiar lessons. They endured the sermon. They embraced the Eucharist. Then they were gone, far more quickly than they had arrived, out into the silent and very dark night and back to God knows where. They would not be seen again soon, certainly not on Christmas morning, which was intimate by comparison, and perhaps not again until Easter day.

Who are they? Why do they come? What do they expect? What do they want? Easter and

Christmas are the two problems that most clergy have the most difficulty in solving.

In my preaching classes I am almost always asked, both by novice preachers and by old hands, "What am I to do with Christmas and Easter?" The problem is real, and for many the answer is, initially at least, clerical violence of a holy, righteous sort, but violence nonetheless. I can remember the pastors of my youth who on Easter Sunday would let out a year's accumulated bile against the "twicesters," as those who came but twice a year were called. One of them went so far as to welcome them at Easter by wishing them a Happy Memorial Day, a Glorious Fourth of July, a Good Labor Day, a Peaceful Veterans' Day, and a Gracious Thanksgiving, and by wishing them as well a Happy Mother's Day, Happy Father's Day, Happy Children's Day, and Happy Birthdays for the year. He did this with a smile, while making the point that not only did he not expect to see them again before the next Easter, but he was annoyed, and so too was God. The large congregation of course blushed and tittered, and waited for him to get it out of his system.

The problem of clerical anger on these great holy days is one thing, but there is an even greater problem, and that is what to say to people who give you at best two opportunities to tell them all they need to know about the gospel. "What do I do with these religious voyeurs?" is the question I often hear. Before I even attempt to answer the question, I force myself and my colleagues to look very closely, very hard, at who comes to these great days, and to speculate, in the absence of a poll, as to what brings them once and what brings them back. Suspending the personal and professional umbrage we may take at their neglect of us and of our services, we should ask not what it is that we are doing wrong on most of the other Sundays and holy days of the year, but what it is that brings them out in such consistently huge numbers on these two occasions.

The analysis is often quite heated, at least at the start. "Rank superstition and primitive, barbaric fear" is one. "Mere social habit, custom, the weight of unexamined tradition" is another. "Lack of imagination; they would not know what else to do on Easter and Christmas" is a third. "Cheap grace, an insurance policy against the possibility that there is a hell and that they may be going to it" is yet another. "Fear and loneliness, perhaps hope and nostalgia as well" is perhaps a more sympathetic view. My experience tells me that it is all of the above, and then some, and this I have found is not a problem but a splendid opportunity, and evidence beyond compromise that people even today seek out those places both deep and thin where they have reason to believe that they will be satisfied. When you are hungry you go to a restaurant. When you are thirsty you seek out water. People are hungry and thirsty, and somewhere in the recesses of their spiritual subconscious they have heard or remember that you can expect to be filled in church. Perhaps they remember from childhood Jesus' words in the Beatitudes in Matthew 5: "Blessed are they who do hunger and thirst after righteousness, for they shall be filled." Or "satisfied," as some translations render it.

They don't come to church on Christmas and Easter because they are cynical. They come because they are hungry and thirsty, and we are told also by Jesus that when a man or a woman is hungry we should not offer stones in place of bread. In Milton's delicious figure in "Lycidas," "the hungry sheep look up, yearning to be fed." It is perhaps inconvenient that they should all want to be fed at once and only twice a year, for it plays havoc with our sense of the seemliness of things, and yet I believe that we should honor and affirm what they know: that these are the right times to be in the right place.

I discussed the problem of the twicesters with some rabbi friends who noted a similar phenomenon in Judaism at the time of the autumn High Holy Days. There is real anger in the congregations, not simply on the part of the rabbis but on the part of those who are always there, who pay their dues and sustain the operation on lean and unfashionable Sabbaths. Then along come all these strangers, taking up pew and parking space, and shoving out the regulars who ought to get some credit for their regular virtue. One of these rabbis said that it was one of his congregation's most vexing problems until someone recognized it as an opportunity, and perhaps even a God-sent one at that. "We see it as an opportunity for what you Christians call 'evangelism.' Except that with you, that usually means you are trying to convert us, but with us, on these Holy Days, maybe we ought to be in the business of trying to convert our fellow Jews." I liked what he said, and half the battle is won by the fact that the people are in the right place at the right time; the rest now is up to us.

Now that we have them, and their attention, what do we do with them? What do we give them? I hope that we don't give them an explanation because certainly on Christmas and Easter the people deserve more than an explanation. That is a hard proposition for the clergy to understand or to accept. Surely we must teach these uninformed, occasional worshipers what it is all about? Well, must we really?! Some of the worst preaching I have ever experienced has to do with the well-intentioned efforts of able and conscientious clergy to "explain" Christmas, or to "make sense of" Easter to their thronged congregations, and these efforts to put people at their theological ease stem, in my opinion, from a profoundly mistaken assumption that people are driven to church on these days by a craving for facts, explanations, and solutions. People don't come to church to seek out truth, as we customarily understand that concept as a form of scientific, rational verification of the facts; rather, the churches are filled with people who are hungry and thirsty for righteousness, satisfaction, and yes, meaning. Unlike American television's Sergeant Joe

Friday of the Los Angeles Police Department, they want, and they deserve, more than "just the facts."

Yet, on Christmas Eve they are given lessons in biology for or against the Virgin Birth. The shepherds, rather than devout apostles of the sleeping Lord, become the victims of an oppressive economic system, and Mary and Joseph become the poster couple in the war against homelessness. Easter is no better. How much clerical jaw-breaking has been expanded upon making reasonable the incredible, and hence the extra-rational, phenomena of Easter morning? Of course it matters that the tomb was empty and the stone rolled away, and that Mary had a chat with an angel and then with the risen Lord. Of course all of that matters, but it is not, at least at that point, about *how* it happened. What use are the functional, mechanical proofs that satisfy our small eighteenth-century minds? These are the wrong questions at the wrong time. People want to know, and have a right to know, both what it means and what it means for them, here and now. Explanations at Easter treat us all in the way the gospel writer describes the disciples' reaction to Mary and the other women when they tell them that the Lord is risen and that they, of all people, had just seen him. The women had had an experience; the disciples wanted an explanation. Since the explanation is always inferior to the experience it seeks to contain and describe, Luke's gospel says of the disciples' reaction to the good news of Easter, "But these words seemed to them an idle tale, and they did not believe them." (Luke 24:11)

Perhaps it is, as the phrase has it, "too good to be true." Perhaps Easter and Christmas are implausible truths, problems that must be solved rather than mysteries to be entered into. Or could it be that shepherds and women, the true worshipers and preachers of Christmas and Easter, know more than we give them credit for knowing, and in fact, know more than we do?

The term "Easter Christians" began as an insult against those who came to church only at Easter, and impugned their motives for doing so only then. Those described by this term more often than not acknowledge sheepishly the truth of the charges made against them, but, wonder of wonders, that doesn't stop them from coming. They have much to teach the rest of us, who, like the elder brother in the parable of the Prodigal Son, protest our faithfulness and object to being supplanted by the wandering absent one, upon whose return the fatted calf is killed and on whose behalf a great party is given.

Surely on Christmas Eve we could wish that those who come to the manger and to the altar would do so on a more regular basis, and would in fact receive the benefit of regular instruction, discipline, and fellowship, but when they do come, we must realize that they have done so not to get a crash tutorial in all that they have missed but rather to obey the most fundamental and unavoidable of all invitations and commands: "O come let us adore Him, Christ the Lord." It is no accident that the carol "O Come, All Ye Faithful," of which this phrase forms the chorus, is perhaps the most beloved and well known of all the most beloved of music. It doesn't invite us to an explanation of a discussion; it invites us to respond with the only human response available in the face of the mystery of the divine condescension: adoration. That promiscuous crowd on Christmas Eve knows a mystery when it sees one, and better than that, it still remembers from its primitive, half-remembered past how to respond to one. Perhaps one of the most sophisticated believers of our age was able to understand, in the only language capable of expressing it, what these Easter and Christmas Christians know:

You are not here to verify,
Instruct yourself, or inform curiosity
Or carry report. You are here to kneel
Where prayer has been valid.
(T.S. Eliot, "Little Gidding")

The Instinct for Mystery

"If it weren't for the miracles in the Bible, I could take it all much more seriously." I have heard this view expressed in a wide variety of forms over the years.

"If it weren't for the miracles in the Bible, I couldn't possibly take what it says seriously." I have heard this view expressed in a wide variety of forms over the years, and from within the very same congregation as the first.

The biblical miracles are in place not so much to confound nature and reason, although they do that quite regularly, but to make the case for the credibility of God in Hebrew scripture, and to confirm the presence of God in Jesus in the New Testament. Their purpose is not so much to do good, although they do that. Their real purpose is to affirm the truth of the proposition that Jesus has within himself and his command the power of God. Miracles are meant to get our attention; they are spice to the gospel's mutton.

Miracles, however, have long posed a problem that we cannot imagine was anticipated by those faithful compilers of them in the gospel record. Rather than telling us more about Jesus and confirming in our minds and hearts who he is, the miracles have for many got in the way, and whatever lack of credibility we place in them now adheres to Jesus. So, for many, a faith that was meant to be advanced by means of the miracles to the Way, the Truth, and the Life, is now inhibited or compromised by those very means. The medium has become the message, and the messenger is held hostage to the limitations of the medium. Miracles, then, like Easter and Christmas, become problems to be solved or at least explained, preferably away or out of the way, and when we speak of a miracle as a mystery, for many that just sounds like a pious old fraud, a problem in search of a solution.

In the summer of 1995, I visited the city of Montreal for the first time. Overlooking that splendid city on a very high eminence atop Westmount Mountain is a quite remarkable place, L'Oratoire St. Joseph, a domed phenomenon, which even from a distance exudes an aura of European French Catholicism. It is a place that demands attention and cries out for exploration, and so a friend and I set out to find its approach, which we did after some preliminary difficulty. The nearer we got the more we were joined by others, and by the time we reached the principal parking lot we were among thousands who had come on that late afternoon from all over the world. Yellow school buses disgorged the young and the old, the fit and the handicapped, and everywhere one looked there were nuns and priests. Standing at the foot of the great basilica one is meant to be dwarfed by the sheer enormity of the building, and the panoramic view of Montreal spread out before one seems second only to God's view of the universe. In the center of the flight of steps to the principal entrance is a set of pilgrims' stairs up which the faithful are meant to ascend on their knees, as an act of devotion, and of course my Protestant sensibilities were both intrigued and horrified by this. There were several faithful who were thus making their way up, but we decided not to wait to monitor their success, and went up in the conventional way and into the enormous ground-floor chapel. The heat within the chapel, from the thousands of flickering votive candles, was almost suffocating, but the most overwhelming sight awaited us in the next room. Upon the walls of this smaller chapel were suspended thousands of canes, sticks, and pairs of crutches lined up from floor to ceiling and leaving no space uncovered; these were the mute yet eloquent testimonials to the cures that had taken place there. Some of them had labels with the particulars of the former owners, some had prayers and thanksgivings, some had scripture verses, but whether they were labeled or not, they all told an incredible tale: People had come here with them and had left without them. This was a place of miracles, and these bits of wood and metal were proof of them. It was the evidence of the curative powers of place that fascinated the average visitor, and drew to the spot thousands upon thousands who were there not to gawk or to visit but to be cured of their afflictions.

As we left, my friend said, "That was scary; impressive, but scary." I agreed, for at first impact it was a little too much for an old Protestant from sober New England, and I remembered what that arch-skeptic David Hume, of whom I had read in my undergraduate Western civilization course, had said about miracles. I admit I was helped in the remembering by John Polkinghorne's excellent summary of Hume's objections to miracles in his *Science and Providence,* where he says that there are four reasons to believe that miracles never happened:

1. There is not a body of credible, intelligent, well-informed witnesses to confirm the

miracle and "secure us against all delusion."

2. The passions of surprise and wonder that arise from miracles are agreeable and pleasant feelings and thus are likely to make us believe in their source as miraculous.

3. Miracles are not to be taken seriously because these supernatural phenomena "abound among ignorant and barbarous nations."

4. All religions claim the miraculous to justify their exclusive claims to truth, and hence all of the claims cancel each other out.

I must confess that those four arguments have some force behind them despite their author's unimpeachable credentials as a dead, white, and very Western male, and an Enlightenment figure into the bargain, and I know many who in a heartbeat could out-Hume Hume and have founded churches in order to do so. As we descended that great mountain, however, for the purpose of obtaining the most self-indulgent French cuisine that our U.S. dollars could buy, it seemed to me that those thousands of crutches and sticks were more compelling than Hume's four points.

Hume did not want an untidy, disorderly world. He wanted what my mother wanted in my boyhood room—a place for everything, and everything in its place—and in such a world miracles simply didn't fit. They introduced a level of arbitrariness and capriciousness on the part of God, and they made of believers gullible dupes who, instead of learning about and sorting out their own problems, would wait and expect God to interfere. The "fixed and immutable laws of nature" that so delighted and reassured the scientific intellectuals of the eighteenth century were there for our guidance. They could be discovered, even revealed, but they could not be abrogated or interfered with.

William Ellery Channing, that early-nineteenth-century preacher who so orchestrated the theology of liberal Christians that it gained coherence in the denomination of Unitarians, of whom he could be said to be the godfather, said in his "Baltimore Sermon" of 1819 that while the Bible is a record of God's successive revelation to us, "Revelation is addressed to us as rational beings." Reason must be used to harmonize scripture with "the human character and will of God, and with the obvious and acknowledged laws of nature." He did not, in that remarkable sermon, address Augustine's remark that "miracles are not contrary to nature, but only contrary to what we know about nature." It was in the company of that provocative remark of Augustine that I left the Oratory and that ghastly, grisly collection of artificial limbs, wheelchairs, crutches, and canes. The question, of course, was not "Are miracles true or even possible?" The question was what was really real: the illness or the cure?

Today, "after modernity," my sense is that more and more people are less and less embarrassed to inquire more closely into those great mysteries and truths of which miracles were both the sign and the signpost. If the rule of life, of nature, of "normalcy" as Warren G. Harding once called it, is really, as that thoroughly premodern curmudgeon, Thomas Hobbes, described it, "nasty, brutish, and short," then something that acts contrary to nature is neither a curse nor a conundrum but a blessing and an act of grace, and welcome as such, for it points us to the source of such blessing and grace with the possibility of more of the same.

The Experience of the Miraculous

My friend Dr. Charles G. Adams, one of America's most distinguished and effective African-American preachers and a fellow graduate of Harvard Divinity School, was once asked to describe the difference between white and African-American preaching in late-twentieth-century America. Dr. Adams said that much white preaching is still very much inspired by the Teutonic origins and principles of what was once called the higher criticism. Here, objectivity and scientific clarity are valued. One takes up a text with tweezers and looks at it from afar, under glass, and from every possible angle, subjecting it to various tests and, like a good medical student performing the tasks of dissection on a cadaver, taking great care to record the results and come to a judicious conclusion or two, supported of course by the evidence. Distance, verifiability, and a scrupulous regard for facts and problems are the hallmarks of this tradition, and many of these values are to be found in the preaching that comes from it.

Black preaching, on the other hand, owes next to nothing to any Teutonic inheritance, although people like Dr. Adams are very much aware of that tradition, and conversant with it. Black preaching, coming out of an oral and aural tradition, is overwhelmingly narrative, and the point of a story is to get into it as quickly and as thoroughly as possible. Rather than taking things apart to see how they work, and if they work, black preaching endeavors to remove as many barriers between the thing preached and those to whom it is preached as quickly as possible, so that the "objective" story becomes with very little effort, "our" story, or "my" story. Distinctions between then and now, while possibly of some rhetorical use, more often than not get in the way. Thus, when the black preacher preaches about the exodus of the Jews from Egypt under the leadership of Moses, he does not dwell on the fact that most black people have more in common culturally with the benighted Egyptians than with the Jews. We *are* the Jews, and their exodus is ours, not by analogy but by participation and experience. At the heart of such preaching is the notion that the "God who spake" now speaks, and it is the same God and the same message.

Does this mean that African-American Christian preachers and believers are essentially fundamentalists and biblical literalists? Hardly. American fundamentalism, as formulated in the 1920s and 1930s, is essentially a white Protestant set of solutions to a set of white secular eighteenth-century problems.

The worlds of the eighteenth-century skeptics and their twentieth-century fundamentalist antagonists were profoundly indifferent, and in America at least, profoundly hostile to the worldview of African-American Christians. Fundamentalism has done nothing for African-American Christianity, and the deepest traditions of African-American piety transcend the historic agendas of American fundamentalism. Why? Because African Americans who read and heard the Bible did not stop to ask if it was literally true, inspired, and inerrant, for they knew that on the authority of their own experience as a people troubled, transformed, and redeemed. The biblical world may be different from the new world to which they had been transported in chains and against their wills, but the view of God was to them the same in both worlds. Hence, what God did for Daniel and the three Hebrew children in the fiery, fiery furnace, God not only would do, but had already done with them. No black Christian ever had to make the necessary racial adjustments to the fact that the crucified Jesus was a white Jew crucified by white Romans in a white Greco-Roman world. Far more than fact-obsessed white Protestant Christians, the African-American believer saw the story whole, saw that it had his face and name on it, and embraced the teller and the tale.

The hermeneutical principle, that is, the principle of interpretation, for the African

American was and always has been the authenticity and hence the authority of his own experience. Redemption was not a theory; it was an experience. Slavery was not a theory; it was an experience. The promises were not just that; they had been and were being fulfilled. Indeed, if the great and ironic truth be known, African-American Christians have infinitely more in common with devout and observant Jews in their view of the workings of scripture and the entrance into the mystery of redemption than they ever have had with their white Protestant co-religionists. For black Christians, miracles are not theories to be tested, or outmoded concepts from the prescientific age of the Bible, to be treated with reverent suspicion. Miracles are the stuff of every day, verified in the experience of the people, and by their very survival among God's chosen and elect. Ask any Jew; he will tell you what I mean.

An Empowering Modesty

I began this chapter with a discussion of mystery and the inherent tendency of mystery to invite us into it, rather than to merely solve it. Problems give us the illusion of power, for in solving them we are able to put them out of the way and to clear the decks for the next problem; but mystery lingers, deepens, and develops—dare we say it?—a meaningful relationship with the one who is drawn into it. Rather than looking for a way out we are enchanted by what we find within, and within the interstices of

484

mystery one has a chance to discover, not to resolve, the greatest mystery of all, which is the love by which we are united to God and to one another.

Nowhere in the Bible are we given to understand that by faithful study and good works, or even with a little bit of luck, we will be able to understand all that we need to know about the fundamental mystery of our relationship to God. Those who think that a careful, painstaking study of the scriptures will reveal all to them in the fullness of time have understood neither the scriptures nor God. If there were to be found such clarity, such a lifting of the veil of ignorance, as it were, there would be no need for all of the extra-biblical devices of theological and philosophical speculation by which we have long sought to make our way from the unknown to the unknowable by way of what we think we know. It always amazes me that certain of my Presbyterian friends think that because the Westminster Confession is so thorough, so eloquent, and so convinced of its own virtuous logic it somehow is able to take them where scripture, unaided by the marginal notes of those seventeenth-century divines, cannot. The Westminster Confession and the Shorter Catechism take the prize for theological immodesty. Thank God for the Bible. It is there, after all, that in II Chronicles 6:1, "The Lord has said that he would dwell in thick darkness." It is in scripture, in that marvelous assault upon virtuous knowledge, in the book of Job, where the great question is asked: "Can you find out the deep things of God? Can you find out the limit of the Almighty? It is higher than heaven—what can you do? Deeper than Sheol—what can you know?" (Job 11:7–8)

The preacher, in Ecclesiastes 3:11, informs us, "He has made everything beautiful in its time; also he has put eternity into man's mind so that he cannot find out what God has done from the beginning to the end."

Jesus, himself a preacher and teacher of righteousness, declares in Matthew 11:25, "I thank thee, Father, Lord of heaven and earth, that thou hast hidden these things from the wise and understanding, and revealed them to babes."

Saint Paul, who seems to know everything, tells us in I Corinthians 4:1, that he wishes us to be regarded as "servants of Christ and stewards of the mysteries of God"; and in case there is any doubt, we are told in I Timothy 3:16, "Great, indeed, we confess, is the mystery of our religion: He was manifested in the flesh, vindicated in the Spirit, seen by angels, preached among the nations, believed on in the world, taken up in glory."

The deep things of God of which the Bible speaks in nearly its every breath are not problems waiting to be solved but a mystery into which we are invited to enter, discover, explore, and indeed to enjoy, forever.

This is an invitation I believe we are able to hear for the first time in a very long time, and this is an invitation that I believe more and more sincere seekers are prepared to accept, and not just for the duration but forever. The evidence of the spiritual hunger and thirst of this generation is around us and on every hand, and so much of this renewal of interest in the deep things of God, this desire to take the mystery of God seriously just as we wish to be taken seriously by that mystery, comes on the part of people who have either been estranged from or never really engaged with the Christian Church.

Many of the people I see fall into one of two categories. Obviously, and first, I see undergraduates in college who, rather than falling away from the faith of their fathers and mothers, in college discover faith on their own and for the first time, and often to the mild bewilderment of their secular parents. A cynic might say that if adolescent rebellion thirty years ago was to drop out of church, adolescent rebellion today is to drop in. There is more to it than that, however. This is not simply the smug cyclical theory of American religion that says that what goes down must turn up again. This is not a renewal of 1950s white-bread American Protestantism, picking up where our parents left off. Too much has happened for that to occur.

No. What we are now experiencing is the end of one world and the birth of another. Now I know how dangerous that sounds with fewer than four years remaining until the millennium and all of the fanciful eschatological predictions that this arbitrary and man-made appointment calendar will induce. The world that is fast coming to a close is a world whose secular assumptions have long proven to be unhelpful and uncredible substitutes for making meaning in a life worth living. The disenchantments of the 1960s were really but the first skirmish in a larger battle against the stifling smugness of a world that had come to believe itself to be the best of all possible worlds. All the social upheavals, the movements for social and political change, the so-called cultural revolutions, and the various struggles for liberation—nearly all of which we can name and envisage whether or not we approve of them—all of these, together with the counterrevolutions of recent years and the attempts to put the cultural genies back into their bottles, have revealed not only a failure of systems generally regarded as unfair, but a profound poverty of spirit, a soulless and spiritual barrenness which godless communism helped conceal; but now that communism has collapsed of its own weight, we are left not to savor our victory but to confront, now thoroughly undistracted, the bleakness of our own interior life and the futility of our terribly threadbare hopes. It is this terrible fear that "there is no there there," as Gertrude Stein once said, that has driven so many into the mean-spirited politics of nostalgia, and so many others to drugs, drink, and self-indulgence on a scale unprecedented since the collapse of ancient Rome.

It is this realization, a sober self-assessment of the limits of human achievement and an acute dissatisfaction with the shoddy, the substitute, and the synthetic, with which we believe we are now condemned to live, that is driving so many people, and not just the young, to an examination of what the Bible calls, in Hebrews 12, "the things that cannot be shaken." Not a few of those who seek such spiritual security now that their social security is threatened are men and women who by the standards of this material world have everything. The churches of America are filling up, but this time not simply with the very young and the very old, but with those whom we might call, for lack of a better term, the deconverted, meaning either those who once had their religious faith and lost it, and seek it again, or those whose faith was in the exchangeable commodities of this world, and who have lost their faith in mammon and are seeking out God. Either way, these are the people with enormous spiritual cravings and an abundance of the experiences of this world, who are now seeking the things that endure. They are not frightened of mystery; they embrace it. Their argument is simple and direct. If there is good news in there, let me have it.

Who of us dares deny that this is the work of God? Are we so content with the glancing shadows on the walls of our Platonic cave that we prefer them to the possibility of something else, anything else, anyone else? The age has lost its nerve, and whenever a culture loses its nerve and its sense of self-esteem, its sense of self-confidence, legitimate or illegitimate, its natural tendency is to indulge itself in diversion. Cultural clutter, a more polite term than decadence, is a sure sign of the culture's attack of acute anxiety. Now we are not afraid of nuclear holocaust or environmental chaos; we are afraid that when we get up in the morning and look in the mirror there will be nothing there. It is in this bottoming out of a once self-confident and self-sustaining culture that people have always turned, first after turning on each other, to the deep things of life.

Theologians are not always very good at reading the signs of the times, largely because they tend to look for guidance into the rearview mirror, and thus always know where they have been, but are neither quite sure where they are or where they are going. Paul Tillich, however, was not one of these. As early as in 1958, in a sermon titled "Behold, I Am Doing a New Thing," based on Isaiah 43:16, 18–19, he said:

Our period has decided for a *secular* world. That was a great and much-needed decision. It threw a church from her throne, a church which had become a power of suppression and superstition. It gave consecration and holiness to our daily life and work. Yet it excluded those deep things for which religion stands: the feeling for the inexhaustible mystery of life, the grip of an ultimate meaning of existence, and the invincible power of an unconditional devotion. These things *cannot* be excluded. If we try to expel them in their divine images, they reemerge in daemonic images. Now, in the old age of our secular world, we have seen the most horrible manifestation of these daemonic images; we have looked more deeply into the mystery of evil than most generations before us; we have seen the unconditional devotion of millions to a satanic image; we feel our period's sickness unto death.

Tillich went on to say, "Nothing is more surprising than the rise of the new within ourselves."

That surprising consciousness to which Tillich refers is what I mean by an empowering modesty. For most of us modesty is not something to aim for, and we are one with Winston Churchill when he said that "modesty is for those who need it," but those moments have past and we stand in enormous need. To know our need is not a concession to weakness; it is the first step in spiritual empowerment, and it is this for which people all over the world, but most especially in this country at this time, are hungering and thirsting. It is as true for those who think that they know it all as it is for those who know that they don't, and who doubt that they know anything at all. This spiritual hunger, this deep poverty of soul, exists in all segments and at every level of the population.

The hope of the Good Book, the conviction of those who have sought to understand it with mind and heart, is that it will help us in the good life, the life that brings us nearer to God and to one another. Such a hope animates us and, indeed, encourages us to use our minds

and trust our hearts. In the English Coronation Service, the Sovereign is presented with a
Bible in these words:

> We present you with this book, the most
> valuable thing this world affords. Here is
> wisdom. This is the Royal law. These are the
> lively oracles of God.

These lively oracles of God are a living word,
from a living God for a needy people. It is indeed the Good Book.

AFTERWORD

THIS book began with the concerned conviction
that to many people the Bible is a confusing
and difficult book with which they have only a
passing acquaintance. I could not really address
those for whom the Bible is of no interest; I
could not really think of how to persuade those
who had written off the Bible to reconsider it.
My ambition was a bit more limited or, as I
should prefer to say, more focused, for I am
convinced that there are many people, the
children of modernity, as it were, who are
anxious about what they do not know of the
Bible, eager to find a way of introducing or
reintroducing themselves to it, and trying to
reconcile what they know of the Bible with what
they know of themselves and of the world. So,
in the first case I wanted to address what B.
Davie Napier once called the "unbelieving
believers," those whose nominal hold on the

492

Christian faith and its chief book, the Bible, leaves them keenly aware that they do not know enough and want to know more.

In the second case I wanted to address those who want to take the Bible seriously but who feel, or have been made to feel, that the Bible belongs to somebody else, to people more expert, more holy, more central to God's plan than they themselves could possibly be. I wanted those who saw themselves as strangers and outcasts to the Bible—the marginalized and the excluded—to see that the Bible itself included them and was for them, and that the record of its reading and interpretation was an ongoing invitation to come in. For such as these were the biblical words written: "Come unto me, all ye that labor and are heavy laden, and I will give you rest." Thus, I wanted black people, women, and homosexuals, among others, to see and to hear that the Bible was both for them and with them. I wanted them to know that the Bible was theirs by right and intention, and not merely mediated to them by others or wrested from others by social guilt or clever scholarship. I wanted them all to know and to share in the full wealth of conviction.

My third ambition was to encourage those to think again, who think that they know all they need to know about the Bible and what it says and means. This is an invitation not to guilt, although there is much about which to feel guilty, but rather to modesty, one of the more neglected of Christian virtues. One must not use the scriptures as the drunk uses the lamppost—for support rather than for illumination; rather, one reads those inspired words with the very fallible apparatus of fallen human beings. The discussions of anti-Semitism, slavery, women, and homosexuality are not meant to condemn scripture as culturally wrong, or to impugn the faithful ambitions of sincere Christians who may hold differing opinions on these critical matters. These discussions are intended to remind the faithful of the wickedness done in the name of good, of God, and of the Bible, and to make us more cautious and self-conscious of the besetting sin, alas, endemic to the faithful, of confusing our cultural prejudices with the immutable will of God, and of using the Bible as a footnote to our convictions. Orthodoxy must never be permitted to become the protective coloration for the self-interests of the status quo; the entire record of scripture cries out against this utterly sinful abuse.

By this discussion of the hard texts, and the painful circumstances that invariably attend them, I wish also to demonstrate the dynamics of interpretation and culture. The texts, as we know, have not changed. We do know more about them, and by virtue of the discoveries of the nineteenth and twentieth centuries, including the Dead Sea Scrolls and the library of Nag Hammadi, we have more of them; but the canon is the same as that formed and confirmed by the primitive church in the second century. It is tempting to say that the world has changed but the text has not; the slogan so often offered to close debate is that "God's word is changeless," and that change is simply a matter of interpretation. That is a silly argument, substituting a misplaced piety for the hard work of destabilizing thought. "Thy true and lively word," of which the Eucharistic Prayer speaks, suggests that scripture itself, and not merely culture and interpretation, is dynamic and living. In Hebrews 4:12, written in the formative period of the faith, the word of God is described as "living and active, sharper than any two-edged sword, piercing to the division of soul and spirit, of joints and marrow, and discerning the thoughts and intentions of the heart." That "word," of course, does not refer simply to the text of scripture, for "scripture" then would not have meant the New Testament as we know it. That word is the whole disclosure of God, apprehended by the aid of the Holy Sprit, witnessed to by prophets, apostles, and martyrs, made manifest in Jesus Christ, and mediated to the faithful in all ages by the sacraments, and by tradition, reason, and experience. Such a process is hardly static, fixed, unchanging, and it is into that living, lively, dynamic word of God that I invite all of those who hunger and thirst after it.

All of this takes work and effort. I wish therefore to expose lazy Christians, and their even lazier reading and study of the Bible, to their spiritual obligation to use their minds. The Proverbs tell us that "he also that is slothful in his work is brother to him that is a great waster (18:9), and in Philippians, the apostle tells his followers to "work out your own salvation with fear and trembling" (2:12). Lest I be accused of proof-texting, however, by those better at that vice than I, let me remind us all of Jesus' own great summary of the law in Mark 12:30, "And you shall love the Lord your God with all your heart, and with all your soul, and with all your mind, and with all your strength." This means that for the Christian the study of the Bible can be neither a hobby nor a mere act of devotion, and that what passes for Bible study among so many of us is nothing less than a scandal. If we are to do more than "overhear the gospel," in Fred Craddock's memorable phrase, we must read, mark, learn, and inwardly digest both what the Bible has to say and how we may understand what the Bible means. This means that we cannot afford to leave textual, historical, and theological study to the experts but must take the time, trouble, and imagination to learn not only what the Bible says, but what the best minds of the church say and have said about it. Anything less than this on the part of a Christian who professes to take the Bible seriously, is a dereliction of duty.

Some will say that the great ignorance of the Bible began when the Supreme Court forbade the reading of it in the public schools, and they think to improve upon this ignorance by insisting that such readings be reinstated. That is an evasion of the point. It is not for the state, however sympathetic we may want it to be to the interests of religion, to authorize readings of the Bible; it is the clear and unambiguous responsibility of Christians to make the Bible known to themselves and to their own. If we are ignorant of the Bible it is because we Christians have neglected its study for ourselves and for those committed to our care, and that is a responsibility that we must now embrace, or fail to do so at our peril.

This task may be more easily stated, and even more easily accepted, than accomplished. The field of biblical scholarship is enormous, complex, and intimidating, and we have long lived in a culture that celebrates simplemindedness, fears complexity, and has a very short attention span. What has long impressed me about fundamentalism is its high-impact diligence in the study of the scriptures. Contrary to the image of raving anti-intellectualism that still pervades much of evangelical Protestantism, it is largely the churches of this tradition of fundamentalism that have kept the study of Greek and Hebrew alive. Their churches are not just one-stop-one-hour Sunday filling stations, but are busy and filled all week long with intensive lay study of the Bible because they know that their lives depend upon it; and theirs is a model from which the whole church could benefit. Today the average Christian has available, at the nearest bookstore or public library, resources in biblical scholarship which would dwarf those available to Augustine, Calvin, or Luther.

Finally, and above all, I wish my readers to know that the Bible is more than syntax, doctrine, and interpretation, and that it is one of the most available and extraordinary means by which humans are brought into proximity with the divine. Saint John tells us that the "Word became flesh and dwelt among us." In the Bible we come to experience the fact that the flesh also becomes word, and that it too dwells among us, full of grace and truth. (John 1:4) The Bible is not only the account of those who have come to know something of the transcendent love and power of the living God through the experience of human suffering and joy, and for whom this ultimate reality is also the ultimate mystery; the Bible also assures us that their experience of these things may in some measure be ours as well. As God not only "spake" but "speaks," so we too may hear that message that makes sense and meaning of our lives. Who of us does not want this? Who needs it? We do. This is why Charles Wesley says in his hymn "O for a Thousand Tongues to Sing"...

> *He speaks, and listening to his voice,*
> *New life the dead receive,*
> *The mournful broken hearts rejoice,*
> *The humble poor believe.*

It is the moral sense of meaning and not the alleged tyranny of fact that has kept the Bible alive and lively, and it is nothing less that the dynamic spirit of God that has made of its interpretation the liveliest of human spiritual and intellectual exercises. When we speak of the Bible as "the lively oracles of God," a figure derived from four citations in the New Testament (Acts 7:38, Romans 3:2, Hebrews 5:12, and I Peter 4:11), we should be reminded that an essential characteristic of an oracle is that it is not a fact but a transaction between the one who speaks and the one who listens, and that that transaction of necessity involves the listener, or the reader in our case, in the work of interpretation. The Bible and the history of interpretation, therefore, is the precious record of human people's exchanges and transactions with their holy book and with the Holy One. In seeking the good life we seek the one who is good, who not only gives life but gives that life meaning, value, and worth beyond itself. This is the context of hope, and not merely the act of hoping. To read, mark, learn, and inwardly digest, to listen to and for the word of God, is to take seriously the invitation and the command of Hebrews 12:25, "See that you do not refuse him who is speaking."

And Now

Over the years of my teaching, my favorite book upon which to lecture has been *The City of God* of Augustine, a work of grand ambition, enormous complexity, and defining significance for the Christian world. Others may prefer the more intimate *Confessions*, with its hint of "kiss and tell," and the more human portrait the confessions paint of a worldly-wise convert to the faith of Jesus Christ, but I like the enterprise, admittedly flawed, of a man who, very much the captive of one world, seeks to write about another, and who lives on the boundary of one realm and looks toward another. It will not do here to give a potted history of this book, one of the monumental works of Western civilization. If you want to know more about what it says, read it for yourself. What draws me to Augustine now are the words with which he concludes his work, in which he senses, as perhaps all do who write about holy things, that his spiritual reach has exceeded his intellectual grasp. It is with his words, then, that I bring mine to a close:

And now, as I think, I have discharged my debt, with its completion, by God's help, of this huge work. It may be too much for some, too little for others. Of both these groups I ask forgiveness. But of those for whom it is enough, I make this request: that they do not thank me, but join with me in rendering thanks to God. Amen. Amen.

(*The City of God*, XXII:30)

ABOUT THE AUTHOR

Peter Gomes was born in Boston in 1942 and grew up in Plymouth, Massachusetts. He graduated from Bates College and from Harvard Divinity School. After teaching and serving as director of freshman studies at Tuskegee Institute, he came to Harvard in 1970 as assistant minister in The Memorial Church. Gomes has been Minister in The Memorial Church since 1974, when he was appointed Plummer Professor of Christian Morals at Harvard College. He delivered the benediction at the inauguration of President Reagan, and the inaugural sermon for President Bush at the National Cathedral. Gomes has six honorary degrees, is Honorary Fellow of Emmanuel College, Cambridge, England, and was, for many years, president of the Pilgrim Society in Plymouth, Massachusetts. He lives in Cambridge, Massachusetts.